SACRED MONSTERS

ALSO BY EDMUND WHITE

SACRED MONSTERS

EDMUND WHITE

MAGNUS BOOKS

Magnus Books
Cathedral Station
PO Box 1849
New York, NY 10025

Libraary of Congress cataloging-In-Publication Data available. Printed in the United States of America on acid-free paper.

First Magnus Books Edition 2011

Edited by: Donald Weise
Cover by: Linda Kosarin/The Art Department

ISBN: 978-1-936833-11-5

www.magnusbooks.com

To George Pitcher

CONTENTS

PREFACE

In French the expression *monstre sacré* is a familiar one and refers to a venerable or popular celebrity so well known that he or she is above criticism, a legend who despite eccentricities or faults cannot be measured by ordinary standards. A fixture on the cultural horizon. A "personality" of exceptional renown whose fame is secure and never fluctuates. I can't help but picture an enormous century-old goldfish swimming about in a murky pool on the palace grounds, though I think the correct image would be something like the Sphinx, half human (or animal) and half divine. In America Bob Hope in old age would have been a sacred monster; Lady Gaga is our newest one. One of Cocteau's best plays (this one about theater folk) is called *Les Monstres Sacrés*, translated into English as "The Holy Terrors."

It might seem paradoxical to write critical essays about personalities who are above or beyond criticism, but I fall into the category of those cultural critics who appreciate more than they evaluate their subjects, who admire more than they judge, who seek to untangle influences received and given, and hope to place a writer or painter into an artistic landscape and maybe even trace out the shape of a career. Having written three biographies of writers (Genet, Proust, and Rimbaud), I have more confidence than most critics do in the biographical approach. Biography, I suspect, is often the hidden agenda behind abstract critical evaluations presented as pure speculation or theory. The evolution of an artistic career can best be examined through biography; only by seeing a writer or painter among his contemporaries can we judge how original he or she was.

Fifteen of my subjects were gay or bisexual or closeted or conflicted about their sexuality. Glenway Wescott, for instance, lived openly with his partner Monroe Wheeler and their erstwhile third wheel, the photographer George Platt Lynes, but they were all three in the public eye and had to practice a measure of discretion. Wheeler directed publications for the Museum of Modern Art, Wescott was for a long time the president of the American Academy of Arts and Letters, and Lynes one of the most celebrated American photographers; their positions made them subscribe to some degree of caution, especially during the witch-hunting McCarthy years. David Hockney, who first emerged in the 1960s and mainly in the permissive Southern California of those days, lived out his homosexuality as easily as did another British ex-pat in Los Angeles, the writer Christopher Isherwood. Both men made art out of their gay lives. John Rechy is a home-grown novelist of that period whose stories of backrooms, hustlers, and the leather scene marked a new limit of explicitness in American letters.

But even for a homosexual as flamboyant and talented and independent as Tennessee Williams those years were difficult. As his journals show, in the 1930s and 40s he was constantly battling depression, low self-esteem and self-destructive hook-ups with violent "straight trade," i.e. sailors and working men who dallied with homosexuals for money—and who often beat them up. The theme of self-dramatizing sensitive people exploited by brutal men was one that Williams would explore again and again in his plays. John Cheever was a closeted, alcoholic writer, the bard of the button-down set, but when he freed himself of his twin demons, came out and embraced sobriety, he produced *Falconer*, arguably his best novel and an explicit gay love story.

Early on the poet James Merrill employed the "you" strategy, that is addressed his love poems to a "you" that in English is not gendered, whereas someone translating Merrill into a Romance language, say, has to decide whether the adjectives modifying the "you" must be either masculine or feminine. Later, especially in his long epic poem *The Changing Light at Sandover*, Merrill presented his gay identity with ease and humor—and even had his spiritual mentors speculate on its cosmic significance.

Of course, there are some unredeemed heterosexuals among my monsters—Martin Amis and Vladimir Nabokov, Edith Wharton and Marguerite Duras and Ford Madox Ford and Rodin, though in my brief piece about Rodin I meditate on my adolescent obsession with his early sculpture of the Belgian soldier. None of these heterosexuals had an unquestioning or conventional approach to human sexuality. They all wrote extensively and convincingly about passion and often as not they pictured it as more destructive than affirmative.

The essays on Mapplethorpe, Capote, and Nabokov have been collected in earlier volumes, but I've dared to reprint them here partly because I feel they gain by being read in the context of this book and partly because they seem to have been ignored in my two previous collections of essays.

THE BRONZE AGE

When I was fifteen I fell in love with this statue—not as an art fancier or potential collector or historian, but the way a lover would. Literally. I was a lonely gay kid living in the dorms at an all boys' school where I would have been beat up if anyone had guessed my inclinations. I was quietly arty—I listened to classical records over at the music building and on my own turntable during the two fifteen-minute periods when we were free to do what we wanted to. I read novels and by the time I had graduated I'd even written two of them (still unpublished).

My boys' school was Cranbrook, outside Detroit, now long since co-ed but at that time strictly segregated from its sister school, Kingswood, and from the art academy, which was just across the street. The academy trained college-age students in all the arts, from silkscreening to sculpture. In our own small school library I discovered a big book on Rodin with black and white illustrations. I checked it out and took it to my room (we each lived in private rooms).

There I pored over the picture of the statue for weeks on end while I was supposed to be studying and by flashlight after bedtime and lights out. I had no friends, certainly no lovers, but the life-size statue of this twenty-two-year-old Belgian soldier, whose name I learned was Auguste Neyt, became the center of all my fantasies. The statue, at least to the eyes of Rodin's contemporaries, seemed so disturbingly lifelike that he'd been accused of casting it from life, of pressing the plaster moulds directly to the model's flesh, as if he were a George Segal *avant la lettre*. Although Rodin had made a trip to Italy and looked at various Michelangelos while working on *The Age of Bronze* (the neutral, mysterious title he gave to the work when it was eventually cast in bronze and exhibited in Paris), nevertheless the figure is less heavily muscled than the sculpture of the Renaissance—and modeled in such a way that it made the light falling on it shimmer.

There is something tragic about the statue and some of Rodin's contemporaries thought it must show someone about to commit suicide. This and other interpretations were licensed because the sculpture, oddly for the period, had no visible pretext. The statue was completed after eighteen months of work in 1877, when Rodin (a late bloomer) was already thirty-seven. The French had recently suffered a humiliating defeat at the hands of the Prussians and perhaps this terrible reversal was in everyone's minds at the time. For me the pose of the raised arm and the parted lips looked both melancholy and sensual, as did the impressionistic modeling of the body surface. The figure was obviously a fine specimen of maleness but the face expressed great vulnerability, and the combination made me think of the photos I'd seen of Nijinsky dancing the role of the Favorite Slave in *Scheherazade*, pictures I'd devoured when I read his biography written by his wife, who was surprisingly frank about her husband's affair with his impresario, Diaghilev.

Of course, our formalist critics today teach us not to confuse art with life, but when I was an adolescent Rodin's art—this one sculpture—had replaced life. I wanted somehow to marry him, to live with him the rest of my life. Since Auguste Neyt had already been dead for half a century, surely, my union with him was preposterous, impossible—something that took me out of time and history and propelled me into an ideal world of timeless desire. That conundrum—how to marry a man already dead for half a century when the statue was Rodin's invention and not the soldier, and marriage to any member of the same sex was unthinkable—was my introduction to the ideal and excruciatingly improbable realm of art.

THE HOUSE OF EDITH

The main impression one has of Edith Wharton after reading
Hermione Lee's full-scale biography, *Edith Wharton*, is what a dyna-
mo she was. Whether she was writing her novels or organizing her
research for them, setting up hospitals in France during World War
I, motoring or sailing about Europe with friends, laying out impressive gardens, building or rebuilding houses and writing about
it, entertaining, reading Dante in Italian or Goethe in German or
Proust in French, looking at paintings, arranging for her own divorce, putting everyone in his or her place, sweetly or maliciously
but always firmly—whatever she was doing, she was inexhaustible.
She admired steadiness of spirit and self-discipline in others and
could vouch for her own rigorous virtues. She had two aspects: for-
bidding in public, the perfect dowager; and light-hearted and amusing in private. But even with friends every moment of the day was
calibrated down to the second. When she became too exacting and
bossy, one of her indulgent friends would say she was "Edith at her
Edithest."

Hermione Lee's triumph lies in rendering the dynamism and integrity of this sometimes remote and always willful and stoic woman without leaving out the nuances, the soft exceptions and endearing contradictions. For instance, who would have guessed that Edith Wharton was so funny—even campy? One of her characters, a female novelist, says, "A keen sense of copyright is *my* nearest approach to an emotion." In writing about the excessive use of draperies in American houses, Wharton complains of "lingerie effects." She kept a commonplace book and a *donnée* book all her life and extracted from them some of the more pointed remarks in her novels. In one manuscript she wrote, "She wore the most expensive gowns with a penitential air, as though she were under a vow of wealth."

Wharton could be terribly snobbish. She dismissed America as a land where people ate bananas for breakfast. When one rich American lady was showing off her house and said, "And this I call my Louis Quinze room," Edith supposedly raised her lorgnette and murmured, "*Why*, my dear?" In speaking of some neighbors in Lenox, Massachusetts, she said that they had "decided to have books in their library." Once, looking at a publicity photograph of herself, she said it made her look like "a combination of a South Dakota divorcée…magnetic healer." Of Americans in Europe she said they were all "in the same attitude of chronic opposition to a society chronically unaware of them."

Few biographies could have been more difficult to write. Wharton destroyed all the letters she received and begged her correspondents to destroy those she had sent them. Unfortunately almost all cooperated, but her caddish lover Morton Fullerton kept her letters, which were written with a passion no one had suspected. She wrote a memoir, *A Backward Glance*, but she was extremely reticent in it. She mentioned few of her close friends, nothing about her lover, little about her husband or divorce. But the problem of writing about Wharton is not only that she covered

THE HOUSE OF EDITH

her traces. Another challenge arises from the fact that she lived such a big life, went so many places, knew so many people, and was such an ambitious culture vulture. Biography is usually the revenge of little people on big people (the application of the biographer's petit bourgeois campus morality, for instance, to uncautious international high flyers), but Lee is subtle and big-hearted enough to understand her subject.

Lee isn't alarmed by the fact that toward the end of her life Wharton had twenty-two servants in two houses; at the same time she refuses to turn Wharton into a sort of American duchess, which is what Percy Lubbock did in his hostile, pioneering biography. Wharton was obviously very fair and generous to her staff; they stayed loyal to her over the years and she gave them pensions when they retired.

Lee is careful to point out that Wharton could be anti-Semitic but in the conventional way characteristic of her class and epoch— and she is less virulent in her novels than in her letters (though there is a caricatured Jew, Rosedale, in *The House of Mirth*). In a letter to Scott Fitzgerald about *The Great Gatsby* she complimented him for his *"perfect* Jew," Gatsby's crooked friend Meyer Wolfsheim; but she was decidedly for exonerating the Jewish scapegoat Alfred Dreyfus, whereas her earliest French friend, the novelist Paul Bourget, and most of the French and American members of her Paris circle were violently anti-Dreyfusard. In her pro-Dreyfus sentiments she was like Proust, another anti-Semite (though half-Jewish), but she refused to meet Proust precisely because she'd heard that *he* was snobbish to a fault. (Her social reluctance did not keep her from reading Proust and praising him in print over the years and sending Henry James the first volume of the *Recherche* soon after it was published.) She drifted toward Catholicism after World War I, but the attraction was as much aesthetic as devotional, and she said, "I don't believe in God, but I believe in his saints." This was the sort of (frivolous? honest?) comment worthy of her friend the society priest the Abbé Mugnier, who, when asked if he believed in hell, replied that he had to believe in it since it was a matter of doctrine, but that he didn't think anyone was in it.

Lee is equally good about the novels. She points out that Wharton ignored many of the great movements and issues of her day and wrote nothing about immigration to America, industrialization, the robber barons, or the amazing technological innovations of the turn of the century. What she did write about were a host of small social questions: "How would a weekend on the Hudson differ from one in Newport or on Long Island? When did lawn tennis supersede archery as the fashionable Newport sport? Why would no one except an eccentric dream of giving a party in Newport on Cup Race Day?" Wharton also shows the rough-and-ready manners of the *nouveaux riches;* Undine Spragg in *The Custom of the Country* is greedy and relentless and strangely cold. In one breathtaking passage she thinks about her son Paul, whom she has abandoned and left with his father: "It was dreadful that her little boy should be growing up far away from her, perhaps dressed in clothes she would have hated..."

Lee never reduces Wharton's books to veiled autobiography, just as she is never reluctant to interpret them in the light of Wharton's life. She shows how over the course of her long, if late-starting, career (Wharton published forty-eight titles) she returns again and again to the themes of her own life—repression, sexual hypocrisy, hidden longings. In the 1930s, at the very moment Wharton began to be seen as old-fashioned and excessively ladylike, she was simultaneously rejected by the mass-market magazines, according to Lee, for being "too shocking and grim for optimistic American post-war readers." By reading Wharton's entire oeuvre attentively, Lee is able to point out previously unsuspected continuities and sudden ruptures and departures. Lee devotes many pages (for my taste too many) to Wharton's building and furnishing of houses and her ambitious gardening, and she shows how her early books *The*

Decoration of Houses (written with Ogden Codman) and *Italian Villas and Their Gardens* demonstrate her concern with the "ethics of style." For Wharton rooms and gardens were never merely pretty or convenient. "Structure conditions ornament," she wrote with typical severity, "not ornament structure."

The moral preoccupations of living arrangements merged into similar ethical concerns in her fiction. In this way Wharton is indisputably a descendant of Hawthorne and a niece to Henry James. But whereas James, for instance, keeps the exact nature of the contested antique pieces of furniture deliberately vague in *The Spoils of Poynton* ("the array of them, miles away, was complete; each piece, in its turn, was perfect to her; she could have drawn up a catalogue from memory"), Wharton is able to spell out every horror (the cabbage-rose-garlanded carpets, the looped-back yellow damask portiere) and does so with relish.

Lee isn't reluctant to say which of Wharton's books she likes and why. She considers *The Custom of the Country* to be Wharton's masterpiece (not the more obvious choice, *The House of Mirth*) and she champions the late novel *The Children* (1927) and states unequivocally, "Though it has its flaws, it is the most remarkable and surprising of the novels that came after *The Age of Innocence.*"

Lee is so immersed in Wharton's life that she sees even the writer's inferior novels as variations on successful themes developed elsewhere. No one today reads Wharton's *Glimpses of the Moon*, for instance, but Lee makes a case for it as a way of converting the tragic situation of *The House of Mirth* into comedy. Wharton saw it as in the vein of Browning's elegy for hedonism, "A Toccata of Galuppi's," in which the question is posed, "What of soul was left, I wonder, when the kissing had to stop?" For Wharton's callous young lovers, Venice was simply regarded as a place "affording exceptional opportunities for bathing and adultery."

Even in the best of Wharton, I'd hazard, there is always something slightly trashy—*not* in the sex scenes, which are usually convincing and deeply felt and shockingly intimate, but in the melodramatic plot twists, as though Henry James and Wilkie Collins were always struggling over her soul. For instance, in the beginning of *The Reef* a penniless American ingénue, Sophy Viner, has a romantic and sexual fling in Paris with the wealthy, worldly George Darrow, and these are some of the finest pages Wharton ever wrote. Darrow has put the girl up in a luxurious hotel, her room next to his, and when she enters her room from the corridor he can picture it all:

> Everything in it rose before him and pressed itself upon his vision with the same acuity of distinctness as the objects surrounding him. A step sounded on the floor, and he knew which way the step was directed, what pieces of furniture it had to skirt, where it would probably pause, and what was likely to arrest it. He heard another sound and recognized it as that of a wet umbrella placed in the black marble jamb of the chimney-piece, against the hearth. He caught a creak of the hinge, and instantly differentiated it as that of the wardrobe against the opposite wall...

This is the language of desire, hallucinatory and precise.

But then, as if her readers would be disappointed with nothing but a persuasive rendering of sexual excitement, Wharton follows it with the rusty machinery of coincidence and social convention. Darrow is engaged to Anna, a rich American, the widow of a French aristocrat. Sophy has by chance been hired by Anna to work as a governess in the same château; Owen, Anna's son, falls in love with Sophy. Anna is in love with Darrow but she learns that he's been sleeping with Sophy, her son's fiancée—and on and on, through the heavy-handed twists and turns. For me at least this artificial "author-manipulation" (as it's called in creative writing manuals) spoils the very naturalness of the opening.

Edith Jones was born on January 24, 1862, at 14 West Twenty-third Street in New York City. Her father had extensive Manhattan land holdings and her mother was from an old, prominent family, the Rhinelanders. Throughout her girlhood Edith was known as "Pussy Jones" and intimate friends always called her "Pussy." Two of her great-aunts (daughters of John Mason, one of the founders of the Chemical Bank) built impressive houses in what was considered the wilds above Fifty-seventh Street; the urge to rival them supposedly gave birth to the expression "keeping up with the Joneses." One of these two great-aunts was the model for Mrs. Manson Mingott in *The Age of Innocence*—a *grande dame* who ruled her world "with a kind of haughty effrontery." Pussy was red-haired with intense eyes but by no means a beauty; she was not "good-featured." She was a withdrawn child with an icy, disapproving mother named Lucretia; she would often be called "cold" and "inexpressive." Edith once said of her childhood, "I had two absolutely inscrutable beings to please—God and my mother." She gave up believing in either of them.

Edith had the run of her father's library and was always reading; in fact one of her relatives warned his child against reading too much lest she come to resemble "weird cousin Edith." She was very shy and once as an adult in England when she was reluctant to come indoors to meet the elderly novelist George Meredith she explained that she was opposed to "human sight-seeing." This reluctance did not extend to places; she said she wanted to travel everywhere and "eat the world leaf by leaf."

When she was just four her family moved to Europe and stayed there for the next six years, until 1872. Her early exposure to German, French, and Italian meant that she was extremely proficient in these languages (much later she wrote the first draft of her most American novel, *Ethan Frome*, in French as an exercise), though it seems she spoke French with a strong American accent, which made her public speeches in that language painful to listen to.

As a small child she had a curious practice of what she called "making up." Before she could read she would sit for hours with a book in her lap and pretend she was reading a story from it. The blacker and denser the print the better. She would walk up and down rapidly and enter into a sort of ecstasy of spoken composition; once her mother tried to take down what she was saying but couldn't keep up. When a child came to pay a call, she asked her mother to "entertain that little girl for me. *I've got to make up*." Later, when she learned to read, her delving into real texts continued to parallel these obsessive inventions.

As a teenager she began to read serious writers—Herbert Spencer, Darwin, and Nietzsche. She received little instruction but taught herself how to read and to write; one of her friends used to say that Edith Wharton and her friend Teddy Roosevelt were "both self-made men." Despite her precocious reading and the private publication of her verses when she was sixteen, she was slow to develop her talent. She was thirty-seven before she became a professional writer.

In the interim she married (at age twenty-two) and immediately fell into twelve years of depression and daily bouts of nausea. During that long period she suffered from continuous ill health and mental lassitude. She and her husband, Teddy Wharton, had little in common. Sexually, their relationship was a disaster from the start—separate bedrooms, no children, much frustration. Teddy was at first blush a joking, easy-going clubman, but it turned out he had inherited the mental illness that had driven his father to suicide. Teddy seems to us like a classic bipolar case: he would go on wild, aggressive tangents and then subside into mute depression. He had almost no culture, little money, few interests beyond motoring, and no judgment at all; what he did possess was a good pedigree. Maybe he was the only eligible man to propose marriage to the odd, chilly Pussy Jones.

In 1888, three years after they were married, Edith inherited a substantial legacy and decided against everyone's advice to spend $10,000 of it on a three-month cruise of the Mediterranean in a

167-foot-long steam yacht with her husband and a crew of sixteen. No casual tourist, she came armed with scholarly works in several languages and applied herself to every Greek isle and Italian port with formidable energy. All her life she would be what Henry James called a "passionate pilgrim."

Edith's twelve years of unhappiness came to an end when she and her husband at last moved away from Newport (and the proximity to her mother and other relatives) and took up living in Lenox, Massachusetts, also a "social" town but one with more scope for Edith. It was there that she built a thirty-five-room house, The Mount, which Henry James described as "a delicate French château mirrored in a Massachusetts pond." At last she was able to get rid of the clutter and ill-sorted bric-a-brac of her Victorian girlhood. Her book on decoration was so successful that it banished forever the practice of having in the same house various rooms from different cultures and epochs (the Turkish corner, the Gothic dining hall, the Louis XVI bedroom, etc.).

But if the building and decorating of her house (and entertaining artistic and intellectual friends) pulled her out of her long slump, what finally saved her was writing, "making up" short stories and novels and nonfiction books. In 1899 she published *The Greater Inclination*, her first collection of stories. The next year she brought out a novella, *The Touchstone*, and soon after, in 1902, a historical novel, *The Valley of Decision*, set in eighteenth-century Italy. Henry James read this book, complimented Wharton on it, but told her to turn to "the *American Subject*. There it is around you. Don't pass it by—the immediate, the real, the only, the yours, the novelist's that it waits for. Take hold of it and keep hold and let it pull you where it will...*Do New York!*"

She followed his advice and at age forty-three published *The House of Mirth*, which was both a critical and commercial success (it sold 140,000 copies in its first year). In fact, she'd been scribbling unsuccessfully for some thirty years; in this way, as in so many others, she resembled Proust, who also had a very long, if nearly invisible (to his contemporaries), apprenticeship. As she put it, she had now become a citizen "of the Land of Letters." In Lily Bart she'd created, as Lee justifiably claims, a tragic heroine of the stature of Isabel Archer and Emma Bovary. Lily has no money but is beautiful and charming and well connected, though she "cannot quite turn herself into a commodity." Slowly she slips down the social ladder and ends up killing herself in a rented room. Though Lee is quite right in saying that Wharton was hostile to feminists, nevertheless she was an expert in dramatizing "the politics of sexual injustice."

Once she was launched with *The House of Mirth* in 1905, Wharton began to publish at the rate of a book a year, more or less. As she prospered her husband became increasingly crazy and sometimes unmanageable, subject to sudden rages or just drunken sprees. During these stressful, if artistically fulfilling years, Wharton came to depend on her closest friend, the cultivated lawyer Walter Berry. She had realized straightaway after meeting Berry in Newport in 1883 that his friendship would mean much more to her than any potential flirtation. He disappeared from her life for more than a decade but then reemerged in Paris, where she and her ailing husband settled full-time in 1911 (though they had been living there off and on from 1906 on). Berry, who specialized in Anglo-French legal dealings, was known as the "first American citizen of Paris."

Wharton loved France and its culture and her admiration served as a theme in her writing as well as a useful counterexample to the rawer American experience. In 1906 she and her husband bought their first car and began to make their "motor-flights" with friends throughout France, England, Italy, Germany, and Spain. Again, these tours were rapid, highly cultured, and tightly organized. They were driven by a chauffeur and the maids and other staff members were sent ahead on the train to prepare for their arrival. In 1908 she published *A Motor-Flight Through France*.

One of her frequent passengers was Henry James, with whom she enjoyed a strong literary friendship until his death in 1916. James introduced her to his circle of younger, admiring gay men (Percy Lubbock, Kenneth Clark, Howard Sturgis) and for the rest of her life she counted many gay and bisexual men in her intimate circle. As Hermione Lee writes: "This was the only family where Wharton felt secure." It stood in contrast to her formal French world of the Faubourg St. Germain and the mindless, selfish world of her New York set. One of her friends called Wharton's gay friends her "male wives."

But as Lee puts it, "Hugging and yearning went along with satire and malice." James liked to present himself to his other friends as the impoverished country cousin whom the demonic lady would swoop down on, drive around in her roaring car, and then drop when he was exhausted and wrung dry. In a letter to a friend, James (referring to himself in the third person) complained "that such fantastic wealth and freedom were not *his* portion—such incoherence, such a nightmare of perpetually renewable choice and decision, such a luxury of bloated alternatives..." James called her Panhard-Levassor the "Vehicle of Passion" and turned it into a metaphor for Wharton herself, "the wondrous cushioned *general* Car of your so wondrously India-rubber-tyred and deep-cushioned fortune." That was to her face, but behind her back James referred to her as "The Angel of Devastation" or "The Firebird" (after the new Stravinsky ballet).

From the beginning of her career Wharton was always discussed by critics as a sort of poor man's version of Henry James. Of course, there are strong resemblances: the subject of the young woman obliged to make crucial decisions about her future in a society where she is kept mostly in the dark; the combination of melodramatic plots, witty and refined dialogue, and a richly nuanced narrative voice; a point of view restricted to one or two characters; the shared interest in ghost stories and the uncanny; and, most importantly, the international theme. Like James, she was more a great romantic like Balzac than a modern ironist like the Flaubert of *A Sentimental Education*. Characteristically, when she read poetry she marked the romantic passages, whereas when she read fiction she underlined the epigrams.

There are also great differences. James usually stays true to his "super-subtle fry" as he called them, whereas Wharton tried to deal with the proletariat in her novels *Ethan Frome* and *Summer*, both based on her desire to imagine her way into the lives of the poor she observed in or near Lenox, Massachusetts. James's heroines are nearly always pure and innocent compared to the schemers who surround them (Milly Theale in *The Wings of the Dove*, Isabel Archer in *Portrait of a Lady*), whereas Wharton's women are less idealized and more disabused, even frankly opportunistic (Undine Spragg in *The Custom of the Country*). In the late James novels (*The Ambassadors*, *The Wings of the Dove*, and *The Golden Bowl*—books that Wharton considered unreadable) the moral point of view can seem perversely, excruciatingly remote from everyday experience. Perhaps because Wharton had actually grown up in an elite New York family, had married and eventually divorced, had had a lover, hidden her passions, and played a big part on the Paris social stage, she was more informed about—and more interested in—the nuances of the rich and the powerful; her very knowledge made her less likely to rethink social realities and use them as allegorical tropes. Still, Wharton always recognized James as the master he was, and he in turn praised and encouraged her, despite the sometimes hypercritical remarks he made to her about her work.

Edith was married to Teddy Wharton for twenty-eight years. When she was fifty-one she divorced him after he had speculated disastrously with $50,000 of her fortune, lived riotously in Boston with another woman, and returned to Paris to subject her to violent abuse. She wrote patient and prudent letters to Teddy and made copies that she carefully set aside and marked "For my biographer."

As she entered into painful divorce proceedings (unusual and scandalous for the period), she relied more and more on her friendships with Bernard Berenson and Walter Berry. Her divorce became final in 1913.

The high point of her romantic life was her affair with Morton Fullerton. Henry James had sent him to her door in Paris in 1907, when Edith was forty-six, though James had warned her that Fullerton was unreliable ("He's so incalculable"). Fullerton was a forty-two-year-old American, a Paris correspondent for the London *Times* since 1891, and a magnetic bisexual (he had an affair with Lord Roland Gower, the model for Oscar Wilde's Lord Henry in *The Picture of Dorian Gray*). After a "motor-flight" with Edith, Fullerton sent her a thank-you note and a branch of witch hazel. Immediately she began a secret erotic journal, which she called "The Life Apart: L'Âme Close." They became lovers, ate in bad restaurants on the Left Bank where they would be sure not to see anyone they knew, snatched moments together in America and France. As Lee observes, "Happiness made her sad." Wharton confided to her journal, "Now I am asking to be happy all the rest of my life."

As is the case with so many writers, Edith "dramatized her love-affair and watched herself having it," in Lee's phrase. She longed to unpack for Fullerton her inner treasures but feared they'd seem to him like "the old familiar red calico beads of the clever trader." Wharton based some of the inexplicit but steamy sex scenes in her novel *The Reef* on her affair with him (a book he not only inspired but advised her on). Fullerton, despite his affairs with men such as Bliss Carman, the American poet, was a tireless bachelor womanizer; he took up with Wharton while he was living with a French actress who blackmailed him (she had incriminating love letters from Lord Gower), and Edith and Henry James helped him pay her off.

As Lee summarizes, "So, when Morton Fullerton met Edith Wharton in 1907, he had a potentially scandalous homosexual past, a French wife whom he had divorced with startling rapidity, a blackmailing mistress, in whose house he was still living (for convenience, not as a lover), and a frustrated career." Why did James send such a man to Edith? Richard Howard in his poem "The Lesson of the Master" suggests that James had some complicated game up his sleeve. But he cannot say what it was.

Edith Wharton is a splendid biography, extremely rich in social and historical detail, a telling picture of the many years Wharton's life spanned (she died in 1937), and the source of almost everything I've mentioned in this review. (Full disclosure: I'm mentioned in the acknowledgments along with scores of others.) As in Lee's excellent biography of Virginia Woolf, the order here is roughly chronological but everything about a given subject (Fullerton, the war, Henry James, Teddy Wharton, for example) gets grouped together in individual chapters. Sometimes this thematic approach leads to repetitions and a moment of confusion. At other times secondary and even tertiary characters get the full treatment, which can slow things down.

No matter. There is no sense in quibbling with a sophisticated, finely written portrait of a woman who embraced the modern age but dismissed modernism in art, who, so far as we know, maintained her dignity but wrote passionate pornography (one story, "Beatrice Palmato," is about incest between a father and a willing daughter), who could be vulnerable but who also dealt with adversity late in life: "At my age, and with a will-to-live (& to work) as strong as mine, one comes soon, I find, to accept sorrows and renunciations, & to *build* with them, instead of letting them tear one down." Edith Wharton would have been horrified by the "indiscretions" in this biography, but it is the balanced, richly detailed, and researched portrait she deserves.

THE STRANGE CHARMS OF
JOHN CHEEVER

Stendhal once said that writing should not be a full-time job, and John Cheever's unhappy life seems to lend substance to his remark. He had too much free time, too much creative energy, too many hours to feel lonely or to drink or to get up to sexual mischief that he immediately regretted. He was both a reckless hedonist and a starchy puritan, just as he was also a freelancer with pretensions to being a country squire, both unfortunate combinations. Oh—and have I mentioned that he was bisexual? And a self-hating little guy who was always ripping his clothes off at parties and plunging into the pool, then mourning his exhibitionism and small penis in his journals the next morning?

There are many other inner contradictions and cruel paradoxes in Cheever's life (cruel to himself and to his family). For instance, he had grown up in fairly genteel but deep poverty with a bossy "castrating" mother (that Freudian harridan in the imagination of the period) and a flaky alcoholic father, but Cheever was not much better as a parent. He railed at his daughter Susan for being chubby (he wanted her to be as sleek and blond and country clubbish as the daughters of his neighbors), criticized his son Ben for being a sissy, and seemed to love only his youngest child, Federico (born in Italy). In his novel *Bullet Park* the uncomprehending but powerful love of Nailles for his mixed-up son Tony parallels Cheever's love for Federico (the fact that Tony is also loosely a portrait of the young Cheever makes this family romance all the more grippingly narcissistic).

Living in Italy for extended periods was the great geographical adventure of Cheever's life and a foil to his obsession with American exurbia. Many of his stories and much of *The Wapshot Scandal*, his second novel, are set in Italy; depending on their mood his American characters are bewildered by the language and the crowding and the thieving criminality of the Italians, or they are seduced by the Italians' beauty and pagan amorality, or they are beset by homesickness and long for hamburgers and baseball. Italy is a theater in which Cheever could stage his inner conflicts. In one of his stories, "The World of Apples," he dramatized the struggle between his licentiousness and his acute moralizing. An aging expatriate poet, laden with honors, lives in the Italian countryside. But every time he begins to write something new it comes out as an obscene scrawl, a banal but offensive piece of pornography: "Filth was his destiny, his best self, and he began with relish a long ballad called "The Fart That Saved Athens." Later he's onto "The Favorite of Tiberio" and "The Confessions of a Public School Headmaster" and "The Baseball Player's Honeymoon."

Every day he destroys what he's written earlier. He finally saves himself from all these obscenities by plunging into a pool. These European stories are never as subtle as Henry James's or Mavis Gallant's, partly because Cheever, unlike these other two North Americans, seems incapable of imagining himself into *being* European, nor can he think beyond the usual American preconceptions about Italians.

Although Cheever's excellent biographer Blake Bailey, author of *Cheever: A Life*, doesn't set much store by it, one of Cheever's most intriguing and experimental stories is "Boy in Rome," which could be read as his answer to a book he despised (and envied), *The Catcher in the Rye*. The narrator in Cheever's story is an American boy whose father has died in Rome and is buried in the Protestant Cemetery there:

> So some Americans live in Rome because of the income tax and some Americans live in Rome because they're divorced or oversexed or poetic or have some other reason for feeling they might be persecuted at home and some Americans live in Rome because they live there, but we live in Rome because my father's bones lie in the Protestant Cemetery.

The casual, run-on narrative might vaguely recall Holden Caulfield, but what Salinger would never have written is the strange "release" toward the end of Cheever's story. The narration has all been in the believable and highly circumstantial voice of the boy, but suddenly another voice altogether intrudes within a long parenthesis, almost as if we shouldn't trust his boy in Rome but realize he's the pure invention of a desperate prisoner:

> (But I am not a boy in Rome but a grown man in the old prison and river town of Ossining, swatting hornets on this autumn afternoon with a rolled-up newspaper. I can see the Hudson River from my window. A dead rat floats downstream and two men in a sinking rowboat come up against the tide. One of them is rowing desperately with a boat seat and I wonder have they escaped from prison or have they just been fishing for perch and why should I exchange this scene for the dark

streets around the Pantheon? Why, never having received from my parents anything but affection and understanding, should I invent a grotesque old man, a foreign grave, and a foolish mother? What is the incurable loneliness that makes me want to pose as a fatherless child in a cold wind and wouldn't the imposture make a better story…? But my father taught me, while we hoed the beans, that I should complete for better or worse whatever I had begun and so we go back to the scene where he leaves the train in Naples.)

This passage is very weird, since it tucks into an extended parenthesis a whole new life of a skilled but previously invisible narrator and even his father who hoed beans! It also, curiously, alludes to Ossining, where Cheever lived, and foreshadows his interest in Sing Sing, the local prison, the model for the site of his last and most successful novel, *Falconer*.

In his little book on Gogol, Nabokov writes of Gogolian metaphors in which a whole distracting world is contained, perhaps a sign of the immense influence of *Tristram Shandy*, with its perpetual digressions, on Russian literature. In one of his texts Gogol inserts a major diversion in a metaphor that compares something to a bather; as Nabokov remarked:

Who is that unfortunate bather, steadily and uncannily growing, adding weight, fattening himself on the marrow of a metaphor? We never shall know—but he almost managed to gain a footing.

Cheever, probably in an original and unrelated impulse, cannot resist spawning one story from another; his is the fertile imagination of the born storyteller. He doesn't have the *spirit* to write convincing novels, though he wrote five fascinating ones; they indicate someone who could spin almost any concatenation of events into a tall tale, though he lacked powers of development. He could, at the most, place his stories in alternating episodes, but counterpoint is not the same thing as *progression d'effet*, that smooth, slow, seamless build so prized by Flaubert and Conrad and the true hallmark of the novel. In his inability to construct a coherent novel, Cheever was similar to that other great storyteller, Chekhov, who worked for two years on a never-completed novel called, symptomatically, *Stories from the Lives of My Friends*.

Chekhov's "failure" to write a novel could be attributed, especially in the context of the philosophical novels of Dostoevsky and Tolstoy, to an inability to work up any great ideas. (Though he was an ecologist *avant la lettre* and concerned about women's rights and prison reform and of course public health, even after a summer combating a cholera epidemic as a doctor he enraged progressive critics by using the epidemic in his next story only as a background to a romance.) As a doctor-observer who kept notebooks and was more interested in recording than prescribing behavior, Chekhov remarked at age twenty-eight to a friend:

> I still lack a political, religious and philosophical world view—I change it every month—and so I'll have to limit myself to descriptions of how my heroes love, marry, give birth, die, and how they speak.

Cheever could have written that sentence. And both would have been more than a little proud to be condemned to express no ideas but in things. This appetite for narrating through quick sketches was something that John Updike, a much more deliberate and slow-paced, if no less eloquent, writer, addressed at Cheever's death:

> One could not be with John Cheever for more than five minutes without seeing stories take shape: past embarrassments worked up with wonderful rapidity into

fables, present surroundings made to pulse with sympathetic magic as he glanced around him and drawled a few startlingly concentrated words in that mannerly, rapid voice of his.

Cheever's knack for working up vaudeville routines based on the anecdotes drawn from his everyday life explains his complaint once in a restaurant that the tables were too far apart. When asked why that bothered him he said, "Now I can't eavesdrop on any of the conversations." Overhearing other people's talk was essential to his art; his was primarily a comic talent for improvising.

The comparison with Chekhov, so often made, should not be pushed too far. In much of his work Chekhov was genuinely neutral morally; it's almost impossible to guess which character he sides with, whereas Cheever clearly takes sides and sometimes explicitly condemns a man or a woman. Cheever loved to write lush, ingenious nature descriptions of a rare beauty, whereas Chekhov sent this polite admonishment to the young Gorky:

Your nature descriptions are artistic; you are a true landscape painter. However, your frequent comparisons to humans (anthropomorphism)—the sea breathes, the sky looks on, the steppe basks in the sun, nature whispers, speaks, weeps, and so on—these kinds of personifications make your descriptions somewhat monotonous, a touch saccharine, vague; in descriptions of nature, vibrancy and expressivity are best produced by simple techniques, for example: using simple phrases such as "the sun set," "it got dark," "it started to rain," and so on.

Again and again, Cheever nests one story into another. One of his first successful stories, "The Enormous Radio," is about a young wife in New York who listens to a new radio all day that, strangely enough, is tuned in not to broadcasts but to the conversations going on in the adjoining apartments. When her husband comes home one day she's a wreck. She sobs:

They're all worried about money. Mrs. Hutchinson's mother is dying of cancer in Florida and they don't have enough money to send her to the Mayo Clinic. At least, Mr. Hutchinson says they don't have enough money. And some woman in this building is having an affair with the handyman—with that hideous handyman. It's too disgusting. And Mrs. Melville has heart trouble and Mr. Hendricks is going to lose his job in April and Mrs. Hendricks is horrid about the whole thing and that girl who plays the "Missouri Waltz" is a whore, a common whore, and the elevator man has tuberculosis and Mr. Osborn has been beating Mrs. Osborn.

The consoling husband has the radio removed—other people's stories may be gripping but they can also have such a sad cumulative effect that they make one's own life impossible to live.

Cheever's canvases, like Breughel's, are always crowded with incident and minor characters going about their activities oblivious to the pink legs of Icarus poking up from the sea where he has fallen. Plots are as productive and cartwheeling as dreams. In *Bullet Park*, Melissa falls in love with the teenage grocery boy Emile, but they are found out and Melissa takes her son and moves to Italy. Emile is fired from the grocery but gets a job with a new supermarket. In order to attract customers the supermarket bosses decide to hide Easter eggs around town that can be redeemed for prizes—the biggest being trips to Rome, Paris, and Madrid. But Emile's mother gets on the phone and gossips about how the eggs are hidden in her son's car.

Just after midnight, many alerted housewives in their nighties descend on Emile's car and even let the air out of his tires. Panicked, he lowers the window and throws all the eggs into a field. When he's fired again he signs up in the merchant marine and ends up in Naples, where he jumps ship and enters a male beauty contest that turns into a slave auction. Someone bids a lot of money on Emile; it's Melissa, and the two of them enjoy a lustful idyll in Melissa's Italian villa. This is just a short section of *Bullet Park* but suggests the odd, serendipitous quality of the plot inventions.

Cheever is, of course, famously a writer about upper-middle-class life in stories, usually first published in *The New Yorker*, that are set on Sutton Place or at summer resorts or in the well-to-do suburbs and that involve cooks and nannies and private schools. Almost always this glossy world is looked at from a jaundiced perspective. In "The Housebreaker of Shady Hill," a suburban man is going broke and begins to rob the unlocked and unprotected homes of his neighbors. In "The Swimmer," a man decides to swim the considerable distance home by traversing all the pools of his neighbors and friends, but as he makes his progress the seasons change, he ages, the neighbors become more hostile, and his house, when he reaches it, is boarded up. In "The Wrysons," a seemingly bland suburban husband can only regain his equilibrium by secretly baking a Lady Baltimore cake at midnight.

In the opening pages of *Bullet Park*, Cheever for a moment assumes the point of view of a "zealous and vengeful adolescent" who surveys the village and thinks:

Damn the bright lights by which no one reads, damn the continuous music which no one hears, damn the grand pianos that no one can play, damn the white houses mortgaged up to their rain gutters, damn them for plundering the ocean for fish to feed the mink whose skins they wear and damn their shelves on which there rests a single book—a copy of the telephone directory, bound in pink brocade.

The houses are then shown to their advantage by a real estate dealer—and all the prices are given by the omniscient narrator as he describes them. Like dollhouses, their walls can be removed and their contents and denizens studied. Everything is mercilessly catalogued, even the Advent calendar, and reduced to the quotidian banalities of the weather:

> St. Paul meant blizzards. St. Mathias meant a thaw. For the marriage at Cana and the cleansing of the leper the oil furnace would still be running although the vents in the stained-glass windows were sometimes open to the raw spring air...he trout streams open for the resurrection. The crimson cloths at Pentecost and the miracle of the tongues meant swimming.

Why has no one ever discussed Cheever as the great humorist he so clearly is, an American rival to Evelyn Waugh (who explores in *The Ordeal of Gilbert Pinfold* the same paranoid fears of being exposed as a homosexual that so beset Cheever)? Everything in this passage is perfect, even Cheever's decision not to capitalize the biblical events. In lowercase they become so killingly matter-of-fact, which is the whole joke.

Howard Moss, the poetry editor of *The New Yorker*, once said that fiction should be a combination of fairy tale and newspaper report. Cheever is sometimes discussed as a sociologist of the suburbs, but in fact a gold dust of fantasy touches everything he writes. In one of his best stories, "The Country Husband" (the story that made Hemingway wake up his wife in the middle of the night so that he could read it out loud to her), a man named Francis Weed survives a plane crash and hurries overland to his Dutch colonial house in Shady Hill. His children are squabbling, his wife preoccupied, and no one seems capable of registering his near brush with death. Francis falls in love with the baby-sitter; his wife threatens to leave him not because of his adulterous yearnings (which she doesn't know about) but because he's inconsiderate and has jeopardized their social standing by insulting the doyenne of Shady Hill. Francis sees a psychiatrist—and the whole suburban pastoral ends with the mysterious, irrelevant, but transfiguring lines: "Then it is dark; it is a night where kings in golden suits ride elephants over the mountains."

Cheever's first novel, *The Wapshot Chronicle*, is full of such poetic excursions. Even the basic premise of the book is right out of a fairy tale: a rich maiden aunt, Honora, will leave her considerable fortune to her penniless Wapshot nephews Moses and Coverly but only if they get married and produce male heirs. This stipulation sends the boys off to New York and Washington to make their way and to find suitable partners—and triggers all the subsequent action, as in a Hellenic romance. Throughout the book, though, those fascinating little fleeting portraits of extras keep boiling up. When Coverly, who's serving in the army, wants to get permission to leave the tropical atoll where he's stationed to rush back to New England to his dying father's side, he's advised to approach the chaplain, who's quickly established:

He wore steel-rimmed GI spectacles on a weak and homely face, and he was a man who belonged to the small places of the earth—to little towns with their innocence, their bigotry and their devilish gossip—and he seemed to have brought, intact to the atoll, the smell of drying linen on a March morning and the self-righteous and bitter piety with which he would thank God, at Sunday dinner, for a can of salmon and a bottle of lemonade.

Many of the wondrous features of Cheever's style are on display in this passage. The surprising series that begins with "innocence" and goes on to "bigotry" and "devilish gossip" not only keeps the reader off balance but also seems unaccountably accurate, as does the catachresis "bitter piety." And the complexity of contrasting sentiments is matched by the syntactical sinuousness of that one long sentence.

In his early stories the sentences sounded quite different. They were written under the influence of Hemingway; the grammar is simple, the nouns unadorned, the emotions implied but never analyzed. But when Cheever found his own voice in the late 1930s—as it is heard in his masterful 1950 story "Goodbye, My Brother"—the emotions are so subtle that they are hard to parse and the nature descriptions provide a majestic correlative to the action. Even the point of view in this story is equivocal; perhaps the narrating brother, who so charmingly takes us into his confidence, is the real villain of the piece. Just before the narrator strikes his brother Lawrence, the setting is already foreshadowing the feelings:

That beach is a vast and preternaturally clean and simple landscape. It is like a piece of the moon. The surf had pounded the floor solid, so it was easy walking, and everything left on the sand had been twice changed by the waves. There was the spine of a shell, a broomstick, part of a bottle and part of a brick, both of them milled and broken until they were nearly unrecognizable, and I suppose Lawrence's sad frame of mind—for he kept his head down—went from one broken thing to another.

The use of the word "milled" brings the whole muted passage into crisp focus.

Cheever's fiction is often exuberant, sometimes heady, even when the plot would seem better served by dreariness. Whereas aestheticians from Aristotle on have insisted that figurative language should redouble and underline the thrust of the anecdote, it turns out that exactly the opposite is what often appeals to us in great works of art, a strange and even mystical discrepancy between the natural drift of the story and the contradictory impulses of the metaphors and similes and descriptions. It was the Russian thinker Lev Vygotsky in his 1925 book *The Psychology of Art* who first pointed out that the reason Ivan Bunin's story "Gentle Breath" has a paradoxical impact of lightness and airiness despite its sad plot is that all the details are moving in the opposite direction from the anecdote. Cheever no doubt never heard of Vygotsky but his stories demonstrate persuasively the truth of the Russian's observations about the importance of such tension at the heart of a story.

The exuberance and humor and charm and energy of Cheever's fiction constitute a powerful and heroic incantation to ward off the unrelenting bad luck of his life. As Blake Bailey presents that life in his thorough and brilliantly researched biography, Cheever was born in 1912 in Quincy, Massachusetts, into a *nouveau pauvre* family disgraced forever (according to Cheever's prickly male supremacist notions) by his mother's having opened a gift shop. His father was a drunk and a layabout: Cheever had to wait many years before he could recast his shamed feelings toward his father into his portrait of Lysander, the delightfully whimsical patriarch in the Wapshot books. Cheever's mother never hesitated to tell him that while she was carrying him his father invited an abortionist to dinner; only at the last moment did she decide to go through with the pregnancy.

A poor student, Cheever attended Thayer Academy but was expelled for not studying. He took his revenge in 1930 at age eighteen with one of his first published works, "Expelled," in *The New Republic*, accepted by the young Malcolm Cowley (who would become a lifelong friend and mentor and whose son would marry Cheever's daughter).

Cheever, who was immensely likable, met and befriended many of the leading writers and artists of the day, became quite close to E.E. Cummings, and even had a guilt-ridden affair with the usually heterosexual photographer Walker Evans. Yaddo became his favorite retreat, an important refuge during the Depression, and the director, Elizabeth Ames, invited him back many times. In 1941 Cheever married Mary Winternitz, whose father had been the dean of Yale Medical School and whose grandfather, Thomas A. Watson, had been a coinventor of the telephone. Cheever, working hard to support a wife, began to publish in the "slicks" such as *Harper's Bazaar*, *Collier's*, and *Mademoiselle*. In 1942 he enlisted in the army and tested low-normal on the government IQ test. In 1942 he published his first short-story collection, *The Way Some People Live*, which wasn't very good but may have saved his life since it impressed a major in the army who was also an MGM executive. He withdrew Cheever from his unit, which suffered terrible casualties in Europe in the last months of the war. Cheever was transferred as a writer to the former Paramount studios in Astoria, Queens.

After the war he began his twenty-year struggle to produce his first novel, which would finally take shape as *The Wapshot Chronicle*. In the meanwhile he supported his growing family by writing many, many stories for *The New Yorker*. Although people today revere *The New Yorker*, in the past it was something of a liability; I can remember in the 1950s how dismissive it was to call something a "typical *New Yorker* story," by which people meant something slight, stylish, and vapid.

Although Cheever's life looked from the outside like a string of successes (literary prizes, steady publications, the esteem of his peers), he was tormented by two possibly related problems: alcoholism and homosexuality. He seems to have been genuinely bisexual in that he often had affairs with women outside his marriage, notably with the beautiful actress Hope Lange. But he was also powerfully drawn to men, including the superb novelist Allan Gurganus, who was a student of Cheever's at Iowa. Many of these crushes (like the one on Gurganus) were not reciprocated, which depressed him; those that were consummated upset him even more.

In 1971, Cheever began to teach writing to inmates at the nearby prison of Sing Sing in Ossining. The seemingly preppy WASP author was quickly accepted by the convicts; he became especially friendly with his student Donald Lang, who when he was paroled lived in a room near Cheever's house, went on binges with him, and kept him constant company. Cheever's inner circle thought that Lang had become his lover, if only intermittently.

By 1972, the drinking had taken on such epic proportions that Cheever was writing only one story a year, more or less. In 1975, after a spectacular meltdown while teaching at Boston University, Cheever was persuaded to enter the Smithers Alcoholism Treatment and Training Center in New York City. After a month there he never took another drink and by Good Friday 1976, he had finished his finest achievement, *Falconer*, which landed him on the cover of *Newsweek*. The book is about Farragut, a white, middle-class convict, sentenced to Sing Sing for fratricide, who falls in love with Jody, a Puerto Rican prisoner:

> They met two or three times a week. Jody was the beloved and now and then he stood Farragut up so that Farragut had developed a preternatural sensitivity to the squeak of his lover's basketball sneakers. On some nights his life seemed to hang on the sound.

What was remarkable was that Cheever finally had the sobriety to think through a novel and sustain its unified design. No longer were his pages inspired riffs held together with paper clips and chewing gum; now he'd turned out a shapely novel. Moreover, there was a calm wisdom in this *Falconer*, his masterpiece, and in it he had quietly come to terms with homosexuality.

Cheever's marriage, which had become Strindbergian in its rancor and spleen, never recovered from the violence and disorder of his decades of drinking. Mary, his wife, to be sure, had her own flaws; she talked and acted like a little girl into old age and was anything but forgiving, but she did stick with her husband through his final battle with cancer and alcohol-related illnesses, which led to his death on June 18, 1982. During the last five years of his life Cheever had also come to terms sufficiently with his homosexual impulses to be able to sustain an affair with a student he'd met at the University of Utah.

The vitality and fantasy of Cheever's writing, even when he is at his most serious, stand in complete contrast to the despair and loneliness and boredom of his life. What was it that allowed him to transform all this dullness into art? My own answer may sound trivializing but I would say it was his knack for writing seductively about the world of the senses—its colors and associations, its sexiness and its smells (above all, its smells!), not to mention its suave beauty, at once transitory and eternal in a way that Wallace Stevens understood in that paradoxical line of "Peter Quince at the Clavier": "The body dies; the body's beauty lives."

THE LOVES OF THE FALCON

I met Glenway Wescott in the fall of 1970. Richard Howard and I were spending a weekend with Coburn Britton, the founding editor of *Prose*, a thick, beautifully produced "little" magazine that was publishing reminiscences and meditations by Wescott. "Coby" had an old apple farm in New Jersey where we were staying, not far from Haymeadows, where the whole Wescott clan was living. Glenway's handsome brother Lloyd had married a banking heiress, Barbara Harrison, and they'd bought the property. Lloyd and Barbara were in one house; Glenway was in another with his lover, Monroe Wheeler. Glenway and Lloyd's parents lived in yet another house. There were cooks and farmhands everywhere, though the atmosphere was casual and friendly.

In those days, I was a resentful young man since I was very poor and though I'd written several books I hadn't managed to get any of them published. Richard Howard had already won the Pulitzer Prize for poetry and had translated dozens of the most important modern books in French. Coby was rich from his Cleveland industrial family and in the winter lived in a house on St. Luke's Place in New York City. Although the Wescotts had started out as subsistence-level farmers in Wisconsin, they now lived in luxury, thanks to Barbara's generosity. Glenway was nearly seventy but still tall and handsome and tweedy and celebrated in his own elite world. He was perhaps best known for his novella *The Pilgrim Hawk: A Love Story*, which was sometimes ranked as one of the best American short novels along with William Faulkner's *The Bear*, Katherine Anne Porter's *Noon Wine*, Herman Melville's *Billy Budd*, and Henry James's *The Turn of the Screw*.

When I met him I hadn't yet read anything by him and he struck me as intolerably urbane and amiable, someone who had lived in France for ages and who had dashed off a few books but then fallen into a silence that had already lasted decades and that was broken only by occasional belletristic essays. He seemed most concerned with his social schedule and his activities connected with the National Institute of Arts and Letters (now called the American Academy of Arts and Letters), where he was an officer for years. He entertained foreign writers at his East Side apartment. He might have lectured on topics such as "Whither the Novel?" Everything I loathed. He wasn't a real writer—he was a clubwoman! Moreover, though he'd touched on homosexuality as a theme, he was pretty much in the closet in his published work, I gathered.

A bad first impression, perhaps all the worse because I could see myself giving up writing before I'd even started and substituting committee work for painful hours at my desk, though I supposed you had to publish something before you could retire. He had a light, "fun" manner that seemed very Parisian and *mondain* —and totally repellent. Now, all these years later, I'm a member in good standing on the awards committee at the American Academy, I write belletristic essays such as this one, I've spent sixteen years living in Paris far from my native Ohio, and my own manner is probably as flutey and "frivolous" as Wescott's, even if I'll never be as handsome or have such a mellifluous voice. Or write such a perfect piece of prose as *The Pilgrim Hawk*.

I suppose the main difference between us is that I have dealt with homosexuality openly and at length, for better or for worse—a freedom that was handed to me by the times, rather than one that I seized. And this freedom has made me far more productive than Wescott, as has my eternal scrambling after money: I live from one advance to the next.

In the meanwhile I've read most of Wescott and come to recognize his immense talent, which of course erases all my earlier doubts. A new biography, *Glenway Wescott Personally* by Jerry Rosco (a title that echoes the name of Wescott's essay "Katherine Anne Porter Personally"), sets forth clearly the public triumphs and private sufferings experienced during this long and interesting life. A biography of a "minor" writer such as Wescott is always a labor of love and readers can only be grateful to Rosco for his curiosity and eloquence.

Wescott was born in Wisconsin on a farm in 1901, the older son of an overworked couple. He was sickly and a sissy and had no aptitude for rural chores, though he must have poured a lot of energy into observing the men and women around him, since they would provide the literary capital he would draw on for many years to come in three major books, *The Apple of the Eye*, *The Grandmothers*, and *Goodbye, Wisconsin*. Although he was troubled by his homosexuality, as anyone of his era would have been, he nevertheless had an affair when he was only thirteen with a fifteen-year-old neighbor boy— and the remarkable thing is that it lasted for a while, until Earl discovered girls.

By the time he was fourteen Wescott was publishing stories in the school magazine, *The Megaphone*. His parents were so poor that he was passed around among relatives—and at sixteen he earned a scholarship to the University of Chicago. At first he didn't get along at the big university:

I lived all the way on the West Side. I was small. I was bad tempered. I was homosexual. I was poor. And I had a very bad tongue, if you provoked me. I was not afraid of anybody.

Fortunately he met Yvor Winters, a very young mentor in search of an even younger disciple. Winters, who would later teach for many years at Stanford and influence students such as Thom Gunn, Donald Hall, and Robert Pinsky, took an interest in Wescott and pushed him toward the principles of Imagism. Winters was opposed to Romantic rhetoric and believed in understatement and strict forms; perhaps he usefully curbed some of Wescott's natural exuberance. Wescott always credited Winters with turning him into a poet. Though Winters was completely heterosexual and even a bit homophobic, he was willing to shape the talent of the sixteen-year-old sissy from Wisconsin.

Two years later, Wescott met his life companion, Monroe Wheeler, who was only twenty himself. Wheeler had decided to skip college and had gone to work for a Chicago advertising firm. He was from a middle-class family of bibliophiles in Evanston; when Monroe asked his father for a motorcycle for his eighteenth birthday his father gave him instead a small printing press, a prophetic present since years later in Paris, Monroe would publish beautiful limited editions and still later become the director of publications at the Museum of Modern Art.

Glenway, after working a few weeks at the only conventional job he would ever have, as a shipping clerk in a department store, took off and accompanied Yvor Winters to Santa Fe, where Winters was sent by his parents for his health. Urged on by Winters, Wescott wrote many poems and became friendly with Vachel Lindsay and Marsden Hartley as well as other local writers and artists. He flirted with lots of men and was condemned by some of them for being too "obvious." As he later recalled:

I really was a very heady brew—I was too good looking, too pretty, with a pout like Rimbaud, and very flamboyant. I talked and talked and some people adored me, and others got irritated.

According to Jerry Rosco's biography, "by the end of 1920, Wheeler and Wescott began to form the bond that would produce one of the great relationships of the century." It wasn't particularly sexual but it did promote their shared social and artistic ambitions and it was full of an enduring tenderness and mutual esteem. For a while Wescott lived back in Evanston with the Wheeler family, until Mrs. Wheeler drew him aside and said his presence was an undue economic burden on them. Wescott moved out and became an office boy for *Poetry*, the celebrated little magazine edited by Harriet Monroe. There he met Margaret Anderson and Jane Heap and charmed most of the local literati except Carl Sandburg, who thought Wescott's obvious homosexuality was disgraceful. (Years later even Sandburg came around.)

Wescott and Wheeler spent the summer of 1921 in the Berkshires house of an artistic patron, which had been the birthplace of William Cullen Bryant. There, Wescott wrote the first part of his first novel, *The Apple of the Eye*. When this novel was eventually published in 1924 it proved that he was a regional writer of both great delicacy and strength. The delicacy lay in the language and the descriptive details and even the moral observations. The strength consisted in the unforgettable presentation of characters, particularly women.

The Apple of the Eye, praised by Kenneth Burke and Sinclair Lewis, was an auspicious beginning, although it seemed more a series of accomplished character sketches than a unified narrative. The first third of the novel is dedicated to Bad Hannah, a woman who has a dalliance with a young handsome farmer who gets her pregnant—and then abandons her to marry an heiress. Hannah drifts off to a nearby town, Fond du Lac, and becomes a casual prostitute. When Jule (her ex-lover) and his wife find out what has become of Hannah they give her a farm and invite her to move back among them. Hannah becomes a useful if eccentric nurse and midwife to the local farming families. She is even something of a witch, though a sympathetic one who smokes a pipe and looks after her animals. The unspoken understanding that Jule and his wife come to with Hannah defies most readers' preconceptions about narrow rural prejudices. In fact the novel provides its characters with a generosity of spirit that is completely unexpected and convincing.

In 1921, Wescott tried to make love to a Chicago writer, Kathleen Foster, with a view toward marrying her:

> I took her in my arms and kissed her and—I almost jumped out the window. It was a very extraordinary panic—not disgust but an experience so foreign, the physical sensation so foreign, that it really was the limit.

At least he did not go so far as George Eliot's young husband, John Cross, who actually did leap from their hotel window during their honeymoon in Venice.

After the failure of his attempt at marriage and heterosexuality, Wescott and Wheeler moved to Europe. They became friendly with the Sitwells and the novelist Mary Butts (a follower of the satanic Aleister Crowley and the woman whom the gay composer Virgil Thomson in his tell-nothing memoir pretends to be in love with). As if being tempted to jump out the window while kissing Kathleen Foster were not enough of a sexual trauma, Wescott next contracted Spanish flu and had to have a testicle removed. No wonder years later he hesitated before letting sexologist Alfred Kinsey film him masturbating:

> I couldn't stand my horrid little penis, and then I lost one of my testicles at the time of the writing of my first book, and

so on. And I've got a malformed chest, and I've never wanted to be looked at or paid attention to.

As to his boyish bottom he remarked, "Much ado about nothing. My ado especially." Of course, this self-loathing was a psychological problem, not primarily a physical one, since he was considered by many to be one of the best-looking men of his generation.

His next book was *The Grandmothers*; writing it struck him as "terrifying" since he'd already begun to develop a massive writer's block that could be dynamited out of his path only with more and more effort and at longer and longer intervals. Perhaps it didn't help that Wescott was living in Paris with Wheeler and hobnobbing with such productive writers as Somerset Maugham and Jean Cocteau. Nevertheless he was able to finish this autobiographical novel about his relatives and ancestors and to publish it in 1927. It won the prestigious Harper Prize and earned him the envy and enmity of Ernest Hemingway. Hemingway said to a reporter from the *Herald Tribune* in a Paris bookshop as he picked up a copy of *The Grandmothers*:

Would you like to know what's wrong with this book? In the first place, every sentence was written with the intention of making Glenway Wescott immortal. And in the second place—but what's the use of telling you what's in the second place. You work for a kind of family newspaper and you couldn't print it. Your editor wouldn't let you.

In *The Sun Also Rises*, Wescott had already appeared as a gay man "from New York by way of Chicago..." Like many a macho writer, Hemingway was convinced that he was being out-earned and upstaged by the pansy brigade—in his case a trio of gay writers: Glenway Wescott, Thornton Wilder, and Julian Green.

In *The Grandmothers*, Wescott invented a mild-mannered stand-in for himself named Alwyn Tower, whom he would use several times in later books. The focus, however, is on his parents and grandparents and other Wisconsin relatives. A poignant gay love story between two uncles is set in the Civil War and told in a circular, never very precise fashion. Uncle Hilary is in love with his older brother Leander. Hilary is happy during the war, even during the hardships of the battlefield, because he doesn't have to share Leander with anyone. But when he sees Leander contemplating a portrait of his fiancée, Hilary becomes desperate:

"I wish," he said with great difficulty, "that I'd never been born—your brother. I'd rather—be dead. I don't—count. The war won't—last. You'll go back—to her. What'll I do? I want, I can't—"

Hilary rushes out into the night and soon is missing in action. Leander realizes too late that he has failed to recognize the great love that has come his way. After the war Leander doesn't marry, but becomes a postman and lives alone. Finally he adopts a beautiful, lazy, shiftless nephew named Timothy and pours all his regret and thwarted love onto the boy. Even his pleasure in Timothy leaves him exhausted: "Joy proved its reality by leaving scars on his face, smaller but deeper than those of sorrow."

Wescott's success as a writer continued with the publication in 1928 of an introductory essay and ten short stories called *Goodbye, Wisconsin*. In that collection, he writes in "Adolescence" about a younger boy, Philip, who has a crush on an older, tougher boy, Carl. Of Philip, the narrator says, "He came from the country, and was sensuous and timid." During a Halloween party Philip dresses in women's clothes he finds in an attic. As he sits up in a tree he looks at his flounces and tries to feel his boy's body inside them; he shook himself from head to toe, and decided that wearing women's clothes was like being tucked into a luxurious, portable bed. A whalebone in the old corset hurt him and had to be pushed back into place.

Philip watches his beloved Carl pursuing a girl in a Turkish costume "with boisterous but somber violence." Suddenly Philip is alone with another boy, this one dressed as a soldier who obviously doesn't recognize him. When the soldier tries to kiss him, Philip gives him a kick and flees. He leaves the party and hurries home, afraid that some of the men coming out of bars will attack him if they think he's a woman alone—or if they recognize he's a boy in women's clothes. As he returns to the miserable boardinghouse where he lives, he wishes he had rich parents as Carl does. The landlady calls out, "Who's that?" but Philip, still in his rumpled and torn finery, doesn't answer and hurries upstairs: "She would think that one of her other boarders, the undertaker's assistant or the patent-medicine vendor, was receiving company in the night."

In each of his first three books, all of them about Wisconsin, Wescott frequently returns to the theme of poverty and thwarted desire. Sometimes he writes about women disappointed in love and sometimes about sensitive boys who have yet to figure out their homosexuality, though they are already in the grip of a passion for another, older young man. In a sense the writing itself is in drag—modern psychological studies of gender ambiguity in the guise of regional studies of struggling, impoverished men and women. The reviews of the day did not recognize the gay themes in his work. To be sure, sexuality is fairly muted in all three books. Perhaps the most passion is lavished on the descriptions of nature and the rendering of the hardscrabble lives of his poor farmers. These are certainly lyrical, forceful works of fiction that deserve to be more widely read.

When Wescott and Wheeler moved to Paris in 1928, they were living with the American photographer George Platt Lynes. Though Wescott and Wheeler were devoted lifelong partners, they each began to take up with new lovers. Lynes (one of the most talented photographers of his generation, famous for his pictures of nude men, celebrities, fashion models, and ballet dancers) was first Wescott's lover and then Wheeler's. Theirs was a bohemian milieu in which people often played romantic musical chairs. Even Wescott's handsome brother Lloyd, a famous womanizer, slept at least once with Lynes. In Paris Lynes pursued his affair with Wheeler and simultaneously with the brilliant young Surrealist novelist René Crevel, who seven years later would commit suicide. Author of *Difficult Death*, Crevel was not only the leading Communist among the Surrealists but the only prominent French Surrealist homosexual (André Breton was deeply homophobic). When the International Communist Congress irrationally expelled the Surrealists in the mid-1930s, calling them "pederasts," Crevel killed himself in part because of this double rejection.

One of Wescott's lifelong lovers was the wealthy book collector and perfume manufacturer Jacques Guérin. Later, after World War II, Guérin would become a patron and benefactor of Jean Genet—and Wescott (perhaps out of jealousy) would fail to see Genet's genius. In his journals Wescott writes with a weary philistine sense of superiority, "Jean Genet, a kleptomaniac assassinophilic pornographic writer, is the great celebrity in Paris now." When I interviewed the ancient Jacques Guérin in the 1990s for my biography of Genet, Guérin was still talking about Wescott with ardor and affection.

While in Paris until their return to New York in 1934, Wescott and Wheeler would socialize with many rich and fashionable people, including Pauline Potter, a Paris-born American fashion designer who would eventually marry Philippe de Rothschild and become known as one of the women of her generation with the best taste— surely an elusive distinction but one that has often been repeated. Wescott seemed to have a genuine gift for friendship. Among his many friends he counted Marianne Moore, Katherine Anne Porter, Somerset Maugham, the Russian painter Pavel Tchelitchew, the American poet Charles Henri Ford, and many others less well known. People often treat the gift of friendship as mysterious, yet (as in Wescott's case) it comes down mainly to charm but also to energy and persistence.

Wescott was a talented and persevering letter writer. He remembered birthdays and made a great occasion out of every festivity. He was a confidant who also confided in others (intimacy is not always a two-way street, which egotistical friends don't notice at first but come to resent in the long run). In fact he was fairly indiscreet, but in the beau monde that counts more as a virtue than a vice, while in the scientific world of Kinsey's sex research, Wescott's gossipiness was a bad habit he was forced to shed, at least while he was in Bloomington.

Maugham was a difficult friend because he was always demanding that Wescott write more. Maugham was not only prolific but also a bestseller, though snobs dismissed his work as middlebrow (a category that few people worry about in our day but that once was anathema). When Wescott wrote his masterpiece, *The Pilgrim Hawk*, in 1940, Maugham (perhaps a bit envious) warned him:

You haven't any business writing things like *The Pilgrim Hawk*...You've got to choose right now. You can either be the American Cocteau, or you can be the American Trollope, and what you ought to do is be Trollope.

At the time, of course, Trollope was held in considerably less esteem than he is now and Cocteau was far better known than he is today, though *The Pilgrim Hawk* is a tighter, more closely worked book than even Cocteau's best novels, *Les Enfants Terribles* (sometimes called in English *The Holy Terrors*) and *Thomas l'imposteur*. In any event, Maugham's comment was off the mark since Wescott was always more likely to achieve a Coctellian concision and epigrammatic wisdom than a Trollopian fluency and sociological breadth.

The Pilgrim Hawk is one of the neglected masterpieces of twentieth-century American literature. It was Wescott's first novel set not in the Midwest but in France, though the characters are an American man and woman, her servants (a couple from Morocco), and a visiting Irish couple and their dashing chauffeur. Wescott is no longer writing about poor farmers but about rich idlers just before the Depression who have too much money and too much time on their hands.

It takes place in one long afternoon at a house in a village next to a large landscaped park (in fact based on Barbara Harrison's house in Rambouillet). Alwyn Tower, the first-person narrator based on Wescott, is quite clear about being an observer as sexless as Isherwood's "Herr Issyvoo." He's also a disappointed writer. While thinking about mental and sentimental human hungers, he reflects on

my own undertaking in early manhood to be a literary artist. No one warned me that I really did not have talent enough. Therefore my hope of becoming a very good artist turned bitter, hot and nerve-racking; and it would get worse as I grew older.

The point is that the unsuccessful artist is like the aging falcon, which weakens and loses its eyesight and is no longer able to hunt and dies of starvation and humiliation. Paradoxically, Wescott is taking this self-defeated tone at the very moment he is writing his strongest book.

The distinctive element in this novella is also its occasional flaw—
its "wisdom," all the apothegms that sometimes are unconvincing
or too obvious or downright sententious, though most of the
time they are pithy and as effective as the epigrams in Elizabeth
Bowen's novels. One unconvincing comment is: "Women who have
been spoiled by the many, tormented by one, often have an air of
innocence." That observation is so retrofitted to the specific case
that it seems unsuitable as a generality. And here's a bit of starstruck
Wisconsin sententiousness: "But not even aristocracy can be
expected to give good examples of itself all the time."

When the generalities are convincing, they can have a peculiar
poetic rightness about them; for example, when Wescott writes
about the character of Madeleine Cullen, the owner of the falcon,
an Irish landowner who must keep traveling restlessly to distract
her alcoholic and greedy husband from his drink and food. At
the moment, they are passing through Paris to shop and heading
to Hungary to hunt. The husband, who is both uxorious and
philandering, seems besotted with his wife and horribly jealous of
the bird she's protecting.

And although the falcon, Lucy (named after Sir Walter Scott's
heroine), is a symbol and an emblem and is seen in many different
lights as many different things by the narrator, nevertheless it is
a wonderfully wild and pagan presence throughout the book.
Wescott has done his homework and refers knowledgeably to the
whole vocabulary of falconry: "croaks" (a disease birds get) and
a "haggard" (a falcon that has already hunted on its own before
capture) and "mantling" (standing on one leg and spreading its
wings) and "bating" (suddenly turning upside down) and the bird's
"mute" (shit). In describing the bird he rises to great heights:

I expected her to scream, aik! But the only sound was the
jingling of her bell and the convulsion of her plumage, air
panting through her plumage. The tail feathers and the

flight feathers, shooting out rigidly, threshed against herself and against her mistress from head to foot. Mrs. Cullen, not the least disconcerted, raised her left arm straight up over her head, and stood up and stood quite still, only turning her face away from the flapping and whipping. Her equanimity impressed me as much as her strength.

The poor woman will need both equanimity and strength when her husband becomes violent—but I won't give the story away.

Four years later, Wescott wrote his last real book, *Apartment in Athens*, an anti-Nazi novel published in 1945. The times were so different from ours that Wescott was able to complain that whereas he'd hoped his book would be a best-seller the first edition sold "only" 500,000 copies in its first year! It is a powerful story of an upper- middle-class Greek couple whose apartment is requisitioned by a Nazi officer. He turns the couple into his servants and terrorizes them. When he shows a bit of vulnerability, however, after his two soldier sons are killed in battle and his wife is burned to death, the Greek man forgets himself (his own son has died in battle) and mutters something against Hitler and Mussolini. The German officer has the Greek thrown into prison—and then commits suicide, but stages it in such a way that it will look as if he's been murdered by the Greek couple, whose relatives are known to be in the Resistance.

The plot is melodramatic but no more than the times were. Wescott was in reality too good a writer to be an effective propagandist. Monstrous as his Nazi officer is, he is nevertheless a well-rounded, all-too-human character—we end up understanding him and nearly forgiving him. The only flaw is that the officer's rhetoric sometimes sounds too much like Schopenhauer (minus the pessimism) to be true. He tells the Greek that whereas ordinary mortals want to win and win now, Germans are indifferent to victory: "You naturally are afraid of fate. We are not afraid, because we have identified ourselves with it, we are active in it, we are it."

In 1947, Wescott was elected to what was then called the National Institute of Arts and Letters and began four decades of work for the institution. In this period Wescott and Wheeler and Lynes all passed young lovers around, including a Russian named Yuri of whom Wescott said, "It was like going to bed with sweet butter and toast." E.M. Forster visited Wheeler and Wescott in New York with his married policeman, Bob Buckingham.

Wescott's terror of writing grew with every year—exactly why no one seems to know. Some people suggest that he feared failure. That he'd written himself out. That he was too closeted to tackle his real subject, homosexuality, though in fact he did write in 1938 an entirely successful long short story called "A Visit to Priapus" that he refused to have published till after his death. It's a sad and comic story of someone who hears about an extraordinarily well-endowed man living in a New England village. The narrator goes far out of his way to meet this prodigy—but in fact Priapus, after spending a lifetime servicing straight men as the town queer, doesn't want to be serviced himself and has no use for his huge organ. In this way Wescott was like Forster, who would let *Maurice*, his queer novel, be published only posthumously (Wescott and Isherwood were the literary executors who shepherded it into print).

Perhaps the most interesting and unexpected chapter in Wescott's post-artistic life was his collaboration with Alfred Kinsey, the great sexologist. Wescott, who became a friend (and even occasional sex partner) to the bisexual Kinsey, spent long periods at his research center in Indiana, sorting through the largest pornography collection in the world outside of the Vatican. Kinsey took sexual histories of Wescott and all his friends. Kinsey was even invited to a gay cocktail party in New York for two hundred young men given by one of Wheeler's lovers. Kinsey was certainly one of the most intelligent and least conventional people of his era and Wescott learned to like himself a bit more because of their friendship (and sexual camaraderie).

Over the years, Glenway Wescott wrote some extraordinary literary essays—"mere appreciation," as literary theorists would say, which of course is the best kind of writing about writing and the only kind the general public likes to read. In Wescott's case these essays were intimately tied to his friendships. He wrote on Katherine Anne Porter, on Somerset Maugham, on Thornton Wilder, and on people he admired but knew only casually (Colette, Thomas Mann, and Isak Dinesen). These essays were collected in *Images of Truth* (1962). Although the Colette essay has been largely superceded by Judith Thurman's definitive biography, at the time it introduced many readers (including this one) to the French novelist's superb oeuvre.

Robert Phelps (who had edited Colette's writings in order to piece together an autobiography, *Earthly Paradise*) excerpted Wescott's journals to produce *Continual Lessons: 1937–1955* (his co-editor was Jerry Rosco). The book, as arranged by Wescott, was published only in 1990 after his death. It is full of gossip. Wescott says he is avoiding Thornton Wilder because of his dirty fingernails and his hypocrisy about his homosexuality. As early as 1949, he is expressing guilty despair over having written no fiction since *Apartment in Athens*. Again and again he speculates about the causes of his own silence, which obviously torments him. He is at once complacent and hypercritical of himself:

I haven't any great strength of character even for art's sake; only a certain persistent subtlety. I haven't great inspiration; only a lifetime's know-how, and accumulated subjects.

Susan Sontag declared in a late essay, "Where the Stress Falls," that *The Pilgrim Hawk* belongs among the treasures of twentieth-century American literature, however untypical are its sleek, subtle vocabulary, the density of its attention to character, its fastidious pessimism, and the clipped worldliness of its point of view.

It seems that at one moment, just as the war was beginning, Wescott was able to look back at the expatriate twenties in France, the period he clearly had liked the most, his glory days "before the revolution," and write about it with all the moral seriousness of his Wisconsin forebears and the fluidity and sophistication of his adopted Parisian milieu. He produced many beautiful pages and only one short masterpiece—but a great piece of fiction of any length is a cause for celebration, not regret.

THE LINEAMENTS OF DESIRE

David Hockney took on gay subject matter before almost anyone else—and the amazing thing is that he got away with it. What was it that tranquillized people's objections—the stylized figures, the nearly empty rooms, the tension between abstraction and representation? The clarity of the California light and the straightforward, almost innocent depiction of the body? Or was it that Hockney was showing us a moment of domesticity rather than a lurid fantasy? Just as Proust's lofty, philosophical style, always moving from the particular to the general, made readers accept his outrageous descriptions of cruising, gay promiscuity, gerontophilia, male bordellos and sado-masochism, in the same way Hockney's cool detachment and our sense that he has other, strictly artistic designs on us direct our attention away from all these smooth, bare buttocks.

Hockney took up gay subject matter with his earliest work. *Queer, 1960* is the first gay painting, done while he was twenty-three and still a student at the Royal College of Art. In the same year he executed a series of drawings called collectively *Fuck*, based on obscene graffiti in public places. At the same time he also executed *The Third Love Painting*, which centers around an abstract phallic form and contains the words "When I heard at the close of the day," the title of a poem by Walt Whitman written exactly a hundred years before in the ultra-gay "Calamus" section of *Leaves of Grass*. In this poem, the poet writes, "And when I thought how my dear friend my lover was on his way coming, O then I was happy…" and later, "In the stillness in the autumn moonbeams his face was inclined toward me, / And his arm lay lightly around my breast— and that night I was happy."

In 1960-61, Hockney did a painting about a gay idol, Doll Boy, in which he used Whitman's secret code, "3.18" to stand for "C.R.," the initials of Cliff Richard, who had just come out with his song "Living Doll" in 1959. In a 1961 painting, *The Most Beautiful Boy in the World*, Hockney used a secret code to allude to Peter Crutch, a fellow student he had a crush on. In the same year, he painted *We Two Boys Together Clinging*, which is also the title of another Whitman "Calamus" poem, verses about two boys, both vagabonds, cutting a wide swath through the world in a ribald, anarchic way. Between the two abstracted figures in the painting tentacles of desire are stretched, as if in reference to Whitman's concept of "adhesiveness," the principle of attraction that draws young men together, which Whitman foresaw as the energy that would weld the United States together in the future, "annealed into a Living Union." From the very beginning, literature, homosexual desire, and tributes to friends came together as sources of Hockney's work. He would remain true to these three influences until the present.

To be sure, saying that Hockney was a pioneer of gay subject matter is a bit of an exaggeration. Photographers and artists long before him had shown men together, but their work was usually offered under the counter to rich "amateurs." It is easy to forget that the photographs of naked men who posed in the 1930s and 1940s for the German photographer Herbert List or the American George Platt Lynes were not exhibited until twenty or thirty years after they were shot. Similarly, Cocteau's dirty drawings in the 1930s of sailors were so controversial he never directly acknowledged them. By contrast, Hockney's first show was in a New York gallery and it sold out. Context determines the reception of an artistic enterprise—the same dance staged on Broadway or presented in a gallery will be experienced in entirely different ways, just as the same words, say, that are printed out as poetry or read as an advertising slogan will have a radically different effect. Hockney wasn't painting "feelthy pictures" (nor are his paintings stimulating). He was entering the lists of high culture with all the dailiness of male-male couples or with the appealing insouciance of a sleeping young man's exposed bum. We aren't voyeurs because, somehow, we are the young man's partner. We are looking at him as Hockney must have done, familiarly.

Picasso's companion, the painter Françoise Gilot, once said that when she was first living with Picasso he asked her to undress and sit facing him. For an hour he studied her in a clear-eyed, focused way—a searching, not a veiled, erotic way. After that, though he rendered her dozens of times, she never posed for him again, since he had "understood" her body. We know that Hockney, by contrast, does like to draw from life, and in his etching *Artist and Model, 1973-4* he shows us Picasso (who died on April 8, 1973) in his trademark sailor's shirt studying a youthful, idealized Hockney in the nude. Hockney's work, moreover, is a tribute to all of Picasso's many paintings of the artist and his model (usually a naked woman).

We're not quite sure what Picasso is holding in his hand—is he verifying a sketch of Hockney against the man himself? Hockney is completely naked, except for his glasses, which emphasize his own act of observation, whereas Picasso is almost glowering at his model with satanic concentration. If Picasso, the master draughtsman, was a continuing inspiration for Hockney, Picasso as an innovator was an unsettling challenge, someone who could continually cross back and forth from distortion to realism, from figuration to something near abstraction.

Early in his career Hockney had been impressed by the abstract expressionists' need to emphasize the flatness of the canvas, to abrogate the illusion of perspective. Somewhat like the American painter Larry Rivers at the same time, Hockney in his first works attempted to combine luscious brushwork, beautiful color, and the flat canvas with fairly primitive or half-effaced figuration or numbers or words—a compromise between realism and abstraction. Rivers also painted a startling nude of the gay poet Frank O'Hara in boots a few years before Hockney took up gay subjects. Both Hockney and the bisexual Rivers were attempting to re-establish figurative art after the total domination of abstract expressionism and just before the triumph of Pop Art. All of Hockney's work (like Picasso's) can be read as a dialogue between a fascination with the way the world looks in all its individuality and a more philosophical drive to find general, overarching principles of construction in it (often through pastiche).

This dialectic gave Hockney's work with homosexual themes an unexpected depth—a saving subtext. He had to fit his work into a culture that accepts female nudes as classical but abhors the naked male body, if it is adult and contemporary and not inspired by the religious repertoire nor by classical mythology (neither Christ nor St. Sebastian nor Apollo). The naked adult male is in and of itself transgressive. Think of the scandals in the nineteenth century launched by Frédéric Bazille's naked male swimmers (he had to add swimsuits) or by Thomas Eakins' bathers (he lost his Philadelphia Art School teaching job because of it) or Caillebotte's fore and aft paintings of a man drying himself off or Henri-Edmond Cross's painting of a similar subject. *Baigneur s'essuyant*, which could never be shown at a Salon (though Manet's shocking Olympe of a female prostitute could be exhibited publicly). Renoir's mouthwatering painting of a naked boy seen from behind playing with his cat atop a pillar was never shown during the artist's life. Potentially Hockney was even more daring—he was showing two men together in one early painting, one showering while the other washes his back.

This canvas, *Domestic Scene, Los Angeles 1963*, was painted months before Hockney's first visit to California, a place evoked in his imagination by a telephone, a pot of flowers, a deeply tanned body, and gym socks. Curiously, the bather is standing in something that resembles a giant flower pot as if he, too, were a transportable plant; this illusion of a private and magical space around the bather is dramatized by the curving zone of water, pale and lightly streaked, that seems to be projected like a waterfall out of the ceiling and not out of the overhead faucet. Only his companion's hand is able to invade this magical space.

Hockney had borrowed the pose from *Physique Pictorial*, a California-based gay magazine of the period that printed black-and-white photos of carefully oiled young men in posing straps, gym shorts, or Grecian tunics. In some shots nudity was shown, though never erections. For the times, however, these magazine pictures were considered racy, certainly titillating. Though these magazines sometimes resorted to the alibi of classical Greece or boxing or javelin throwing, they also contained articles pleading for tolerance towards sexual deviation.

Hockney had already "quoted" *Physique Pictorial* in 1962, when he did *Life Painting for a Diploma*. The Royal College didn't want to award him his diploma because he had not done enough work from a live model nor enough art historical study. In this picture he cheekily paired a drawing of a skeleton (which he'd drawn during one of his first courses at the College) with a beefcake pose from the magazine. In a subsequent 1962 work, *Life Painting for Myself*, Hockney pictured his friend Mo McDermott nude—perhaps this was his first recognizable portrait. In another painting of 1962,

Picture Emphasizing Stillness, Hockney shows a naked man and a clothed man unconcerned by the attack of a tiger (the idea, as in Keats' "Ode to a Grecian Urn" was that a menace can never be realized in a static work of art).

No wonder Hockney was attracted to California and its beefcake magazines. In fact the beach communities in California after World War II were the nurseries of modern homosexuality, and it is no accident that Hockney imagined the place before moving there (for just a year the first time). As he later told a French journalist, "I was drawn towards California, which I didn't know…because I sensed the place would excite me. No doubt it had a lot to do with sex." Sex and exoticism, for as he also said, "It's very British to go about to see something unusual and paint it. I'm always excited by the unlikely, never by ordinary things." This predilection is proved by how few English landscapes or cityscapes he has chosen; typically he will paint a room in Morocco or California or the Riviera, almost never one in Belgravia.

During the war millions of sexually segregated young men had been taken far from home, given a bit of money and lots of enforced idleness—and they faced an imminent death that made a mockery of timidity and prudery. It was a now-or-never atmosphere and many youngsters in uniform followed their instincts, straight as well as gay. After the war many of these newly liberated gay servicemen settled in California precisely because it was far from their families in the Midwest or on the East Coast or the South. They chose to live in beach communities such as Santa Monica, Catalina and Santa Barbara dedicated to hedonism, the body and the cultivation of the self.

Hockney, as we have seen, had already daydreamed about this world of sunlight and pleasure, so reminiscent of Matisse's Nice with its palms, bathers, simple forms, striped awnings, bright colors and patterns on patterns. Hockney was no doubt equally attracted to the strange fact that during the war Los Angeles, thanks to the arrival of so many distinguished European exiles, had become the cultural capital of the world, a legacy it was still living off. In this one city could be found Thomas Mann, Bertolt Brecht, Igor Stravinsky, Aldous Huxley, Arnold Schoenberg...

One of the wartime exiles was Christopher Isherwood, the great English novelist (*The Berlin Stories*) who had been flirting with gay subject matter for years but at last dealt with it explicitly in one of the founding texts of the modern gay movement, the novel *A Single Man* (1964). When Hockney arrived in Los Angeles in January 1964 he sought Isherwood out; Hockney had a letter of introduction from Stephen Spender. Eventually, Hockney would draw all three members of this famous British triumvirate (W.H. Auden, Stephen Spender, and Isherwood). Hockney and Isherwood were the two most "out" of this group. As Isherwood exclaimed at the time, "Oh David, we've so much in common; we love California, we love American boys, and we're both from the north of England." To Isherwood their shared geographical origin outweighed the fact that Hockney was from the working class and Isherwood was a member of the gentry.

Isherwood and his young California lover, the artist Don Bachardy, eventually became the subjects of one of Hockney's best known paintings. Hockney worked for six months in 1968 on a double portrait in which Isherwood is shown looking anxiously at Bachardy, whereas Bachardy is pictured looking out at the painter. Although there were strains in the relationship (Bachardy was much of the time in London, doing commissions as an illustrator and portrait painter and Hockney had to work from photographs), nevertheless Hockney was intent on portraying the two men not just as friends but as lovers. Bachardy's full-frontal curiosity about the world and Isherwood's worried concern about his lover capture the complex dynamics of this relationship. It is a relationship as intimate and as edgy as the double portrait of Los Angeles art collectors Fred and Marcia Weisman, painted the same year, or the eerie portrait of 1969, Henry Geldzahler and Christopher Scott, or the 1970-71 portrait of the British fashion designer Ossie Clark and his wife the fabric designer Celia Birtwell, and their white cat, Percy. Hockney's strategy of alternating gay couples with straight couples served to "normalize" the male-male relationships and place them in a context of ordinariness and intimacy. No one else so well known was doing such gay "activist" painting.

In every couple, there is a disturbing element. Ossie Clark and Celia (whose marriage was short-lived) occupy separate shadowy spaces, backlit and divided by a wide, sunny balcony. Both partners seem more interested in the observer than in each other. His body language is relaxed but his facial expression is sullen; he's barefoot and smoking, a self-conscious study in ease, whereas she is posed in a formal dress, her hair and face rendered with all the grace of an Ingres. Geldzahler, a curator of the Metropolitan Museum, is seated imposingly in shirtsleeves, whereas his younger, thinner boyfriend, Christopher, carries himself like an older man and is buttoned up in a raincoat as if he is just stepping into the room. Hockney has said that someone once told him that his double portraits are like Annunciations: "There is always somebody who looks permanent and somebody who's kind of visiting." In the picture of the Weismans, Fred seems to have just returned from the office whereas Marcia is in a robe. They stand stiffly at right angles to each other, her stature unnaturally tall, her teeth and height an echo of the totem pole to the right, his pharaonic pose as stark as those of the modern sculptures by Henry Moore and William Turnbull. Man and wife are placed in the framework of a different doorway. The mood and emotion of each double portrait is expressed not so much by the faces as by the overall composition. In every case, a comparison of the finished painting with the photos on which it is based points up how the real-life clutter has been simplified into an imagined space of just a few, often carefully balanced objects. This simplification (in the Isherwood-Bachardy portrait two piles of matching books, a corncob, and a bowl of fruit) makes the paintings look timeless, whereas the photos look definitely as if they were of a particular and long-gone era.

That Isherwood was a writer—and one who had lived through the first, German gay liberation movement of the 1920s in Berlin and the new movement that was emerging in the 1960s in the States—was crucial to Hockney's interest in him. In fact Hockney has said that Isherwood was the first writer he truly admired whom he came to know as a friend. Literature—and especially queer literature—has always played a key role in Hockney's work. For instance, one of his projects in the 1960s was a series of fourteen etchings to accompany poems by Constantine Cavafy, the early twentieth-century Greek poet from Alexandria. At that time Cavafy had recently been translated into English by Rae Dalven (and into French by Marguerite Yourcenar), had appeared in E.M. Forster's history and guidebook, *Alexandria*, and figured as a character in Lawrence Durrell's highly popular *The Alexandria Quartet*. The Dalven translation was introduced in enthusiastic terms by Auden, though Hockney ended up using new translations done by Stephen Spender and by Nikos Stangos, Hockney's friend and editor at Thames and Hudson.

Cavafy had written two kinds of poems—historical and modern—and the modern verses were almost entirely dedicated to the fugitive and sometimes doomed love between various pairs of young men. Often they are from good families but have been rejected by their parents. Their lust is described as "tormented" or "unhealthy" or "perverse," but the reader can't help but think that Cavafy admires their powerful sensuality as well as the dark glamour of their ephemeral unions. The admiration is even more marked in Hockney's etchings, which parallel but do not illustrate the poems.

In order to get a feel for the world of the poems, Hockney astutely traveled not to modern Alexandria (which no longer resembled the city Cavafy had known) but to Beirut. He even did a portrait of Cavafy that included a contemporary car, for historical recreation was never his goal. As Marco Livingstone puts it in his perceptive critical book, *David Hockney*: "Only a small number of the Cavafy etchings...depict a particular place or scene as described in the poem. The prints demand, instead, to be appreciated as a group of recollections or visions which in their totality provide an experience similar to that suggested by the poems. This is attested to by the fact that Hockney did not have the poems by his side while he was working and did not conceive of each image as an illustration of a particular poem; the reverse is, in fact, the case, for instead of choosing the poems first, he and Nikos Stangos assigned poems to the etchings only after the prints were done...The Cavafy prints are not literal depictions of the subject-matter of each poem but a visual equivalent to the mood and theme of all Cavafy's homo-erotic poetry, just as the later Grimm etchings are evocations of a particular world rather than illustrations of events described in the narrative." Hockney has not only illustrated Grimm's Fairytales but also Wallace Stevens' long poem, "The Man with the Blue Guitar," which in turn was inspired by Picasso's Blue Period painting.

In the summer of 1966, Hockney was teaching a drawing course at the University of California at Santa Cruz, where he met a seventeen-year-old student, Peter Schlesinger. They soon became lovers—and Peter became Hockney's muse. As Schlesinger put it, "On the first day of class the professor walked in—he was a bleached blond; wearing a tomato-red suit, a green-and-white polka-dot tie with a matching hat, and round black cartoon glasses; and speaking with a Yorkshire accent. At the time, David Hockney was only beginning to become established in England, and I had never heard of him."

For Hockney the memory was just as striking: "It was incredible to meet in California a young, very sexy, attractive boy who was also curious and intelligent. In California you can meet amusing and intelligent people, but generally they're not the sexy boy of your fantasy as well. To me this was incredible; it was more real. The fantasy part disappeared because it was the real person you could talk to."

Peter quickly became Hockney's favorite model and the line drawings Hockney made of him, the first he did after the Cavafy pictures, reveal a new suppleness and elegance of line—as well as a reduction of marks on the paper. Hockney has always returned to the same subjects again and again—his parents, his friend Mo, the various writers he has known, Celia Birtwell, Ossie Clark, Henry Geldzahler, his dealer Nick Wilder, George Lawson and his ballet dancer lover Wayne Sleep. In fact he never did commissions in the first two decades of his career and when he did undertake one (*Sir David Webster, 1971*) he considered it something like an artistic experiment—and to be sure Sir David, the retiring General Administrator of the Royal Opera House, was a wonderful old camp, very much part of the world in which Hockney moved. (I can remember that once when someone at a party said that a pretty rent boy had left in a huff, Sir David remarked to me, "A huff? Hired, no doubt".)

By the same token Hockney rarely did self-portraits in those early years, as if he, too, were a stranger. One of his few self-portraits is a bit of legerdemain. At his London studio in 1977, he was working simultaneously on *Self-Portrait with Blue Guitar*, which he included in an unfinished state behind a picture of a sleeping young man; the finished work is, paradoxically, called *Model with Unfinished Self-Portrait*. The model and the furniture and objects in the foreground are all presented in a three-dimensional, realistic fashion whereas Hockney in the background at first looks as if he is behind the model but in the same space until we notice that the table and chairs near him are schematic—"unfinished."

Curiously, the model is based not on one but two people. Hockney's lover Peter Schlesinger had left him in 1973 and by 1974 Hockney had taken up with another young man, Gregory Evans.

In the 1977 *Model with Unfinished Self-Portrait*, Gregory started out posing but the finished face was based on Peter, who happened to be visiting while Gregory had to absent himself. Heterosexuals, with their strange values, always have a hard time understanding how gay relationships survive even a messy break-up, but this curious hybrid portrait of the "Model" attests to the role of the Lover that sometimes assumes more importance than the individual who happens to be filling the role for the moment. This doubleness of individual and role links up with Erwin Panofsky's classic definition of a portrait:

> A portrait aims by definition at two essentials…on the one hand it seeks to bring out whatever it is in which the sitter differs from the rest of humanity and would even differ from himself were he portrayed at a different moment or in a different situation; and this is what distinguishes a portrait from an "ideal" figure or "type." On the other hand it seeks to bring out whatever the sitter has in common with the rest of humanity and what remains in him regardless of place and time; and this is what distinguishes a portrait from a figure forming part of a genre painting or narrative.

Peter Schlesinger has left us a photographic record of many of the people Hockney painted. Whereas the camera snaps people moving about in their lives and everything happens under the sign of the arbitrary, Hockney in his paintings banishes the confusion, poses his sitters, chooses the revealing pose and emblematic objects that are at once symbolic and mysterious. Photos are anecdotal; paintings are, at least in Hockney's case, as hieratic as official portraits though now the artist and not the sitter controls the image. And, as Hockney has remarked, "I can often tell when drawings are done from photographs, because you can tell what they miss out, what the camera misses out: usually weight and volume, there's a flatness to them."

Hockney's portraits have been painted during different periods in his life. From 1968 and for the next few years he painted friends and lovers and relatives just under life size and in pictures that gave good likenesses of his subjects. Hockney's own presence is often implied, since the lines of perspective converge to suggest the artist's point of view. In his next period, he revolted against portraiture and naturalism in favor of set designs for operas and ballets and of cubistic investigations of space. When he returned to the figure, as in *Model with Unfinished Self-Portrait*, he was exploring a tricky *jeu d'esprit* that contrasted a "direct" rendering of a model with a painting within a painting of himself. In the early 1980s, he began to do composite Polaroid portraits that were intended to give the multiple perspectives that Braque and Picasso had achieved in their analytical Cubist period. These Polaroid photos inspired him, even in his drawings, to put Cubistic heads on simply rendered bodies.

From the early 1980s until the present, Hockney has been engaged by several new technologies—Xerox prints, photo collage, and the use of the camera lucida being the most significant. The camera lucida is essentially an early form of the photographic camera. An image is refracted through a lens and artists, including the incomparable Ingres, have long used it to draw people quickly and with precision. Hockney began to experiment with camera lucida portraits in 1999. Even when he abandoned the procedure a year later, he retained an interest in detail and quirkiness that it had made him aware of. No matter how strange the results of his various experiments with technologies may appear, they are all governed by a quasi-scientific urge towards realism, with answers to the all-important question, "How do we see?" The static nature of the traditional portrait he wants to forego in favor of canvases that emphasize movement—the movement of the eye as it dollies in to take possession of a room or a face or a landscape, and the movement of the body as, for instance, a young man crosses and recrosses his legs impatiently while posing. Chinese pen and ink drawing techniques, a new return to watercolor (a technique that is unforgiving of mistakes and permits no pentimenti), a shift in predominating color toward a glowing Van Gogh palette—all these technical variations have prompted Hockney into new bursts of activity.

Most innovations in art come from either a scientific interest in how the world really looks or from a rediscovery of the vision and technique of an artist of the past. Art is inspired either by nature or by previous art. Hockney relies on both sources. Picasso has been the major artistic influence of his career, though someone as cultured as Hockney can submit to the attraction of painters as diverse as Hokusai and Matisse, Lucien Freud and Fragonard. His scientific explorations of multiple perspectives, movement, and true likeness (as made possible by the camera lucida) have given him new imagery and an increased exuberance. He is a painter driven by opposing interests in the particular and the abstract, in tradition, and science—and he has enlisted all his observations in the service of his terribly human portraits of his parents, his lovers and his friends, the people for whom he has most powerfully felt the pull of adhesiveness. As he has remarked, "I'm quite convinced painting can't disappear because there's nothing to replace it. The photograph isn't good enough. It's not real enough."

THE CONSOLATIONS OF ART

No matter how strange Proust's life might have been, it has been subsumed, as he hoped, into the radiant vision of it that he presented in his writing. Nevertheless, the intensely intimate, if not always personal, quality of Proust's novel makes him more and more popular in this age of memoirs. Whereas other modernists—Stein, Joyce, Pound—rejected confession in favor of formal experiment, Proust was a literary Cyclops, if that means he was a creature with a single, great *I* at the center of his consciousness. No matter that the first-person narrator is only occasionally the literal Marcel Proust. Every page of Proust is the transcript of a mind thinking. Not the pell-mell stream of consciousness of a Molly Bloom or a Stephen Dedalus, each a dramatic character with a unique vocabulary and an individuating range of preoccupations, but rather the fully orchestrated, ceaseless, and disciplined ruminations of one mind, one voice, the sovereign intellect.

Proust may be more available to readers today than in the past because, as his life recedes in time, and the history of his period goes out of focus, he is read more as a fabulist than a chronicler, as a maker of myths rather than the valedictorian of the *Belle Epoch*. Under this new dispensation, Proust emerges as the supreme symphonist of the spirit. We no longer measure his accounts against a reality we know. Instead we read his fables of caste and lust, of family virtue and social vice, of the depredations of jealousy and the consolations of art not as reports, but as fairy tales. He is our Scheherazade.

Of course, Proust is also popular because he wrote about glamour, rich people, nobles, artists. And he wrote about love. It doesn't seem to matter that he came to despise love, that he exploded it, reduced it to its shabbiest, most mechanical, even hydraulic terms. By which I mean he not only demystified love, he also dehumanized it, turning it into something merely Pavlovian. The love Swann feels for Odette is in no way a tribute to her charms or her soul. In fact, Swann knows perfectly well that her charms are fading and that her soul is banal.

Modern readers are responsive to Proust's tireless and brilliant analyses of love because we too no longer take love for granted. Readers today are always making the personal public, the intimate political, the instinctual philosophical. Proust may have attacked love, but he did know a lot about it. Like us, he took nothing for granted. He was not on smug, cozy terms with his own experience. We read Proust because he knows so much about the links between childhood anguish and adult passion. We read Proust because, despite his intelligence, he holds reasoned evaluations in contempt, and understands that only the gnarled knowledge that suffering brings us is of any real use. We read Proust because he knows that in the terminal stage of passion we no longer love the beloved. The object of our love has been overshadowed by love itself. Proust writes: " . . . and this malady, which Swann's love had become, had so proliferated, was so closely interwoven with all his habits, with all his actions, with his thoughts, his health, his sleep, his life, even with what he hoped for after his death, was so utterly inseparable from him, that it would have been impossible to eradicate it without almost entirely destroying him." As surgeons say: his love was no longer operable. Proust may be telling us that love is a chimera, a projection of rich fantasies onto an indifferent, certainly mysterious surface. But nevertheless, those fantasies are undeniably beautiful, intimations of paradise, the artificial paradise of art.

I doubt whether many readers could ever be content with Proust's rejection of rustling, wounded life, in favor of frozen, immobile art. But his powerful vision of impermanence certainly does speak to us. The rise and fall of individual loves on the small scale, and of entire social classes on the grand, the constant revolution of sentiments and status, is a subject Proust rehearsed and we've realized. Proust is the first contemporary writer of the twentieth century, for he was the first to describe the permanent instability of our times.

THE PANORAMA OF
FORD MADOX FORD

Ford Madox Ford was a man full of contradictions. His name sounded thoroughly English and he considered himself to be the last Tory; during World War I he said that he never felt so calm as when he wore the King's uniform. In fact, however, his father was a German émigré, Francis Hueffer, and Ford himself was known as Ford Madox Hueffer until he changed his name to Ford Madox Ford by deed poll on June 4, 1919 as a way of downplaying his German origins. He was obsessed with ideas of what gentlemen do and do not do and he sometimes claimed that he was descended from German barons, but in fact his Münster family members were (and still are) publishers and printers.

He was an inveterate liar—or rather what the French call a *mythomane*, which suggests someone who exaggerates for the love of the legend and not for any direct personal gain. Or perhaps he "lied" only because he wrote so fast that he couldn't recall what he'd already said about someone or an event. His politics were confusing. He wrote of "the true Toryism which is Socialism," he opposed liberal democracy because it promoted plutocracy, and he had a sentimental, literary attachment to feudalism.

In many ways he can be seen artistically as the last and greatest heir to Henry James, who was a friend. Like James, he often dictated all or part of his novels. He loved to play with point of view and the underlying motives of his narrator. His plots, like those of James, can sound melodramatic when summarized but in the actual telling they become so gauzy with subtlety that at moments the reader isn't sure what exactly is going on. His characters, like James's, are obsessed with jousting for position and often use sexual allure to gain the advantage, but they are just as likely to throw over everything out of excessive idealism.

The international theme, which fascinated James for the first half of his career, was also of great interest to Ford. After all, the narrator of Ford's best novel, *The Good Soldier*, is an American who uses his American origins as an explanation of his not-quite-believable naiveté as he interacts with the wily English. There is a lot of dialogue in the fiction of both James and Ford and sometimes there are tense dramatic exchanges, full of sudden reversals, that sound scripted for the theater. One of Ford's deepest regrets was that neither Conrad nor James, the two writers he most admired, had much respect for his work.

But if Ford is at the end of one tradition, the Jamesian, he is also at the beginning of another. As a poet he was an "imagist," which meant that he often relied on free verse and direct sensory impressions presented in brief bursts, haiku-like, without interpretation. In prose he said he was an "impressionist," which meant several things to Ford, though he and Joseph Conrad, who worked out their ideas together, believed that fiction is primarily a visual art and that the writer should be more concerned with the vividness of his remembered or invented images than with facts. Ford wrote:

Impressionism exists to render those queer effects of real life that are like so many views seen through bright glass— through glass so bright that whilst you perceive through it a landscape or a backyard, you are aware that, on its surface, it reflects a face of a person behind you.

For Ford experience was rarely ordered or hierarchical. It was all a jumble and the function of literature was to reproduce that confusion, though in a fashion that was clear and intentional, never random. Simultaneity was one of his artistic strategies, which is most clearly seen in his novel *Parade's End*.

Ford could be airily dismissive of factual accuracy, which he considered "pedantic," but he remained scrupulously faithful to recording his exact sense memories. His inaccuracies got him into trouble with the literal-minded, especially since he wrote several different versions of the same events in his various memoirs. As he said in the introduction to his first volume of reminiscences, *Ancient Lights*: "This book, in short, is full of inaccuracies as to facts, but its accuracy as to impressions is absolute." Further on he adds: "I don't really deal in facts, I have for facts a most profound contempt."

He wrote easily, sometimes fatally so, and he turned out more than eighty books, including a mammoth *March of Literature* late in life. He wrote book-length studies of Henry James, Conrad, Rossetti, the Pre-Raphaelite Brotherhood, his grandfather the painter Ford Madox Brown, and Hans Holbein, two books about New York, literary reminiscences (including *It Was the Nightingale*, about Paris in the 1920s), a suffragette pamphlet in 1915 (*Monstrous Regiment of Women*), books about Provence, books about London, books about the English character, two World War I (fairly mild) propaganda attacks on the German character, collections of poetry, literary critical essays, anthologies he edited—and of course his great and not-so-great novels.

Ford thought of himself as an experimentalist, and as an editor he championed the avant-garde, though he always feared he was older than most of his modernist friends and was being outstripped by them. In the 1920s in Paris, he founded *the transatlantic review*, which published Ezra Pound, T.S. Eliot, James Joyce, E.E. Cummings, Jean Rhys (his lover for a while), Ernest Hemingway (who worked as his assistant editor), Gertrude Stein, Basil Bunting, and many others—so many Americans that he later claimed that more than fifty percent of his contributors were from the Midwest or West (including Pound, Stein, Eliot, and Hemingway). He published James Joyce, who, Ford said, made "little jokes, told simple stories and talked about his work very enlighteningly." Throughout his career Ford was so generous to other writers that Pound remarked that when someone else wrote a good book in London there was only one person, Ford, who was genuinely happy about it, "one man with a passion for good writing."

Early on in Pound's career, before World War I, Ford had played a decisive part. Ford was living in a village in Germany and Pound came to visit with his first real book of poems, *Canzoni*. Pound was twenty-five and arrived in Giessen wearing a green shirt with glass buttons. Ford was thirty-eight. The older man couldn't bear the artificiality and pretentiousness of Pound's poetic diction. As Hugh Kenner puts it in *The Pound Era*:

The summer was the hottest since 1453. And into these quarters marched jocund Ezra Pound, tendering his new book that chaunted of "sprays [to rhyme with 'praise' and 'rays'] of eglantine above clear waters," and employed such diction as "hight the microcline." Ford saw that it would not do. The Incense, the Angels, elicited an ultimate kinesthetic demonstration. By way of emphasizing their hopelessness he threw headlong his considerable frame and rolled on the floor. "That roll," Pound would one day assert, "saved me three years."

Ford fervently believed—and persuaded Pound—that a writer should write "nothing, *nothing*, that you couldn't in some circumstance, in the stress of some emotion, *actually say.*" Indeed Ford's prose, more than that of any other writer of his period, sounds spoken. As he said in 1938 about his much earlier collaboration with Conrad, he tried to evolve for himself "a vernacular of an extreme quietness that would suggest someone of some refinement talking in a low voice near the ear of someone else he liked a good deal." This could just as easily be a Jamesian precept and in our own day Colm Tóibín (especially in *The Master* and *Brooklyn*) seems to be subscribing to this hypnotic practice.

Ford was born in 1873 in Merton, Surrey, now part of London. His German-born but fiercely pro-British father, the music critic for the *Times*, died when Ford was just fifteen years old. The boy went to live with his maternal grandfather, Ford Madox Brown. When he was eighteen he published his first book, *The Brown Owl*, a fairy tale for children; when the very shy Ford was introduced to Thomas Hardy, the great, much older writer thought it must be a nature book, questioned the musicality of the title, and reduced Ford to stammering silence.

The next year Ford converted to Catholicism to please his German relatives, though he seems to have been interested in the church more as a force for order than as an invitation to religious ardor. By 1898 Ford was married to Elsie Martindale, a childhood sweetheart, and was collaborating with Joseph Conrad, with whom he co-authored three novels, *The Inheritors*, *Romance*, and *The Nature of a Crime*. In letters to friends Conrad could be catty about the much younger Ford, but Conrad—who was always broke, often blocked, and terrified of missing serialization deadlines—needed the ever fluent Ford. Not many novelists before Conrad and Ford had collaborated (one thinks of the Goncourt Brothers and Dickens and Wilkie Collins, but few other pairs of literary authors come to mind), and indeed their work together produced nothing memorable beyond their theorizing about the novel, though each of them did extraordinary independent work during their years of collaboration.

Conrad wrote, among other things, *Nostromo* and Ford wrote a trilogy of historical novels about Henry VIII and Katherine Howard, *The Fifth Queen*, *Privy Seal*, and *The Fifth Queen Crowned*. Conrad praised him for leading the historical novel to its apotheosis, but the trilogy suffers from the usual Monty Python–sounding "period" dialogue: "Ignoble, ignoble, to twit a man with that Eton villainy," or "Oh moody and suspicious artificer. *Afflavit deus!* The wind hath blown dead against Calais shore this ten days." Nevertheless the trilogy is often counted as one of Ford's (few) enduring works.

Although Ford was physically awkward and wheezed and was obese and looked like a seal with his limp blond hair and mustache and liquid eyes, he was a successful womanizer and moved from Elsie to her sister to Violet Hunt, an ex-lover of H.G. Wells, and on to half a dozen other women, and each time he was convinced he was in love. Elsie, his first and only wife, refused to divorce him; if she had done so, Ford would surely have married at least two of his subsequent loves. For the most part his women were writers, often of note. He was usually nearly penniless and living on the cheap in falling-down cottages in the English countryside, and once he even declared bankruptcy. *The Good Soldier* went into a second printing but earned only £67. Nevertheless he traveled extensively, to America and to his beloved Provence in particular, and appeared to be cheerfully bohemian in his values.

In 1915 he wrote *The Good Soldier*. Although in the same year he published two books of war propaganda, *The Good Soldier*, despite its title, is distinctly about the privileged pre-war world of rootless invalids, real or imaginary, visiting Continental spas and entering into dangerous amorous intrigues. A case can be made that Ford was dramatizing in this novel if not the events at least the tensions underlying his own messy love life. The plot undergoes so many surprising reversals that halfway through the reader can't imagine what possibly could come next—and is he or she surprised!

Ford had a very difficult war. He was forty-one when he volunteered in July 1915 and not in good shape. He was under fire for ten days during the Battle of the Somme and was so traumatized that he lost his memory for a long period—an infirmity he ascribes to his principal character, Christopher Tietjens, in his tetralogy about the war, *Parade's End*, written in the 1920s. Even during the war Ford was very cynical about how it would be perceived afterward. As he said to Wyndham Lewis:

One month after it's ended, it will be forgotten. Everybody will want to forget it—it will be bad form to mention it. Within a year disbanded "heroes" will be selling matches in the gutter.

When Ford recovered he moved to France, alternating between Provence and Paris, where he edited *the transatlantic review*. Curiously enough Ford ended his long and restless life as writer-and-critic-in-residence at the tiny Olivet College in Michigan, where he organized the first writers' conferences ever held anywhere. He must have liked the admiration of undergrads, since as Stella Bowen, one of his mistresses, said, he needed "more reassurance than anyone I have ever met. That was one reason why it was so necessary for him to surround himself with disciples." He had intense friendships with older and younger men, all of a literary sort. He died in 1939 (at Deauville in France) and was thus spared the second Great War.

Although Ford wrote some excellent, rather prosy poetry, his heart was given over to fiction. Even in praising Pound's great

Cathay poems, Ford wrote words that only a novelist could have penned: "Beauty...is the most valuable thing in life; but the power to express emotion so that it shall communicate itself intact and exactly is almost more valuable."

Max Saunders, Ford's splendid biographer (*Ford Madox Ford: A Dual Life* in two volumes), is one of the editors of a new four-volume edition of *Parade's End*. The first (rather expensive) volume, *Some Do Not...*, has now appeared. It comes with Saunders's very useful introduction and copious notes giving variants as well as explanations of now obscure references. Saunders has also reconstructed Ford's dramatic original ending. The second volume has also appeared, edited by Joseph Wiesenfarth. The final two volumes will be edited by two other editors.

Published in four parts between 1924 and 1928, *Parade's End* leads its bumbling Tory of a hero, Christopher Tietjens, into the war—and presents a parallel struggle between him and his beautiful, rich, aristocratic bitch of a wife, Sylvia. She may well be one of the most monstrous women in fiction. She tries to subvert Christopher at every point, even on the battlefield with his commanding officer. When an American woman cuts down the centuries-old tree on her husband's estate, she condones it; Groby Great Tree has long symbolized the strength of rural England. She beats a pet dog to death. She cheats on Christopher constantly (his son and heir is another man's child), yet she is fiercely jealous of Christopher's (entirely pure and innocent) love for a penniless girl, Valentine Wannop, and does everything to ridicule and undermine it. Sylvia even tries, unsuccessfully, to convince Christopher's brother Mark that Christopher is a cad and should have his allowance cut off.

There is nothing Sylvia will not do to humiliate her long-suffering, virtuous husband. Since he does not believe in divorce, he is powerless against her. In any event his ideas about what an English gentleman will and will not do prevent him from striking back. I suppose today we'd say she is a sadist and he a masochist, though such terms flatten out the complex moral subtlety of these characters. Sylvia has contempt and respect for her husband's unassailable goodness in almost equal measure.

Rather than narrating long sweeps of history (as Flaubert does in *Sentimental Education*) through short scenes, one after another in chronological order, Ford sets up shop in a key moment and thoroughly explores it (somewhat as Edward St. Aubyn more recently does in his dark, fascinating trilogy, *Some Hope*). Then months or years go by and another crucial moment is presented in slow motion. In *Some Do Not...*, several years pass between Part I and Part II, for instance. The slowness of the storytelling gives Ford room for his famous impressionism. He has the space for giving Tietjens's thoughts, for rendering bits and pieces of overheard dialogue, for describing the scene (a perfectly appointed Edwardian train compartment in the opening pages; later, a sumptuous English breakfast interrupted by the appearance of the mad host; still later, a ride through the countryside all night long through a pea-soup fog).

This fog-bound night is one of the most striking moments in the whole book and the one scene I remembered thirty years after an initial reading. Madly in love with Valentine and yet scientifically observant of the light effects produced by the silvery fog, Tietjens goes through a night at once ecstatic and calm. Although nearly medieval in his devotion to Valentine, Tietjens is also a lightning calculator and a repository of so much knowledge, trivial and grand, that he spends his off hours mentally correcting the Encyclopedia Britannica.

One of Ford's best friends, Arthur Marwood, had this same breadth of knowledge. He was a descendant of a king and the first cousin of Lewis Carroll. Ford considered Marwood to be at once his double and his opposite, and as the embodiment of a type, "the heavy Yorkshire squire with his dark hair startlingly silver in places, his keen blue eyes, his florid complexion, his immense, expressive hands and his great shapelessness." After Marwood died an early death from tuberculosis, Ford based many of his aristocratic characters on him, especially Tietjens. As Max Saunders summarizes, Marwood's "traits can be glimpsed in characters from most of Ford's novels after 1905." These include, among others, Henry VIII in The Fifth Queen trilogy; Dudley Leicester in *A Call*; Mr. Luscombe in *The Simple Life Limited*; both the Duke of Kintyre and Lord Aldington in *The New Humpty-Dumpty*; Ashburnham in *The Good Soldier*; George Heimann in *The Marsden Case*; and Hugh Monckton in *The Rash Act* and *Henry for Hugh*. Of course Tietjens is the most extended portrait. In real life Ford even began to impersonate many of Marwood's peculiarities. The whole of *Parade's End* can be read as an homage to this larger-than-life quixotic figure and to Ford's obsession with him.

In the last volume of the tetralogy, *The Last Post*, the entire action takes place in just two days. Tietjens's brother Mark is dying and is nearly speechless, either from a stroke or from choice. The war is over and the family is living in reduced circumstances since Christopher Tietjens has decided not to draw on his family's money. Mark is married to a Frenchwoman; Christopher is living "in sin" with his beloved Valentine and she is very pregnant, about to give birth to their child. He is earning a living selling old furniture; his partner is an American who refuses to pay Christopher his due. Groby, the family estate, has been rented out to an insufferable American woman who claims to be descended from Louis XIV's mistress (and later wife), Madame de Maintenon.

Almost as in a Cubist painting our final notion of Tietjens is built up through different points of view. We are privy to Valentine's thoughts and to Mark's and to those of Mark's wife and of Sylvia, who has had a change of heart and becomes a more benign presence. Valentine is afraid of losing her baby at the last moment or of having its life cursed by Sylvia's presence (Valentine sees her as a huge, beautiful statue). The Americans come off very badly—

grasping and dishonest and besotted with European titles and old things they're not willing to pay for.

Mark is almost a caricature of the English gentleman—more rigid and considerably less intelligent than Christopher but just as decent. In an earlier volume Sylvia has started the rumor on the battlefield that Christopher wants to be Christlike—an idea that shocks and appalls his general. As Mark thinks:

That had seemed horrible to the general, but Mark did not see that it was horrible, *per se*...He doubted, however, whether Christ would have refused to manage Groby had it been his job. Christ was a sort of an Englishman and Englishmen did not as a rule refuse to do their jobs...

A few pages later Mark is identified with the ultimate English gentleman's credo:

Mark's horror came from the fact that Christopher proposed to eschew comfort. An Englishman's duty is to secure for himself for ever, reasonable clothing, a clean shirt a day, a couple of mutton chops grilled without condiments, two floury potatoes, an apple pie with a piece of Stilton and pulled bread, a pint of Club médoc, a clean room, in the winter a good fire in the grate, a comfortable armchair, a comfortable woman to see that all these were prepared for you, and to keep you warm in bed and to brush your bowler and fold your umbrella in the morning. When you had that secure for life you could do what you liked provided that what you did never endangered that security. What was to be said against that?

If Ford can enter into this absurdity so thoroughly it's partly because he believes it or at least can appreciate it. He was an outsider and half German, just as for most of his life he was poor and living outside England and outside marriage with various artistic women. But at the same time he admired Marwood and emulated him, revered his German father's notions of being an English gentleman, embraced Catholicism and his identity as a Tory. In this way he was like the half-Jewish Proust, who devoted huge amounts of energy to studying the French aristocracy and memorizing its eccentricities.

But Proust was not only an apostle of snobbism but also its most observant and fervent critic. Perhaps Proust's disappointments in love and friendship made him lose his faith in the values he'd once embraced. Certainly the Dreyfus Affair thoroughly disillusioned him and his sexuality further alienated him, as did his bad health.

Ford was less hysterically and more genuinely sociable than Proust. He was a robust survivor. He was much more casual about controlling the quality of his oeuvre than Proust, though Ford took a justifiable pride in *The Good Soldier* and *Parade's End*. Since, unlike Proust, Ford does not have a narrator who hovers over the entire book, there is much less attempt at "wisdom" in *Parade's End*, and all the thoughts and aperçus can be ascribed to particular characters in unique dramatic moments. Proust contrasted family love (the only genuine form of love) with the illusions of romance; nothing comparably bleak appears in Ford. Proust saw in the Great War the collapse of all social values; Ford did not go so far. Tietjens is an emblem of all that was great about the old pre-war England and at no point does Ford suggest that he must be downgraded in the reader's esteem. Because Ford was a complex and divided personality, his look at the English character is always shaded, if never disillusioned.

If *Parade's End* is due for a revival it's not for its large historical or philosophical truths but because it is panoramic and beautifully written. It is a condemnation of the brutal senselessness and stupid waste of war. Through its fascinating scenic technique it paints detailed, intimate pictures of tents on the French battlefield, spa towns in Germany, the Inns of Court in the City, and English country estates, and it peoples these places with convincing characters who stay in the mind, especially Sylvia and Christopher Tietjens.

SWEATING MIRRORS

It was ninety-nine degrees in New York, not a breeze stirring, the air yellow and poisonous. Strangers on street corners actually stopped each other to comment on the weather as though it were the first rumblings of an earthquake. That's how menacing the hot smog seemed—not a torpid ambience but an active agent. Cycling through my brain on a loop were the words "What a despairing day."

I was looking forward to the frigid embrace of Truman Capote's apartment in the United Nations Plaza, but when I stepped off the elevator he was standing barefoot in the hallway with a torn pink palmetto fan in hand and a drenched white T-shirt, and he told me that his air conditioner was on the blink. He was thin-lipped and cheerless and so faint that his voice was nearly inaudible as he led me into a small sun room that looked out on the steaming East River and the UN Secretariat, which today looped up more like a static tornado than a building. The huge windows of the sun room were sealed shut, and the only air came from tiny vents ajar below them.

We sat at opposite ends of a large Victorian couch ("My grand-mother's," he said) and looked at the larger adjoining sitting room and its mirrored wall; even the mirror was fogged and perspiring.

I congratulated Capote on his new *Music for Chameleons*, his first book in seven years. It contains a sort of pendant to *In Cold Blood* called "Handcarved Coffins," a short story, "Mojave," and, best of all, effervescent non-fiction portraits of Marilyn Monroe and of a char ("A Day's Work"). In both of these portraits he himself appears as a fully fleshed character—gossipy, elfin, compassionate, doomed. In the introduction to the book he explains that he'd sought a way to employ all his technical skills at once. One might add that the most dazzling "technique" is the stunning personal candor, one that sheds the same mordant brilliance that Nabokov achieved, in a quite different way, by contrasting passionate tenderness toward the beloved with patrician contempt for everyone else.

When I read "A Day's Work" in Andy Warhol's *Interview*, it was so good I called up a dozen friends to tell them about it. In this small masterpiece of journalism, Capote follows his maid, Mary Sanchez, as she goes from one cleaning job to another. The lives of the clients can be deciphered instantly from their apartments: the divorced executive's pigsty piled high with bottles of vodka; the tidy quarters of a young woman with a position in publishing whom Mary, against her Catholic principles but in accordance with the dictates of her heart, had helped during the woman's recovery from an abortion ("from having a baby murdered," as Mary puts it); and finally the overstuffed apartment of Mr and Mrs Berkowitz, where Capote and Mary, high on grass and gorged on sweets, dance around the living room until they are discovered by the irate master and mistress of the house.

Truman Capote's entire *oeuvre* is a shrewd staging of a fairly simple-minded morality play, in which children and loving but sexless eccentrics represent good, and adults represent evil. In his universe, Marilyn Monroe and Holly Golightly are good because they are children (the portrait of Monroe is even called "A Beautiful Child"). The writer Jane Bowles is admirable because she is "the eternal urchin, appealing as the most appealing of nonadults." As children, his heroes and heroines are dispossessed. When Dolly, Catherine and Collin leave home to live in a tree in *The Grass Harp*, the sympathetic Judge Charlie Cool declares, "It may be that there is no place for any of us. Except we know there is, somewhere; and if we found it, but lived there only a moment, we could count ourselves blessed."

I should add right away that such a formulation of experience (the innocence of childhood and nature, the corruption of maturity and civilization) strikes me as no more impoverished than most of the schemes that animate literature, although it does contain little room for development or refinement. The refinement was to come in the style and in the larger strategies Capote wielded, not in his ways of conceiving character or destiny. Consequently, he is regarded in Europe, especially in France, as a major American author (although his last name is the French word for *condom*), whereas in the United States his frequent acerbic performances on television talk-shows, the great ball he hosted in New York in the 1960s, his quarrels with his rich and powerful friends, his later arrest for drunken driving, all gave him a mass celebrity and rendered him more a "personality" than an artist. Capote once described his own writing as "simple and clear as a country creek". Transparent and beguiling it certainly is, with the magnificently dour exception of *In Cold Blood*, a black agate set among the other diamonds.

"In my other journalism, like *In Cold Blood*," Capote told me, "I kept myself scrupulously out of the picture, but in *Music for Chameleons* I've made myself visible for the first time. I realized that in most reportage, including my own, the writer is telling only half of the story. What was *really* said is missing." The personal, even confessional note of this book certainly gives it a new electricity. Capote also comes across as a charmer, a character as winning as he is honest, as impertinent as he is down-home.

"How did Mary Sanchez react to 'A Day's Work'?" I asked.

Capote threw back his head and gave his startling, mirthless laugh. "She loved it. I read it to her out loud, because I wanted to make sure it didn't lose her any jobs, get her into trouble."

A wave of anxiety suddenly overcame Capote. He stood, paced around. His hand was trembling. He excused himself and left the room. When he re-emerged in a few minutes he seemed calmer, more focused, and he came trailing a question: "Do you ever read your own books? I do. Every year I reread *In Cold Blood*. I don't mean to. I just pick it up and quickly become engrossed. I don't remember any of it—it's as though someone else wrote it. It's *enthralling*." Loud, barking laugh.

Capote's works are as elegant and calculated as those of Prosper Mérimée. Like Capote, Mérimée traveled widely, worked at his best in miniature forms, despised the avant-garde, cultivated the powerful (Mérimée was a friend to the Empress Eugenie, just as Capote was a companion to Empress Jackie and Princess Lee), loved a good yarn, took an anthropological interest in the violent lives of the poor *(Carmen, In Cold Blood)* and, though highly intelligent, wrote not for intellectuals but for that now-vanished creature, the invention of humanists and bourgeois liberals, the Common Reader.

Both Mérimée and Capote justly prided themselves on being stylists, not in the Proustian sense (elaborating syntax, rhetoric and metaphor in order to assimilate the most disparate elements into a single sentence), but in the older sense in which "style" meant fashioning the neatest, freshest, most natural classical prose in their respective traditions. Capote is a stylist who never intimidates his reader and whose poetic effects are purely local, never threatening the narrative progression. One lovely phrase follows another. Travel is a state of "alert slumber." Before dawn "drooping stars drift at the bedroom window fat as owls." A nighttime view of Tangier is "like a birthday cake blazing in a darkened room." One can imagine this purist cutting down Proust's usual three adjectives to the single limpid one, with a predictable loss of chiaroscuro and gain in brightness and resolution.

He told me that he thought the story closest to perfection in *Music for Chameleons* was "Then It All Came Down", which records a visit he paid to Robert Beausoleil in prison, the mystery man in the Charles Manson cult. "It's as linear as a fish bone," Capote said, drawing the spine in the air with his fan. "It *moves*, it has narrative energy and drive." To illustrate, he snapped his fingers and sketched a little dance on the rug with his bare feet. "No one understands anything about style, about what I'm trying to do. Now the story 'Dazzle' in *Music for Chameleons*—it's taken me forty years to learn how to write that way, to make it simple. Most writers start simple, then they become more and more complex. Then they have to unlearn everything they've acquired. Simplicity and swiftness: that's what I value.

"Of course, the most *subtle* story, the real *subtlety*—" he lingered on the word as though he had invented it, or as though it were some foreign expression I might not have caught—"the most *subtle* story is 'Music for Chameleons.' Even sophisticated readers don't understand it. They think it's about a visit with a woman; they think it's a *travel* piece about Martinique." Spasm of laughter that stopped on a dime. "But it's actually a meditation on murder, about how our passions flog us." He took off his glasses and stared at me with two perfectly clear blue eyes, the pupils tiny as gnats in the poisonous yellow light.

I asked him how he'd ever remembered the conversation he had had with Marilyn Monroe in 1955 after a funeral—one of the most touching and charming pieces in *Music for Chameleons*. "Well, Marilyn was a *great* friend. I loved her a lot. And *never* have I read anything that has anything to do with that girl at all except the *basic*—" his voice died away and his face sank into a grimace worthy of the Greek mask for tragedy—"...unpleasant...acts..." He suddenly brightened and turned to me; unfortunately the sun was glaring on his gray-tinted granny glasses and I'm staring into two silver dollars. "But, you see, I keep these extraordinary journals. And I *suddenly* remembered I had written down everything we'd said that day. Other people who knew her tell me I've caught the most perfect likeness. She was my first choice to be in the movie *Breakfast at Tiffany's*. She and Maureen Stapleton even worked up a wonderful scene for an Actors Studio class; I saw it, but Marilyn was too afraid to do it in class. Excuse me."

Capote left the room. When he regained the couch, he spoke to me in profile. His voice was high and weak and drawling and his pronunciation slack-jawed, mushy, like a child's—or like Baby Snooks's. As he picked up confidence, volume, clarity, he turned the two silver dollars toward me. He shook the fan at me to cool me off. I stared down at his long yellow toenails, which reminded me of those four-inch thumbnails the mandarins grew to prove they were so rich they never had to pick anything up. Incapacitating nails and bound feet: emblems of regal dependence on others.

Capote is an entertainer who is never dull, who appeals to the reader's curiosity without endangering his or her values, who adds to our store of experience without undermining the categories by which we process that plenitude, whose tales of underdogs and heartbreaking failures only reinforce the political status quo.

Capote's fascinating criminals, lovable maiden aunts, precocious kids and wilted gentry, while appearing to upset the order of things, are in fact the exceptions that prove the rule. They may be rebels but Capote's presentation of them is never subversive. Take this description of a New Orleans eccentric:

My interest in Miss Y. is rather clinical, and I am not, I embarrassedly confess, quite the friend she believes, for one cannot feel close to Miss Y.: she is too much a fairy tale, someone real—and improbable. She is like the piano in her parlor—elegant, but a little out of tune. Her house, old even for N.O., is guarded by a black broken iron fence; it is a poor neighborhood she lives in, one sprayed with room-for-rent signs, gasoline stations, jukebox cafes. And yet in the day when her family first lived here—that, of course, was long ago—there was in all N.O. no finer place. The house, smothered by slanting trees, has a gray exterior; but inside, the fantasy of Miss Y.'s heritage is everywhere visible: the tapping of her cane as she descends birdwing stairs trembles crystal: her face, a heart of wrinkled silk, reflects fumelike on ceiling-high mirrors: she lowers herself (notice, as this happens, how carefully she preserves the comfort of her bones) into her father's father's father's chair, a wickedly severe receptacle with lion-head handrests.

Here we have the pairs of balanced opposites (elegant and tuneless, shabby and rich, wraithlike and eternal, comfortable and severe) that serve to stabilize, even freeze character—which, moreover, is read through the house and its furnishings.

To interpret the self from its possessions is the great nineteenth-century fictional method (and a bourgeois habit of mind). Earlier novels described actions, not belongings; later novels dramatized inner conflicts, so often at odds with the milieu. That Capote found such a tight fit between his characters and their settings reflected his nostalgia for the traditional society of the Old South. His first novellas—*Other Voices, Other Rooms* and *The Grass Harp*—take place in that South of small towns and big pretensions, of genteel manners and savage prejudices.

Capote shuffled out of the room again. I, too, stood up, as though to throw off the heat squatting on me like a nightmare in a Fuseli painting. Art and fashion books sat in the sort of stylish piles decorators used to distribute around rooms to give them a studied "casual" look. The bookshelf itself contained mostly the various editions and translations of Capote's own titles. Puppies, kittens and cobras seemed to be the dominant motifs everywhere. (Now I'm interpreting Capote from his belongings!) All along one wall were drawings, paintings and pastels of household pets, but flung across the coffee table were three snakes, one of them huge and reared up to strike. As I strolled about I spotted other puppies, kittens and snakes on desks, woven into pillows, resting on the window-sill—fitting emblems, I suppose, for a man who celebrated domestic love in "A Christmas Memory" and has written the most detailed modern chronicle of murder, *In Cold Blood.* A dozen calla lilies fresh from the florist crowned the coffee table, but the geraniums along the window looked parched, neglected, a bachelor's plants.

When Capote re-emerged a minute later he'd picked up vitality. The photographer, Robert Mapplethorpe, and his assistant arrived, and Capote and I posed for our picture against a Japanese painting of fish. "The Japanese, of course, didn't paint in oils for the longest time," Capote explained. "This one, which was done in the nineteenth century, is one of the first oils. The artists reached the height and then, naturally, committed suicide. All the best Japanese artists commit suicide."

Mapplethorpe told us to look at each other, at the window, at him and we did so rather stiffly as though we were puppets gloving arthritic hands. The sweat flowed freely over our bodies. Although Capote, as he told all the world, was homosexual, he seemed not even faintly interested in either the handsome Mapplethorpe or in his friend, Marcus Leatherdale, who resembles James Dean. Not the faintest *sexual* interest, that is; he does express his admiration of Mapplethorpe's photographs. Capote let out a sigh and stood: "I can't take it. I can't be photographed one second more," and he hurried down the hall for the third time in twenty minutes.

Mapplethorpe and his friend left. I ambled around the living room and stopped to examine two decorative windows placed on the facing wall. The borders were painted with fruits and birds and the inner surface was studded with abstract shades of tinted glass and mirror. "The Shah of Iran gave those to me," Capote told me as he returned. "They're *very* old and valuable—national treasures. I'm terrified the Ayatollah will send someone to recover them."

Capote was now doing a sort of fan dance, listlessly waving his palmetto and slowly jogging in place. He dropped his fan and rubbed his stomach in long up and down strokes. "The pain…" he murmured. "Barbara Walters was here yesterday for *fourteen* hours. Their equipment broke down. But I have to admire her. She never once complained. She's a real professional."

His tongue flickered over his lips while he complimented me on my own writing, which I was pleased to learn he'd read with such thoroughness. "I love the piece you wrote on Texas, especially the part where you went to bed with your grandfather." He gave me a wan smile. "So *Southern*." He sighed, excused himself and ambled off into another room.

The Grass Harp is narrated by Collin, who at one point startles us by claiming he's sixteen years old and in love with Maude, though the reader finds his age and sexual tastes to be as ambiguous as Marcel's in *Within a Budding Grove*. The loving, harmonious family (which neither Proust nor Capote ever actually knew) cannot be abandoned, nor can the homosexual nature of the narrator's desires (Collin's crush on Riley, for instance) be either abandoned or acknowledged; the bizarre compromise is chronological and erotic shiftiness. Symptomatically, Capote in his early fiction becomes so fussed when he must even allude to homosexuality that his silver tongue becomes instantly tarnished. Take this line from "A Diamond Guitar": "Except that they did not combine their bodies or think to do so, though such things were not unknown at the farm, they were as lovers."

Adrienne Rich once remarked that if Elizabeth Bishop had acknowledged her lesbianism she wouldn't have written better poetry but she might have written more of it. Capote was similarly gifted—and similarly blocked. His output and his range, as measured by his own ambitions, remained strangely limited. One could even say he devoted a great deal of creative energy to avoiding honesty. The relationship in "A Diamond Guitar" is romantic but sexless. *The Grass Harp* casts dangerous longings under the sentimental glow of a fairy-tale atmosphere that, at its worst, turns into pure Disney: "The wine-colored violin, coddled under her chin, trilled as she tuned it; a brazen butterfly, lighting on the bow, was spiralled away as the bow swept across the strings singing a music that seemed a blizzard of butterflies flying, a sky-rocket of spring sweet to hear in the gnarled fall woods."

In "House of Flowers" man-woman passion is presented, but among Firbankian darkies in the never-never land, a Haiti right out of Le Douanier Rousseau. Ottilie leaves Port-au-Prince and the bordello in order to live in a house of flowers with Royal, a beautiful jaguar of a husband. As in Andrew Marvell's "The Garden," the vegetable world is active and the human inhabitants passive. By the end of "House of Flowers," Ottilie has been bound by Royal to a tree, where she happily awaits his return from the sugar fields. She has been quite literally returned to nature. The wound of urban experience has at last healed over.

The fairy-tale aspect of Capote's talent is exquisite but a bit remote, since it seldom rehearses real feelings; the world is all too well banished. At the opposite extreme (but no less efficacious in staunching self-revelation) are his non-fiction experiments—his many portraits and travel sketches, his wickedly comic account of the American *Porgy and Bess* tour of the Soviet Union in 1955 *(The Muses Are Heard)* and his "non-fiction" novel, *In Cold Blood.* In all these writings his own presence is either meticulously eliminated (as *in In Cold Blood)* or scarcely adumbrated.

When he returned I asked him about "Handcarved Coffins," the "non-fiction" novella in *Music for Chameleons.* It's the story of a rancher who methodically murders one by one the members of a committee that had diverted the major flow of a river off his property. "Aren't you worried about libel? I mean, when that rancher reads your story?"

At the mention of the word *libel* the fan stopped. Then it began to waver tentatively. I looked at a row of three pink piggy banks, which I imagined were filled with dimes and silver dollars. As he spoke, the fan beat more and more confidently. "I changed certain things. I'm protected. Whereas I made everything absolutely accurate *in In Cold Blood*. But in 'Handcarved Coffins' I had to touch up the details. Of course there's *no* legal case against the rancher, just supposition. No one believes the rancher is guilty—not even his own cousin, who's the next in line to be murdered. He's in Hong Kong now, and I'm just waiting for his murder." Capote strolled about and I shadowed him with my notebook like a clerk trailing a good customer through a chic shop. "I've been following the case since 1972 and I could have made it longer than *In Cold Blood*, but I think it works better this way."

I mention the dedication of *Music for Chameleons* to Tennessee Williams. "Wasn't Williams irritated," I asked, "by your portrait of him in one of those chapters of *Answered Prayers* that *Esquire* published?" In that chapter, "Unspoiled Monsters," Williams (or "Mr. Wallace," as he was called in the text) was portrayed as a drunk wreck inhabiting a room at the Plaza. The incoherent Wallace has been cooped up for days with his dog, which had left piles of shit all over the carpet. The narrator, a hustler, has been summoned to the room to amuse the delirious playwright. And to walk the dog. Not a very flattering portrait, all in all.

"Tennessee was *furious!*" Capote announced with the first genuine glee I'd observed. Then turning sober, adult, serious, Capote went on: "We've had our ups and downs. We've known each other for a thousand years. I think he's a *genius.* The *abuse* he's been subjected to has been *outrageous.* Can you imagine another country that treats its major artists as terribly as America does? Those *creepy* critics torturing Tennessee, when they don't have the right to lick his *feet*. Well, I didn't ask him if I could dedicate my book to him. It's a surprise. He probably doesn't even know yet. America in general is very disrespectful of its artists," Capote concluded tonelessly, as though this plight were too banal to merit expression.

In the extant chapters of *Answered Prayers*, he depicts some of the jumbled elements of his own life (much as Nabokov does in *Look at the Harlequins!*). The results were so scandalous, the *clefs* rattled so noisily, that Capote lacked the courage to press on. Drink and drugs dimmed his lights. The book's jet-set milieu, however, which he'd first touched on in "Greek Paragraphs," a minor travel piece, appealed to his temperament. At last he was free from his sexless youths and corrupted adults, his fairy-tale romances and objective reportage.

The rich have the means to realize their whims and the effrontery to avow their desires. Sex, travel, gambling and intrigue are their sports, while their itineraries and adulteries provide them with conversation, just as loyalty to the clan, devotion to fashion and the display of perfect manners constitute their virtues. Above all, jet-setters love a good story. Too bad Capote didn't stay sober long enough to betray his friends more thoroughly.

To find the psychic energy to pursue a long career, it seems to me, a writer must juggle between a vigorous, recording curiosity about the world and how it works and the ongoing process of self-creation. It is the imagination, of course, that negotiates between reality and the ego, between the repetition compulsion and the pleasure principle. If the self is utterly eliminated we end up with journalism: if the ego is shamelessly gratified, we have the *longueurs* of the intimate journal. If both the self and the world are held at bay and the imagination is given free rein, then the result would be pure fantasy or tedious sci-fi. The successful novel cleverly adjudicates among these temptations and somehow combines newspaper story, confession and fairy tale.

Capote's most successful response to these various claims is *Breakfast at Tiffany's*, a sort of rewrite of Isherwood's Berlin stories. Holly Golightly plays Sally Bowles, the impoverished and sexless young Capote stands in for the similarly disabled Herr Issivoo, and in both books the various eccentrics, lovable or menacing, parade past like vaudeville performers doing their exotic "turns." Both Sally and Holly are at once wish-fulfillment and object-lesson, real girls and gay boys in drag, as well as innocents playing at adult vice. In both Capote's and Isherwood's tales the results make for very seductive reading.

He excused himself, but when he returned this time he didn't seem livelier but dangerously fatigued. I started to leave. "I've been very anxious," he said. "It's something that's been hanging over me for two and a half years. Partly professional and partly personal. I thought it was over, but it isn't. That's why I'm so nervous. I can't tell you about it—it's a secret. But when you do eventually learn about *it*, then you'll understand why it's been so hard for me to finish *Answered Prayers*. Everything will come clear then."

At the door we started talking about the hazards of the writer's career. "I've had the phones taken out," Capote confided. "I get some —" he raised his eyebrows and trippingly articulated the next words as he bounced up the scale—"some pret-ty weird-o phone calls."

He gave me a cheek to peck, a purely routine gesture, as though we were Gabor sisters air-kissing each other for the benefit of photographers. "Well," he told me, "you'll write some wonderful books, I'm sure, but believe me…" He took off his glasses and stared at me. "It's a *horrible* life."

BEAT MEMORIES

Both Allen Ginsberg and William Burroughs discovered late in life that making works of art is the way to get money. Literature just doesn't do it. Speaking engagements pay, but eventually they become tiring—or one exhausts the market. Neither of the two had ever been money-mad, but old age requires a bit of a cushion. Burroughs turned to painting. He would set up paint cans in front of blank canvases and then shoot at them; the splatter was the art. Although these paintings are his best-known artworks, they make up only a small part of his output: he did twenty-four shotgun paintings in 1982 and a few more before he died in 1997. According to his friend James Grauerholz, Burroughs turned out more than 1,500 artworks between 1982 and 1996—including stencils and targets, which were almost all brightly colored abstractions—and had his work exhibited in several museums and more than eighty galleries worldwide.

As Ginsberg said:

If you're famous, you can get away with anything! William Burroughs spent the last ten years painting, and makes a lot more money out of his painting than he does out of his previous writing. If you establish yourself in one field, it's possible that people then take you seriously in another. Maybe too seriously. I know lots of great photographers who are a lot better than me, who don't have a big, pretty coffee table book like I have. I'm lucky.

Ginsberg had been taking snapshots of friends with a borrowed camera since the mid-1940s. In 1953 he bought a small Kodak Retina camera for $13 secondhand at a Bowery pawnshop, and for the next ten years he photographed all his friends and activities in a casual, spontaneous way. It wasn't until 1983 that Ginsberg rediscovered these pictures among his papers.

As Sarah Greenough writes of Ginsberg in the catalog of *Beat Memories: The Photographs of Allen Ginsberg*:

Long a foe of American materialism and convinced that it was better to give to friends, colleagues, and worthy causes than to pay taxes, he found himself in the mid-1980s sixty years old and without much money in the bank. Until his death in 1997, he presented numerous lectures and workshops around the world on "Snapshot Poetics" and attentively worked with dealers and agents to sell his photographs and reproduction rights.

It was also in the 1980s that he added chatty, affectionate, handwritten captions to his photographs, which explained what was going on in them—and which also added to their value by making them into unique objects.

In 1994 Ginsberg sold his archives to Stanford University for a million dollars, but after all the deductions for the auction house, his agent, and taxes he only had enough money left to buy his New York loft and was back to square one. His photos brought him some income in his last years, though he insisted that most of the profits were plowed back into his work, for hiring an assistant and maintaining a lab.

The pictures are fascinating since few of them are well known and they often show their subjects in their youth—a fresh-faced, toothy, nerdy Ginsberg, for instance, long before he became the bearded guru, and a melancholy, poetic William Burroughs before he became the saurian undertaker seen in his familiar portraits. There's even a shadowy nude of Burroughs in bed during the period when he and Ginsberg were lovers.

Almost all of the Beats were bisexual and one another's lovers. Neal Cassady, the heartthrob of the bunch, slept with everyone, male or female, though he preferred women and was never faithful to anyone. He let Ginsberg sleep with him but mainly as a favor and partly as an experiment; soon after their first New York idyll, Cassady left a lovesick Ginsberg behind and ran off to Denver and to adventures with numerous women. Ginsberg joined him there but was ignored most of the time.

Burroughs had as his female companion a woman named Joan Vollmer Adams; the apartment they shared in New York with Kerouac and his first wife, Edie Parker, was a central gathering spot for the Beats in the 1940s. In 1951, when they were living in Mexico City, Burroughs shot and killed her during a game of William Tell gone awry. He fled back to the U.S. to avoid jail time. About the incident, he later wrote: "I am forced to the appalling conclusion that I would have never become a writer if not for Joan's death... [It] brought me into contact with the invader, the Ugly Spirit, and maneuvered me into a lifelong struggle, in which I have had no choice except to write my way out."

Kerouac was mostly straight but he did drink epic quantities and put out for Ginsberg occasionally. Peter Orlovsky, who was very striking when Ginsberg met him, was straight but slightly mad; he let the inexperienced Ginsberg screw him on their first date and then wept, bewildered by what had happened. They stayed together for the rest of their lives though Orlovsky was often so paranoid and out of control that he had to be hospitalized—and occasionally he was hostile to Ginsberg. Not so many years ago I remember asking a straight friend why he had had sex with Ginsberg and he said, opening his hands palm-up as if it were self-evident, "Dude, he was *Allen Ginsberg.*"

Here they all are in the National Gallery show—and what a handsome group they are, especially the young Kerouac and Cassady and Orlovsky. Perhaps the most memorable photo is of Kerouac wandering down East 7th Street in Manhattan in the fall of 1953 "making a Dostoevsky mad-face or Russian basso be-bop Om," though I like to think his mouth is shaped in a giant O because he's reciting "O harp and altar, of the fury fused," Hart Crane's ode to the nearby Brooklyn Bridge. Cassady is also a natural Marlon Brando stand-in and a 1955 picture shows him and one of his fugitive loves, Natalie Jackson, posing under a San Francisco movie marquee advertising *The Wild One.*

In another image, the eternally elegant Paul Bowles is shown in a seersucker suit and a rep tie between the grubby Gregory Corso and the frankly weird Burroughs in Tangier in 1961. Burroughs is dressed like a court stenographer in a long-sleeve black shirt buttoned all the way up, pleated trousers cinched high around his waist, and a trilby hat shading his drug-wasted face. The long sleeves were necessary even in the semitropics to hide the needle tracks.

One earlier, campy photo from 1953 shows an unexpectedly suave and theatrical Burroughs giving sophisticated advice in the "André Gide" manner to a browbeaten but adorable Jack Kerouac, an All-American boy right out of a Thomas Wolfe novel (Ginsberg's interpretation). According to Ginsberg's caption, written forty years later, Burroughs is saying, "Now Jack, as I warned you far back as 1945, if you keep going home to live with your 'Mémère' you'll find yourself wound tighter and tighter in her apron strings till you're an old man and can't escape…" By the time Ginsberg wrote those words he knew that in the interval Kerouac had in fact become a day-in day-out drunk, moved back to his mother in Lowell, Massachusetts, and died in 1969 with her in Florida from complications due to cirrhosis of the liver. He was just forty-seven years old.

A late photo of 1964 shows, in Ginsberg's words, Kerouac as a "red-faced corpulent W.C. Fields shuddering with mortal horror… and resembling his own father. There are equally devastating late photos of Gregory Corso ("Maestro Poet," Ginsberg notes beneath the image of his bloated friend, "ancient herald's wand pin, messenger-god Hermes Caduceus, near his pen, a quiet afternoon in 'The Kettle of Fish,' an old bar in Greenwich Village under whose sign Kerouac used to drink") and Herbert Huncke ("Old-timer & survivor Herbert E. Huncke," Ginsberg calls him, "Beat literary pioneer who introduced Burroughs, Kerouac & myself to floating population hustling & drug scene Times Square 1945"); only Ginsberg himself retains his warmth and humanity to the end. In fact, one of the most touching pictures is a self-portrait as an old man in the nude, an image that has the dignity and depth and vulnerability of a late Rembrandt self-portrait.

Early on, when they were just inventing themselves and their original brand of writing, Ginsberg and Kerouac decided to turn all their friends into myths. They did so by writing about each other and their holy or zany or heroic or comic exploits, but they also compared each other to famous people of the distant or recent past. In his late captions to his early photos, written by hand at the bottom of new, "museum-quality" prints of them, Ginsberg quite naturally vaunted the epic qualities of his friends. In one picture he has posed Burroughs in the Egyptian Wing beside "a brother Sphinx" in the Metropolitan Museum to emphasize his sepulchral personality. Ginsberg's description of Kerouac's "Dostoyevsky mad-face" is designed to ally his pal with the great Russian.

Their letters and journal entries from that period all reveal that they were convinced they represented something new and monumental in literary history. To be sure, Ginsberg was at Columbia studying literature with Lionel Trilling and art history with Meyer Shapiro and, outside school, hobnobbing with the much older poet William Carlos Williams—this heady intellectual company only reinforced his sense of artistic destiny.

Although Ginsberg was usually enthusiastic, especially about his friends' work, sometimes his faith was shaken. During a spell in a mental hospital, Ginsberg had met Carl Solomon, whose uncle, A.A. Wyn, was the publisher of Ace Books. Carl convinced his uncle to publish Burroughs's early novel *Junkie*, but Wyn was reluctant to publish Kerouac's *On the Road*—and this reluctance gave Ginsberg a temporary doubt. He wrote in his journal: "Carl shook my own self-esteem, threw me into depression. Is there no way we can tell what's good on our own except by personal heart sympathies, going against almost all rational *and* commercial possibility?"

In this early period Ginsberg was working out—as a photographer but primarily as a poet—his doctrine of spontaneity, "First Thought, Best Thought." This principle, which Kerouac probably invented, made *On the Road* a classic work of American literature and "Howl" a daring piece of confessional poetry, so that even established masters such as Robert Lowell took account of it (his next book was *Life Studies*). But the Beats' refusal to edit themselves also led to poems and novels that were repetitious and full of dreary *longueurs*. Ginsberg was always at his best in visionary poems such as the genuinely inspired free-verse "Wales Visitation":

All the Valley quivered, one extended motion, wind
undulating on mossy hills
a giant wash that sank white fog delicately down red runnels
on the mountainside
whose leaf-branch tendrils moved asway
in granitic undertow down—
and lifted the floating Nebulous upward, and lifted the arms
 of the trees
and lifted the grasses an instant in balance
and lifted the lambs to hold still
and lifted the green of the hill, in one solemn wave
A solid mass of Heaven, mist-infused, ebbs thru the vale…

In 1949 Ginsberg wrote about his down-and-out pal Herbert
Huncke. They lived together briefly and Huncke was constantly
arranging the furniture and burning bits of wood to smell their
scent:

> Perhaps he had nothing better to do. But I appreciated these
> activities as touches peculiar to Huncke alone, and therefore
> valuable, lovely and honorable. They were part of his whole
> being and "life force." I also enjoyed mythologizing his
> character. It is a literary trick which Kerouac, the novelist—
> who has written much about Herbert Huncke—and I
> exploited in the past.

Not only in the past but throughout their careers. It's really a very
simple strategy. You have a small group of friends and you declare
them all to be geniuses and you laud all their work and ascribe to
them sweet and stormy qualities worthy of the Greek gods. What
you're selling is not just your writing but your personal legends.

IN LOVE WITH DURAS

Marguerite Duras was a huge presence in the 1980s and early 1990s when I lived in Paris. She was very old—in her seventies—and very alcoholic, and her disintoxication cure in late 1982 at the American Hospital was much written about (not only by journalists—she wrote about it, and her companion Yann Andréa did as well in a book called *M.D.*). Just when people thought her liver or her kidneys would give out, she rose from her ashes and wrote *The Lover* (1984), a story drawn from her youth in Indochina that sold a million copies in forty-three languages and became the inspiration for a major commercial movie.

Before her cure, she was holed up in her house dictating one much-worked-on line a day to Andréa, who would type it up. Then they would start uncorking cheap Bordeaux and she'd drink two glasses, vomit, then continue on till she'd drunk as many as nine liters and would pass out. She could no longer walk, or scarcely. She said she drank because she knew God did not exist. Her very sympathetic doctor would visit her almost daily and offer to take her to the hospital, but only if she wanted to live. She seemed undecided for a long time but at last she opted for life since she was determined to finish a book that she'd already started and was very keen about.

There was always something preposterous about her. When she was feeling well enough she surrounded herself with courtiers, laughed very loudly, told jokes, and had opinions about everything. She was an egomaniac and talked about herself constantly. Almost three years after her cure she created a scandal by speculating recklessly about the most famous (and still unsolved) murder case in recent French history—the case of Little Grégory. This child, Grégory Villemin, had been killed and trussed and dumped into a culvert. He was just four and a half years old. More than a hundred journalists were hovering around the site of the murder, the village of Lépanges near Épinal in the Vosges.

And then on July 17, 1985 (273 days after the murder), Marguerite Duras (once again drinking heavily) visited the town briefly, studied the house where Little Grégory had lived, and published a front-page article in *Libération* announcing to the world that she knew who had done it: the mother, Christine Villemin! Duras's main evidence was that there was no garden around the little house. This proved that Christine was unhappy, that her husband was forcing sex on her, that she was just staring into space all day and sitting about without any occupation at home, dreaming up atrocious crimes. It was a modern tragedy, Duras claimed, in the tradition of Racine. Even though the mother, who had at first been arrested, had been freed because of the lack of evidence and had specifically refused to speak to her, Duras had no doubts that Christine had done it. She was careful to point out that she didn't judge the young woman. Any woman was capable of this sort of violence, Duras assured her readers, especially if she was being subjected by her husband to bad sex.

Serge July, the editor of *Libération*, was so embarrassed by Duras's article that he printed a less heated version of the events beside it—a virtual disavowal that she considered an unforgivable betrayal. Hundreds of readers wrote in, most of them disapproving of Duras's article. Many prominent women, including Simone de Beauvoir and Simone Signoret, attacked the article. Duras never looked back or admitted she'd been intemperate. The title of the article had been "Christine Villemin, Sublime, Necessarily Sublime." Duras said that she was sure that Christine "had killed perhaps without knowing it just as I have written without knowing it." (Since Duras drank in order to write she seldom recognized her own writings when she reread them.)

Immediately afterward (between July 1985 and April 1986) Duras and François Mitterrand (then president) granted several long interviews to the magazine *L'Autre Journal*, discussing among other things their role in the Resistance. (These interviews were later turned into a hit play *Marguerite and the President*.) Mitterrand, after working for the Vichy government, had indeed been a cell leader of the Resistance under the name François Morland; he had organized Frenchmen who had been captured before France's surrender and held as prisoners of war by the Germans and later released (Mitterrand himself escaped his German prison). And Duras had indeed used her apartment on the rue St.-Benoit (around the corner from the Café de Flore) as a meeting place for resistants, and after the liberation by the Allies she'd edited a newspaper, *Libres*, reporting on the whereabouts of French men, women, and children coming back from the camps.

Her husband, Robert Anthelme, had been arrested for his Resistance activities and sent to a concentration camp, Bergen-Belsen. When he was liberated a year later, he could barely walk. As Duras writes in one of the rough drafts reprinted in *Wartime Writings*:

When he weighed his eighty-four pounds and I used to take him in my arms and help him pee and go caca, when he had a fever of 105.8, and down at his coccyx his backbone was showing, and when day and night, there were six of us waiting for a sign of hope, he had no idea what was going on.

What is being reprinted in paperback as *The War: A Memoir* is called in French *La Douleur* (*Suffering*). It is a terse, action-packed, nonfiction notebook hastily scrawled during the war, with no regard to prose style, and published by Duras only in 1985. The notes provide a blow-by-blow account of her fears for her husband's survival, his long convalescence, and her alternating moods of joy and panic. This text fills seventy pages. It is followed by other accounts of Duras's war, including a fairly preposterous one ("Albert of the Capitals") in which she claims that she tortured a French collaborator right after the Liberation. Duras's biographer, Jean Vallier, denies that she ever acted in this way. She wasn't a torturer at the interrogation center, Vallier writes, but a canteen waitress (*une popotière*), which in French doesn't sound very warlike.

In their interviews with *L'Autre Journal* neither Mitterrand nor Duras mentioned their activities earlier in the war. The young Mitterrand had served the Vichy government as a clerk concerned with French prisoners of war and had received a medal—the Francisque—for his activities from Pétain. But by 1942 he was already using his contacts with former POWs to start an underground alliance against the Germans. After he was elected president in 1981, however, he would never explicitly condemn the Vichy government and he had dinner in the Élysée Palace with René Bousquet, an old friend and ally in the Socialist Party who had, not incidentally, ordered the arrest of Jewish children in Paris and their transportation to the death camps (thereby exceeding the demands of the Nazis themselves). Bousquet was welcomed by Mitterrand as a frequent guest until 1986, when a public outcry made their friendship difficult to maintain. Nevertheless, the French government under Mitterrand dragged its feet in prosecuting Bousquet, who was finally shot by a madman in 1993—fortunately for everyone, especially Mitterrand.

Duras never mentioned that she, too, had worked as a minor bureaucrat under the Occupation. When she was a young and aspiring but unpublished author, she accepted a position with the government organization that decided on a book-by-book basis whether a publisher would be given paper with which to produce a given title. Essentially, the service of "paper control" for which she worked from July 1942 to the end of 1944 was acting as a state censor. D.H. Lawrence's *Lady Chatterley's Lover* was withdrawn, as were titles by Freud, Zola, and Colette. Quantities of paper, however, were allotted to the publication of Goebbels's memoirs, Paul Claudel's *Ode to Marshall Pétain*, and the vilest anti-Semitic garbage of the period, *The Ruins* by Lucien Rebatet, who, as Jean Vallier writes, had "a sewer mouth that all by itself was able to dishonor an entire epoch."

It was perhaps because Duras held this sensitive position that her own first novel, *Les Impudents* (which had been turned down by several publishers), was now accepted and received a glowing review from the brilliant collaborationist critic Ramon Fernandez (who also worked for the paper control service and whose wife Betty was Duras's best friend). Duras at least was able to admit it years later:

If my first novel finally appeared…it was because I was part of a paper commission (it was during the war). It was bad…

To be sure, everyone not independently wealthy had to have a job, but her position as censor for the Nazi occupiers was certainly one that Duras was eager to forget. Nor did she want to remember that before the war she had worked in the publicity department representing France's colony in Indochina during the late 1930s, especially at the 1937 International Exposition, the last great manifestation of French colonialism. Most of the French did not object to France having colonies at the time. But Duras, with her considerable powers to mythologize the past, knew how to invent a suitably leftist record for herself.

And she could see her present in a similarly self-serving way. She loved herself, she quoted herself, she took a childlike delight in reading her own work and seeing her old films, all of which she declared magnificent. When toward the end of her life she ran into Mitterrand in a fish restaurant, she asked him how she had become better known to people around the world than he was. Very politely he assured her he'd never doubted for a moment that her fame would someday eclipse his.

It's easy enough to make fun of her narcissism and her prevarications. But her work was fueled by her obsessive interest in her own story and her knack for improving on the facts with every new version of the same event. For instance, in *Wartime Writings* there are some previously unpublished pages (about fifty) that are among the most arresting she ever wrote. Written by hand in a notebook during the war, these pages recall her growing up in Indochina and give the first version of the "affair" with the man who would eventually become "the Lover." There are also fragments that Duras later assembled into her first successful novel, *The Sea Wall* (1950), which is based on her childhood in Indochina as well.

In her notebook (which was published in French only two years ago) Duras writes in an aside to herself:

It was barely thirteen years ago that these things happened and that our family broke up, except for my younger brother who never left my mother and who died last year in Indochina. Barely thirteen years. No other reason impels me to write of these memories, except that instinct to unearth. It's very simple. If I do not write them down, I will gradually forget them. That thought terrifies me.

In this first version of the story, there is as in later versions the initial meeting with the Chinese lover on the ferry from Sadec to Saigon. But in this version, in which he's called Léo, he's ugly, pockmarked, humble, awkward. After two years of his pleading, Marguerite goes to bed with him just once—and she finds him repulsive. Léo invites Marguerite and her mother and two brothers to expensive Chinese restaurants. The brothers barely speak to him, since he is "beneath" them as a Chinese. The mother counsels little Marguerite to get as much money out of him as possible but never to sleep with him. Marguerite herself has contempt for him:

Léo was perfectly laughable and that pained me deeply. He looked ridiculous because he was so short and thin and had droopy shoulders. Plus he thought so much of himself. In a car he was presentable because one couldn't see his height, only his head, which, albeit ugly, did possess a certain distinction. Not once did I agree to walk a hundred yards with him in a street. If a person's capacity for shame could be exhausted, I would have exhausted mine with Léo.

Duras's parents were both teachers in Indochina, employees of the French government. Marguerite was born near Saigon in 1914. She had two older brothers. Her father, sent back to France on sick leave, died there in 1921. After a few years spent with her mother's relatives in the north of France, the family returned to Indochina. Her mother bought a farm near the Gulf of Siam and attempted to build a sea wall against the Pacific. But the wall was destroyed by crabs and the rice fields were inundated and ruined. The collapse of the family fortunes was a theme that Duras would return to again and again.

After the rice fields were flooded and the farm abandoned, the family retreated to a small house where her mother would beat her, and, Marguerite writes, her older brother soon picked up the mother's "habit":

The only question became who would hit me first. When he didn't like the way Mama was beating me, he'd tell her, "Wait," and take over. But soon she'd be sorry, because each time she thought I'd be killed on the spot. She'd let out ghastly shrieks but my brother had trouble stopping himself.

In the notes, we see a family living in poverty, the mother encouraging her daughter to soak her Chinese suitor for money; she was after all conferring a favor on him even to let him spend time with them, since they were, as whites, innately superior. Racism, colonialism, family sadism, extreme poverty, greed—the gritty life of this young woman is quite different from that of the androgynous seductress she becomes in *The Lover*. In this first version she recalls that she was so badly dressed (in a man's hat and gold lamé shoes) that she was almost ridiculous. Léo has to spend a month to convince her that her felt hat is in bad taste and doesn't suit her, so entirely sure is she that her mother (who gave her the thrift-shop hat) knows everything about fashion.

In the first fictional and published version of this story, *The Sea Wall* (in French *Un Barrage contre le Pacifique*), the Lover is called Monsieur Jo. He isn't handsome but he is rich enough to have an elegant car and a big diamond ring. Otherwise, there is nothing desirable about him; the girl's brother dismisses him as a monkey. In *The Sea Wall*, the diamond is very generally described as enormous, magnificent, royal. But by the time Duras has progressed to the very last incarnation of the story, *The North China Lover* (1992), the ring has acquired a history —now the Chinese says:

It could be worth tens of thousands of piastres. All I know is, the diamond was my mother's. It was part of her dowry.

My father had it set for me by a famous Paris jeweler after her death. The jeweler, he came to Manchuria to pick up the diamond. And he came back to Manchuria to deliver the ring.

Most important, the Chinese character in both *The Lover* and the later book, *The North China Lover*, is handsome—a proper romantic hero. The story is no longer one about family abuse and greed, about a desperate mother who exploits her virginal daughter. Now it's become a love story between a European Lolita and a Chinese Humbert, except in this case "the child" (unlike Lolita) is excited by her older lover. Her painful deflowering is carefully recounted, as are the many nights of ecstatic pleasure that follow.

Duras's editor, Jérôme Lindon at Éditions de Minuit, thought that, after the worldwide success of *The Lover*, she was making a mistake to follow it up with another version of the same story. Marguerite was outraged at this hesitation on her editor's part. She switched to Gallimard and brought out the book—again to great success.

The North China Lover bears obvious traces of having started out life as a screenplay. In fact, Duras had been unhappy with the screenplay proposed (and eventually used) to make the film version of *The Lover*. She had her own ideas. After all, she was a distinguished filmmaker in her own right and had created two (strange, static) masterpieces, *The Truck* and *India Song*, as well as many lesser but no less experimental movies. What's remarkable about Duras's entire long career is how often she switched from a novel version of a story to the movie version and then to a play, or moved in a different order among the three modes, or modified the story or bits of it from novel to novel, play to play, film to film.

In *The North China Lover* Duras has combined the movie and the novel forms, while referring explicitly to the preceding novel, *The Lover*. She writes (referring to herself as "the child"):

The man who gets out of the black limousine is other than the one in the book, but still Manchurian. He is a little different from the one in the book: he's a little more solid than the other, less frightened than the other, bolder. He is better-looking, more robust. He is more "cinematic" than the one in the book. And he's also less timid facing the child.

Her prose, always incantatory, has now become the scenarist's shorthand:

Him, he's Chinese. A tall Chinese. He has the white skin of the North Chinese. He is very elegant. He has on the raw silk suit and mahogany-colored English shoes young Saigon bankers wear.
He looks at her.
They look at each other. Smile at each other. He comes over.

In the earlier versions of the "affair" (*The Sea Wall* and *The Lover*), the figure of the Lover himself was left vague (perhaps because these versions were based on fairly cloudy memories). Now that in old age Duras has succumbed to a "cinematic" form of wish fulfillment and given up the shadowy, unflattering reality, the Lover has become distinct, tall, good-looking—and the affair itself has taken on weight and body.

Duras certainly loved to return to the same handful of themes again and again. For instance, she invented the character of a French vice-consul (based on a Jewish fellow student she'd encountered in Paris during her university years and who became her lover—or so she claimed). This man, in real life called Frédéric Max, was supposedly the original of the disgraced French bureaucrat in *The Vice-Consul* (1965) who has been transferred from Bombay to Lahore.

There in the book he falls in love with a married Frenchwoman, the curiously named Anne-Marie Stretter. The story is retold in the 1972 play *India Song* (published in 1973), which Duras directed as a film by the same name in 1975 with a cast including Michael Lonsdale, Matthieu Carrière, and Delphine Seyrig, the star of the earlier, equally stylish, and static *Last Year at Marienbad* (with a script by Alain Robbe-Grillet). That film had been directed by Alain Resnais, who in 1959 had directed Duras's remarkable script *Hiroshima Mon Amour*.

Other events and encounters got recycled in a similar way. For instance, Duras met the much younger (and gay) Yann Andréa (she gave him the euphonious last name) in 1980, fell in love with him, and kept writing again and again about their spiritual closeness and physical frustration until her death in 1996. Her "Yann" books include *L'Homme atlantique*, *La Maladie de la mort* (a frightful attack on homosexuality), *Les Yeux bleus, cheveux noirs* (a truce with her beloved's homosexuality), *La Pute de la côte normande*, and *Yann Andréa Steiner*.

I suppose an entire dissertation could be written about this theme of the older woman artist and her gay sidekick or "walker." I'm thinking of Marguerite Yourcenar and the young gay man she wanted to inherit her fortune, though he surprised her by dying (of AIDS) before her. Or Germaine Greer and David Plante. I'm reminded of the elderly French widow who said to one of my bitchy friends, "I don't really like homosexuals," to which he replied, "That's a pity, Madam, since they are your future" (*"Dommage, Madame, c'est votre avenir"*).

In Duras's case, Yann Andréa was by her bedside taking down her last sporadic ravings, which he published in 1995 as *C'est tout*—a fairly dubious or at least controversial move, a bit like the promotion of de Kooning's Alzheimer paintings. Certainly Duras, while she was still in her right mind, wrote some beautiful pages about Yann, especially in the little book *Yann Andréa Steiner*.

Preposterous, self-obsessed, eloquent, unstoppable, Duras left her mark on French letters, theater, and cinema. She produced a bibliography of fifty-three titles, though some are very short (*La Pute de la côte normande* is just twenty pages long). Elisabeth Schwarzkopf once said that to be a successful opera singer you have to have a distinctive voice and be very loud. By those standards Marguerite Duras was a great diva indeed.

CONCERNING E.M. FORSTER

Aspiring fiction writers have been reading E.M. Forster's *Aspects of the Novel* since it was first published in 1927. I can remember devouring it with real avidity in 1960 or soon after; here was one of the greatest English novelists of the twentieth century, the author of *A Passage to India*, divulging the secrets of the trade—or rather expressing strong but always courteous opinions about the rival merits and methods of the important novelists of the past.

Here we first learned of "flat" (quickly sketched in) versus "round" (fully developed) characters and how every book needed some of both. Here we were told that Henry James' decision in *The Ambassadors* to make his two chief male characters reverse positions by the end of the novel was a bad idea, a shoehorning of human vagaries into the rigors of unbending "pattern," whereas Proust's far better principle of composition was subject to a more fluid and spontaneous sense of "rhythm." Forster gives as an example Proust's constant but never systematic or insistent return to the theme of the "little phrase," a melody that the fictional composer Vinteuil serves up in various forms and that the characters hear at strategic moments. Forster writes of the melody: "There are times when it means nothing and is forgotten, and this seems to me the function of rhythm in fiction; not to be there all the time like a pattern, but by its lovely waxing and waning to fill us with surprise and freshness and hope."

Frank Kermode, who is ninety this year, has brought out a subtle and fascinating book of criticism that obeys the delightful vagaries of rhythm more than the inflexibility of pattern. In *Concerning E.M. Forster*, Kermode sinks probes into Forster's book about fiction (the first chapter is called "Aspects of Aspects") and manages along the way to explore esthetic questions, Forster's life and Forster's links to other writers such as Virginia Woolf and D.H. Lawrence.

We learn that Forster would never have finished *A Passage to India* had it not been for Leonard Woolf's prodding. We read that Forster was, especially in his youth, a devoted Wagnerian and that the leitmotifs influenced his ideas about literary rhythm, though Forster felt his own rhythms were less obtrusive than Wagner's recurring themes. We discover that Forster rejected Henry James in part because he did not want to conform to James' practice of writing an entire novel from a single point of view and in part because Forster wanted to express his own opinions about life and the world in asides to the reader—an old-fashioned practice that James avoided. Giving as an example one of Forster's novels, Kermode writes: "It may be allowed that in *Howards End* the characters are represented as free individuals, with minds of their own, but the book contains a strikingly large amount of authorial reflection, wise sayings about love, class and culture, panic and emptiness, prose and passion, connecting and not connecting, straightforward announcements of the Forsterian way of looking at the human condition."

Although Kermode admires—or is at least keenly alive to—
Forster's prose style, his humanism and his moral elegance, he is
by no means an uncritical admirer. I remember that when I read
Howards End I was put off by Forster's snobbism in his treatment
of an upwardly-aspiring working class character, Leonard Bast, and
Kermode also remarks on Forster's inability to imagine the lives
and the minds of the poor—and his open hostility to Bast and his
wife: "The fact is that Forster could not bear him or his wife, and
made sure they were pitiable, indeed repulsive." This topic allows
Kermode to take a glance at the actual culture of autodidacts just
after the turn of the twentieth century and to demonstrate how
advanced it was in many cases. But for Forster, an unforgiving elitist
despite his democratic sympathies, the fact that Bast's wife makes
grammatical errors proves she is "bestially stupid."

Kermode makes neither too much nor too little of Forster's
homosexuality. He points out that Forster's affection for an Indian
student in England was what initially caused him to travel to India.
He also argues persuasively that Forster's pleasure in writing his
homosexual romantic novel, *Maurice*, which was published only
posthumously, and in penning his gay short stories, many of which
he destroyed as he went along, eclipsed the interest he'd taken in
writing about heterosexual characters. If he stopped writing novels
altogether for the forty-six years between *Passage to India* (1924) and
his death in 1970, it was partly because he was now very comfortable
financially (since his considerable royalties had topped off his
inherited income) and partly because he was convinced he was not
free to explore in print the only subject matter that attracted him.

With great authority Kermode places Forster in the artistic
context of his times. Forster, as I've already mentioned, attacked
James for being too abstracted from common human experiences.
He said that James's characters "are gutted of the common stuff that

fills characters in other books, and ourselves." In addition, Forster (who came from an evangelical family but was not actively religious himself) criticized James because "there is no philosophy in James's novels, no religion (except for an occasional touch of superstition), no prophecy, no benefit for the superhuman at all." Here we can see Forster defending his own turf—his knack for rendering ordinary human concerns with a gift for what he called "prophecy."

In *Aspects of the Novel* Forster discusses prophecy in nearly mystical and certainly eloquent terms. Of Melville he says that he "reaches straight back into the universal, to a blackness and sadness so transcending our own that they are undistinguishable from glory." If Melville was a model and a hero, one closer to hand, as Kermode points out, was D. H. Lawrence. At first glance they would seem to have nothing in common. Lawrence was from the working class and he had none of Forster's sprightly sense of social comedy. But Lawrence had prophetic powers and an ecstatic apprehension of nature—and Forster was perceptive enough to recognize that Lawrence was the greater artist.

As for Forster's own achievement, Kermode reminds us that Forster believed in inspiration (no wonder he went for such long periods without writing!) As Kermode puts it: "His experiences suggests that his own brilliancies derive from a creativeness essentially more intermittent. The music comes from the placing of these intermittent discoveries and their inter-relations. The novel enshrines them in its prose, putting quasi-musical motifs within its realist structures. It is these moments, and not the 'elaborate apparatus' Forster deprecated, that are the means by which novels can be complicated and passionate."

Kermode has a good, clear grasp of literary theory, which he has written about extensively and which he touches on in *Concerning E.M. Forster*. But he also has wide literary experience (one of his many volumes is subtitled *From Beowulf to Philip Roth*) and an ear attuned to poetic nuance (another of his best books is called *Shakespeare's Language*, a subject that—amazingly—is often neglected). Although this new book on Forster is not very long, it is rich and suggestive and written with quiet authority. People interested in all the "aspects of fiction" (cultural, thematic, formal and technical) will find it wonderfully stimulating.

A LOVE TORMENTED BUT
TRIUMPHANT

If you're going to read more than 700 pages of someone's diary covering just a decade, you want him to be a good writer, to know interesting people, to be intensely self-aware and above all to be a fascinating companion. Christopher Isherwood ranks high on every count. He was fifty-six years old when he began these diaries in 1960, an Englishman who'd lived in the States since 1939, mostly in Los Angeles. In his youth he was best known for his Berlin novels, *Mr. Norris Changes Trains* and *Goodbye to Berlin*, on which much later the musical *Cabaret* was based.

In Los Angeles, he wrote his three best books: *Prater Violet*, *Down There on a Visit*, and *A Single Man*. The composition of these last two novels occurred in the 60s, so we get to follow here his frustrations and triumphs in working on them. At the same time, he was writing many film scripts and entertaining almost nightly friends passing through town as well as local Californians. Among his closest friends were Charles Laughton, W. H. Auden, Jennifer Jones, Igor Stravinsky and his wife, Vera. (Isherwood agreed with Aldous Huxley that Stravinsky was "a saint of art," so thoroughly did he dominate the twentieth century—and "love...the act of composing.")

Gerald Heard, the Irish intellectual and eccentric, was another close friend; it was Heard who introduced Isherwood to his Hollywood guru, Swami Prabhavananda, who would play such an important role in Isherwood's life as a spiritual mentor (he is the subject of Isherwood's later memoir *My Guru and His Disciple*). The swami appears on nearly every other page of this book, a sweet, radiant, cheerful presence, demanding but forgiving.

I think what is most striking about these diaries is the combination of the sacred and the profane. Isherwood took his Hinduism very seriously, and *The Sixties* is filled with references to "making japam," or saying the Hindu rosary, every day. During a long period, Isherwood was occupied with the writing of the life of Ramakrishna, the mid-nineteenth-century Hindu holy man; simultaneously, he was working on *A Single Man*, his most openly gay novel and the founding text of modern gay literature. I've always read this novel as Vedanta without the religion—that is, a vision of a thoroughly secular existence in a book that contains not a single Hindu reference but that becomes coherent only if one invokes ideas like maya (illusion), atman (the essential soul) and karma (the moral record that passes on from one life to the next).

This "synchronicity" (a meaningful but seemingly accidental simultaneity—a Jungian concept that Isherwood often played with) between the Ramakrishna book and the novel illustrates perfectly the double life Isherwood was leading. He was getting drunk almost every night, he was living with a youngster thirty years his junior, he was conducting a few extra affairs on the side, he was concerned with money and status—and at the same time he was making a pilgrimage to India with his guru, he was a regular participant in temple activities and he was preparing his soul for old age and death.

Perhaps the best-sustained piece of writing in the book is the travel diary from his trip to India. Isherwood had a great eye. He writes of an example of Hindu Victorian, a house that has "charming old fanlights of colored glass, bottle-green louvered shutters, door handles made in the shape of hands." He is capable of the lofty, devastating brief dismissal: one of the monks "is admirably opposed to the Indian weaknesses; fatalism, love of chatter and indifference to social abuses." His swami is justifiably proud of Isherwood the celebrated writer. But Isherwood is all too aware of his shortcomings and finally announces to his spiritual mentor that he will never again make a public speech in which he holds himself up as a moral example.

The dominant theme of these years was Isherwood's conflictual relationship with Don Bachardy. They had become lovers in 1953, so they have already been together for seven years when this volume begins. Don had been just a typical Hollywood kid when they first met—in love with movie stars and the beach and dancing. But in his years with Isherwood, Bachardy acquired an English accent, complete with the Oxbridge stutter, a great ambition to be an artist—and a very prickly disposition. Bachardy, quite reasonably, was sick of being ignored by most of Isherwood's older famous friends. He wanted to be a personality and a talent in his own right. He wanted to travel (he made frequent trips to London, where he studied and where he had his first gallery show). The much older Isherwood had had many affairs—now Don wanted to catch up.

It's a miracle they stayed together until Isherwood's death, in 1986. I knew them as a couple in the early '80s, and by that point they seemed to be completely harmonious. By then they had written several play scripts and movie scenarios together, and Bachardy's drawings were hanging in the National Portrait Gallery in London. Don himself had converted to Hinduism (the ceremony occurs in the present volume).

Don's resentment and frequent departures for London and New York were among the triggering events behind *A Single Man.* Isherwood had been forced to imagine living alone forever, and in the novel the younger lover dies in a car crash. If Hinduism (albeit as a silent presence) was the second inspiration, the third was Isherwood's rereading of Virginia Woolf's *Mrs. Dalloway*: "Reading 'Mrs. Dalloway,' which is one of the most truly beautiful novels or prose poems or whatever that I have ever read. It is prose written with absolute pitch, a perfect ear. You could perform it with instruments. Could I write a book like that and keep within the nature of my own style? I'd love to try."

I once suggested that Isherwood was the closest thing we had to a secular saint. Now I can see, based on this volume and the previous one Katherine Bucknell has edited so brilliantly, that Isherwood had many faults, the worst one being his casual anti-Semitism. If someone who irritates him happens to be Jewish, Isherwood instantly makes a slur against his religion. But then again, Isherwood is the first to acknowledge his own faults: "Why aren't I wise, like it tells you you will be, toward the end? One is a dull-witted, gluttonous, timid, ill-natured—I was going to write animal, but let's leave the animals out of this; the thing I am isn't fit to touch their hooves or paws."

I get an acknowledgment in this book because Bucknell contacted me about several names in her glossary (I wasn't able to help her). That glossary makes *The Sixties* accessible to everyone, and the book is a true piece of social history. In these pages you can discover so much—about the Anglo-American community in Los Angeles, about the movies and how they get written, about the emergence of the gay literary movement, about a tormented but eventually triumphant love—and you even get to read a lot of good gossip and scurrilous jokes.

MORE LAD THAN BAD

The Pregnant Widow begins as a beautifully poised, patient comedy of manners, in the tradition of the nineteenth-century English novels that Martin Amis's college-age hero, Keith Nearing, is reading; then, in the last third, the narrative skips ahead and thins out and speeds up and starts to destroy itself joyously, like one of Jean Tinguely's self-wrecking sculptures—or like civilization itself in the twenty-first century. It's as if *As You Like It*, after carefully staging explorations of love and gender in a sylvan setting, were to knock itself out in a violent, messy, urban free-for-all right out of *Animal House*. In this respect alone I was reminded of *Gravity's Rainbow*, in which the main theme, entropy, causes the book itself to give up on being, intermittently, a fairly traditional historical novel about World War II and to go to pieces, to run down, and the main character, Slothrop, to vanish.

Amis has definitely given us an example of imitative form. In the first two thirds of the book there are even many direct references to Shakespeare's comedies, and young women are accused of being blokes or even "cocks," and the feminist revolution is piggybacked on the earlier sexual revolution. It all recalls Shakespeare's games with androgyny, his boys playing girls playing boys. Toward the end of the book, Keith suggests to the deeply ambiguous Gloria Beautyman that she dress up as Viola or Rosalind: "She's pretending to be a boy. Passing as a boy. Wear a sword."

After dwelling on a single visit to an Italian castle for a tense, glorious summer in 1970 and working out all the erotic possibilities (the characters even play chess much of the time), the narrator nosedives through the succeeding decades up to the present, losing hopes, loves, friends, and even the lives of the people he (or possibly she) loves along the way in a reckless, pell-mell casting aside of almost everyone he had ever cherished. Very lifelike. That's what aging does to you.

Philip Larkin had declared that "Sexual intercourse began/In 1963," and by 1970, when *The Pregnant Widow* begins, the youngsters have added copious four-letter words to their repertoire as well as saucily direct comments, appalling nicknames, and obscene erotic refinements. At one point Keith thinks: "The word *fuck* was available to both sexes. It was like a sticky toy, and it was there if you wanted it." In spite of all these liberties and acquisitions, the youngsters still seem naive, self-hating, and snobbish.

In his memoir, *Experience*, Amis credits Mrs. Thatcher in the early eighties with having cut through the British obsession with class of those earlier days: "Whatever else she did, Margaret Thatcher helped weaken all that. Mrs. Thatcher, with her Cecils, with her Normans, with her Keiths." It's no accident that Amis has used here the plebeian name Keith, as he has in his past fiction. In *The Pregnant Widow*, Keith, in talking with his girlfriend Lily, tries to defend his Christian name by saying at least it's better than that of their friend Timmy:

"It's impossible to think of a Timmy ever doing anything cool. Timmy Milton. Timmy Keats."

"...Keith Keats," she said. "Keith Keats doesn't sound very likely either."

In *Experience*, Martin Amis, impressed by his posh classmates at boarding school, looks up his own name: "Martin was the forename of half the England football team; and when I looked up Amis in a dictionary of surnames I was confronted by the following: 'Of the lower classes, *esp.* slaves.'"

It's too bad that Keith Keats isn't more promising as a name, since our Keith wants to be a poet. After a brief flurry of publishing in his early twenties, he gives it up and indeed Keith Nearing, we might say, resembles Martin Amis if he hadn't had the drive and talent to become a writer. Keith is addicted to sex, or thoughts of sex, as most men are, with this difference: male writers are also obsessed with dreams of glory and mental games of literary composition. Writers spend free nonsexual moments thinking about their writing and careers. Amis has said that he *enjoys* writing, that doing it is an active pleasure for him, and in *The Pregnant Widow* that pleasure is plain for all to see, even though the book is often world-weary in tone and the main character (for that's what Keith must be called in fairness since, improbably, he turns out not to be the narrator) is so often in poor shape when it comes to sex. Keith has a longish period when women aren't attracted to him and he's condemned to a bilious celibacy; in *Experience* Amis tells us of the real-life counterpart to this dreadful but mercifully short sexual dry spell.

Not that this novel is veiled autobiography. It's really more a kind of alternative memoir about a lesser person, one who doesn't have the stamina and imaginative fire to write. In that way it's a bit like *Look at the Harlequins!* in which Nabokov provides the gullible reader with a fictional autobiography of a Russian cad who has a string of unsuccessful marriages and had seduced a nymphet. In the same vein, Amis in *The Pregnant Widow* is an orphan and thereby sheds his famous real-life father, Kingsley, the beloved and eccentric main character in *Experience*. Keith Nearing's biological parents, we're told, are of the servant class.

In *The Pregnant Widow* there's a large cast of young characters and few adults to supervise them (one chapter is titled "Where Were the Police?"). Keith is at the castle with his girlfriend Lily, who has, alas, become something like a sister to him; when he has sex with her he often has to fantasize she's someone else, even with her verbal help and cooperation. At one point she pretends to be Scheherazade, the shatteringly beautiful sister of the owner of the castle. Scheherazade is so young she has only just grown into her beauty and hasn't yet become fully conscious of it: "There was too much collusion in the softly rippled lids—collusion in the human comedy. The smile of a beautiful girl was a sequestered smile. *It hasn't sunk in yet*, said Lily. *She doesn't know*." At one point Scheherazade sets up a secret rendezvous with Keith until he gets drunk and starts ranting against God; she, as it turns out, is religious (or at least her adored absent fiancé, Timmy, is).

More obliging though also more sadistic is Gloria Beautyman, a triumphant narcissist who looks at herself and declares that she loves herself: "Oh, I love me. Oh, I love me so." There's something mysterious and odd about her, though, which only becomes clear at the very end of the book. Then there's Adriano, the perfect Italian aristocrat, who's rich and flies his own helicopter and plays rugby with *I Furiosi* and speaks several languages and is capable of deep emotions and is altogether perfect—except he's four foot ten inches tall. (He gets called "Tom Thumb" behind his back, a consolation to Keith, who is worried about his own height and has to stand on a drainpipe in order to kiss his girlfriend in the street.) There's the older, wiser gay man Whittaker, who's in love with a very young, difficult Libyan named Amen. Various other young men and women drop into the castle and the narrative, including a viciously uninhibited woman nicknamed "The Dog."

This is a book that is highly conscious of being a book. Keith, of course, is reading all those novels; at one point he says, "Timmy'll be along in a chapter or two." The action often echoes the plots of the novels he's reading. "If Keith paraphrased Mr. Knightley, would Scheherazade realize, at last, that she was in love with him?" Elsewhere, Keith is poolside, perusing *Peregrine Pickle*: "Peregrine had just attempted (and failed) to drug (and ravish) Emily Gauntlet, his wealthy fiancée…" Later Keith will try to drug his girlfriend Lily so that he can ravish the beautiful and wealthy Scheherazade (he fails).

There are many subtle parallels between books and reality. But for Keith the whole experience is literary:

> The Italian summer—that was the only passage in his whole existence that ever felt like a novel. It had chronology and truth (it did happen). But it also boasted the unities of time, place, and action; it aspired to at least partial coherence; it had some shape, some pattern, with its echelons, its bestiaries.

By contrast, life—the life he goes on to live—"is made up as it goes along." This contrast between the rare, well-made, already novelistic experience and the more common, messy, improvised shapelessness of ordinary existence explains the shift from the tidy social comedy of youth to the baffling weirdness of age—and the exploded shape of this book.

Martin Amis is very funny and accurate about aging. In the first few pages we encounter this:

> When you become old you find yourself auditioning for the role of a lifetime; then, after interminable rehearsals, you're finally starring in a horror film—a talentless, irresponsible,

and above all low-budget horror film, in which (as is the way with horror films) they're saving the worst for last.

But Amis has no single theory about age. It's much too interesting (and neglected) an experience to sum up once and for all. Here's an observation about it:

> As the fiftieth birthday approaches, you get the sense that your life is thinning out, and will continue to thin out, until it thins out into nothing. And you sometimes say to yourself: That went a bit quick. That went a bit quick. In certain moods, you may want to put it rather more forcefully. As in: *OY!! THAT went a BIT FUCKING QUICK!!!*...Then fifty comes and goes, and fifty-one, and fifty-two. And life thickens out again. Because there is now an enormous and unsuspected presence within your being, like an undiscovered continent. This is the past.

Over the years, Amis has learned how to notate a superbly comic speaking voice; getting it down on paper is comparable to a good composer's skill in scoring heteroclite sounds never before made by concert instruments. That in this passage a solemn tone brackets a middle section of Borscht Belt humor illustrates perfectly Amis's mastery of the sudden shifts in register that are the peculiar genius of English prose—nearly impossible to translate into Romance languages, for instance.

The nasty depredations of age are items Amis loves to tick off in a comic, lip-licking list of horrors:

> And it all works out. Your hams get skinnier—but that's all right, because your gut gets fatter. Your eyes get hotter—but that's all right, because your hands get colder (and you can soothe them with your frozen fingertips). Shrill or sudden

noises are getting painfully sharper—but that's all right, because you're getting deafer. The hair on your head gets thinner—but that's all right, because the hair in your nose and in your ears gets thicker. It all works out in the end.

Here the rhetorical effects of repetition, the insistence that everything is all right, the parody of cheerfulness in the service of disgust—all these figures dramatize the tragicomedy of one's "late period."

Perhaps Amis's most striking meditations on age and time in this "snuff film" we're all starring in, this move from Club Med (frolicking in the sun) to Club Med (the medicalized final moments), derive from his analysis of age as the one remaining class system. If Thatcher got rid of poshness and feminism got rid of masculine hegemony and political correctness downgraded the status of the white race, then all that remains is age:

> As we lie dying, not many of us will have enjoyed the inestimable privilege of being born with white skin, blue blood, and a male member. Each and every one of us, though, at some point in our story, will have been young.

The people who are currently young, Amis predicts, will rebel against caring for the growing percentage of the population that is old; they "won't like the *silver tsunami*, with the old hogging the social services and stinking up the clinics and the hospitals, like an inundation of monstrous immigrants. There will be age wars, and chronological cleansing…"

The tone of these comments is rendered in Amis's hilarious essay style. Sometimes I wonder why writers who are witty and restless and worldly in their essays become dull narrators, inexhaustibly sequential ("and then, and then") in their novels, grazing every last thing in view. Wasn't it Valéry who said that when he read in a novel sentences such as "The Marquis went out at ten o'clock," he was tormented by how arbitrary the specific time was and realized he could never stoop to the dreariness of fiction? It's as if some essayists go from being fiery, high-stepping horses to digesting bovines, patiently chewing every last bit of grass, once they turn to fiction. If Proust remains the supreme mind in fiction, it may be because he *began* his novel as an essay or rather a Platonic dialogue between his mother and himself about Sainte-Beuve. And George Eliot, another truly intelligent novelist of ideas, turned to fiction only after she'd written numerous essays on fiction. Neither of them merely masticates.

I mention this notion of the essayistic in fiction not because I want pages and pages of ideas transcribed in novels but as a corrective to the American assumption that true novelists are rough-and-tumble brutes *getting it all down*—redskins instead of palefaces, to use the old distinction. Camus said that American writers were the only ones in the world who weren't also intellectuals. I suppose what I'm saying is that writers shouldn't lose twenty points of IQ when they turn away from essays to fiction. They should remain true to whatever it is that deeply engages them in writing, no matter what the genre.

Amis certainly knows how to present dramatic scenes with dialogue and terse descriptions of action. But he has also always known how to analyze action, usually from a comic point of view, how to place it in a chilling-hilarious historical or social setting. Few contemporary novelists would dare to write, as Amis does here, "We live half our lives in shock, he thought. And it's the second half." But this isn't some random apothegm; it is a dramatic thought, provoked by the life situation of the main character and attributed to him; it certainly is not an Olympian idea delivered from on high. Late in the novel the narrator asks:

What kind of poet was Keith Nearing, so far? He was a minor exponent of humorous self-deprecation (was there any other culture on earth that went in for this?)...He was of the school of Sexual Losers, the Duds, the Toads, whose laureate and hero was of course Philip Larkin.

The idea that humorous self-deprecation is unique to the British is not only true (try modesty in an American job interview and see how far it gets you) but also pertinent to Keith's portrait.

This funny essayistic voice is the same one we hear in Amis's amusing and accurate literary essays, collected in *The Moronic Inferno: And Other Visits to America*. In discussing the fame and material success that came to Norman Mailer when his first novel was published, Amis writes: "After an equivalent success, an English writer might warily give up his job as a schoolmaster, or buy a couple of filing cabinets." In discussing the last days of Truman Capote, Amis talks about how the diminutive novelist was hounded constantly by Lawrence Grobel, the author of *Conversations with Capote*: "Towards the end, his life appeared to be a bleak alternation between major surgery and Lawrence Grobel."

In *The Pregnant Widow*, however, the wit and the analysis are used to open up the story, to take a single idyllic summer and trace out its consequences in numerous lives and through four decades. Many of the themes in this new novel echo those sounded in Amis's very first, *The Rachel Papers*: sexual hunger joined to sexual insecurity; Latin tags and literary references used as erotic window-dressing; a twenty-year-old protagonist let loose in a foreign setting where he stalks British birds (Spain in the case of *The Rachel Papers*); intense if ambiguous class consciousness.

Amis has always dealt with lads or cads, amoral pigs (*Money*) or spotty kids on the make (*The Rachel Papers*) or a hateful, petty mobster (Keith Talent in *London Fields*) or an evil, competitive novelist, Richard Tull, determined to destroy his successful rival Gwyn Barry in *The Information*. He understands that evil exists in the world and he knows how to portray it in all its self-justifying, self-pitying luxuriance. When I teach creative writing I have to give a very exact assignment to get my students to sketch a bad person, to render any character other than one who is kind, sensitive, and politically correct. Only once they break the good barrier do these young writers begin to understand the possibilities of fiction. Martin Amis learned this liberating lesson early and well. He knows how to give his characters a short memory of their own misdeeds and a long memory of their grievances. He knows how they can justify any horror they've committed—and even add a little grace note of self-congratulation to the gory recital, and by the end of the book he has clearly matured, if that means to have grown bleak with insight and depressing wisdom. Amis's readers will be delighted by this return to form—that is, a new depth brought to familiar themes. And no one can deny the superb writing throughout, the attention to detail and to language lavished on every sentence. At one point close to the present Keith wonders if beauty has gone out of the world; if it did, it has just reentered literature through this strange, sparkling novel.

NOTEBOOKS OF TENNESSEE WILLIAMS

Tennessee Williams kept notes most of his adult life, although towards the end of it he wrote less and less as he descended more into his addiction to alcohol and drugs. The really fascinating years are those that preceded and accompanied his first two triumphs in the theater, *The Glass Menagerie* (1945) and *A Streetcar Named Desire* (1947). Throughout the 1930s, when Williams was already in his twenties, we see him drifting about from New Orleans to Laguna Beach or down to Florida and always back to his family in St. Louis. He didn't have sex until he was twenty-eight, and then he reeled away from the experience with a feeling of revulsion. He writes on June 11, 1939: "Rather horrible night with a picked up acquaintance Doug whose amorous advance made me sick at the stomach.— Purity!—Oh God—It is dangerous to have ideals." A few days later he adds, "I had the experience Sat. night which confused and upset me and left me with a feeling of spiritual nausea." Williams was, after all, the grandson of an Episcopalian minister and the son of a mother whom he dubbed the "president of the anti-sex league."

Later, during the war years, he made out like a bandit, hauling two or three men a night off the streets or out of the bars to his room in the Manhattan Sixty-third Street Y or his Brooklyn Hotel. Occasionally he was beat up (a violent trick was called "dirt" in the gay lingo of the period). The ideal of that time was not necessarily another gay man (though there were plenty of them) but rather a straight man who wanted to be serviced ("trade" in the gay language of the day—sometimes "straight trade").

Naturally, making propositions to drunken straight sailors or truck drivers could be dangerous. On January 14, 1940 Williams writes: "Probably the most shocking experience I've ever had with another human being when my trade turned 'dirt.' No physical violence resulted, but I was insulted, threatened, bullied, and robbed—of about $1.50 and a cigarette lighter. All my papers were rooted through and the pitiless, horrifying intimidation was carried on for about an hour. I was powerless. I could not ask for help. There was only me and him, a big guy. Well, I kept my head and I did not get panicky at any point though I expected certainly to be beaten. I didn't even tremble. I talked gently and reasonably in answer to all the horrible abuse. Somehow the very helplessness and apparent hopelessness of the situation prevented much fright. I stayed in the room while he was threatening and searching, because my Mss. were there and I feared he might try to confiscate and destroy them. In that event I would have fought, called for help, anything! He finally despaired of finding any portable property of value and left, with the threat that any time he saw me he would kill me. I felt sick and disgusted. I think that this is the end of my traffic with such characters. Oh, I want to get away from here and lead a clean, simple, antiseptic life."

So much is contained in this passage. The self-hatred and the quest for "real" men often put gays into the hands of blackmailers or brutes. The powerlessness was very real, since at that time the police would never have protected a gay man; homosexuality was a worse crime than robbery or assault and battery (it was still a capital offense in some states). Finally, the increased disgust with oneself and a pledge to "reform" after being attacked was typical; the victim blamed himself. The individual note that Williams brings to this scenario is his fierce protectiveness towards his manuscripts, if not to his own person. Also idiosyncratic is the use of elegant Southern turns of phrase ("portable property of value").

Young self-respecting gays today should read these notes just to learn about how much the oppression of the past distorted the personalities of the oppressed. If Williams was always lonely and insecure, if he met so few gay couples, if the other gays he knew all deplored their condition, these lacks and lamentations were characteristic of this period three decades before the beginning of gay liberation. At one point a gay friend of Williams announces that "we ought to be exterminated…for the good of society." Williams argues that gays are some of the most sensitive, humanitarian members of society, but his friend declares flatly, "We ought to be exterminated at the age of 25."

Everything is in this journal—his bouts of crab lice, his palpitations of the heart, accounts of his sudden fits of morbid shyness when he can't get a word out, his dependence on barbiturates and martinis—everything! And especially there are fascinating manifestations of his indomitable spirit, his reckless courage in the face of adversity. Again and again, Tennessee was shaken by anxiety and fear, but after each bout he drove himself to write again.

Year after year, no matter how crippled he was by hypochondria and some quite real ailments, no matter how isolated and defeated he felt, Williams was writing and writing. Plays and poems and stories poured out of him, sometimes at an almost unbelievable rate of one or two a day. If a story was rejected, he answered it by submitting another ten to publications around the country. Sometimes it seems as if he was just tossing his writing out into the world and seeing if anyone would respond to it. In 1940 his play *Battle of Angels* was produced by the Theatre Guild in Boston and closed after two weeks, an expensive and conspicuous flop. Almost any other playwright would never have emerged out of the ashes, but Williams in the same year wrote, "Perhaps I have really burned my daemon out. I don't think so. I think he is still a phoenix and not a cooked goose."

What is especially interesting is the way Williams kept trying out the same themes over and over in various literary forms and returned repeatedly to the same cast of characters, especially to his sister Rose, who had to be institutionalized for her psychiatric problems—and who was lobotomized in 1943. No matter how far Tennessee traveled, he remained true after his fashion to the fragile, vulnerable members of his family, and they haunted almost all of his writing. What becomes clear in these notes is that Williams feared that he himself might sink into the same madness that afflicted his sister. His writing not only extended sympathy to the wounded of the world but also acted as a form of therapy to keep himself sane.

Tennessee Williams gave the American theater more masterpieces than any other writer, plays that are still performed and that actors and audiences alike continue to be drawn to. *The Glass Menagerie, A Streetcar Named Desire, Summer and Smoke, The Rose Tattoo, Cat on a Hot Tin Roof, The Night of the Iguana*—the list is long and distinguished. These notes suggest some of the sources and influences, such as his ardent admiration of the novelist D.H. Lawrence, the poet Hart Crane, the playwright Anton Chekhov, and surprisingly the tough-guy Ernest Hemingway, whom he liked for his "fearless expression of brute nature." *Notebooks* is a thick volume elaborately annotated and copiously illustrated; the apparatus is more than justified since it gives us a look at the shoddy backstage of real life that permitted Williams to devise his unforgettable and perfect dramas.

THE MAKING OF JOHN RECHY

John Rechy's latest book is a memoir that reads like a novel, complete with cliff-hanging chapter conclusions, long dialogue scenes, a regularly repeating leitmotif (of a mysterious, glamorous woman), and a clear progression of accumulated effect. Fair enough, since he's stated that he believes there's something fictionalized about any memory. And he has dealt with many of the subjects in this book in previous novels. Rechy has said that the autobiographer is the biggest liar for claiming, "This is exactly how it happened." The biographer is on the next level down of lying for arguing, "I am capable of knowing another's life." The most honest writer is the novelist, who says, "This is a lie, a fiction, but I'm going to try like hell to make you believe it's true."

Rechy was born Juan Francisco Rechy into a Mexican family in El Paso, Texas, on March 10, 1931. His paternal grandfather was a Scottish pharmacist and physician who had settled in Mexico and then in 1910, for political reasons, emigrated to Texas. John Rechy's father, Roberto, had been a prominent musician and conductor in Mexico, but in El Paso his fortunes declined. This angry, frustrated father, given to violent rages, is one of the main characters in *About My Life*.

Roberto's second wife, Guadalupe Flores, was a long-suffering and very pious woman. Rechy was a mama's boy and his devotion to Guadalupe has been a major theme in his oeuvre. In his memoir he never gives us much of her background nor does he analyze her. No, he plunges right from the beginning into dramatic scenes— initially, those surrounding his sister Olga's wedding into a Mexican-American family a notch above the Rechys. That Olga is already visibly pregnant adds to the ire of her father-in-law, known simply as "Señor." The irate patriarch promises to interrupt the wedding and denounce the participants, but in fact he never does stage such a disruptive scene though he frightens everyone in the church. To add to the drama, his daughter Marisa, the "kept woman" of the title, has vowed to come up from Mexico City to attend the ceremony. Her father has disowned her ever since she began to live openly in sin with one of Mexico's richest and most powerful men, Augusto de Léon.

This sleek, elegant, fearless woman, Marisa, braving society's scorn and her own father's wrath, becomes a fixed point in Rechy's private cosmology. As he grows up and eventually becomes a male hustler, he summons up Marisa's courageous, coolly independent image every time he feels under assault by his father or by the law or by other scornful heterosexuals. Marisa, the kept woman, is his guiding spirit, protecting him from the anathemas hurled at him.

At the wedding little Rechy's fascination with the kept woman helps him to overcome his feelings that his sister is abandoning him by marrying and running off with this other man. In Rechy's books, feelings are always close to the surface, and bruised pride, desperate possessiveness, wild elation and wilder despair, lust and chagrin are usual emotions in his universe. And shame. Shame may be the strongest emotion of all. Shame at his family's fall in the world, shame at his own homosexuality, at least as he experiences it in the years before gay liberation, though often shame takes the form of an alienating distance from other men.

Rechy has always struck his readers as a lonely, remote figure—and his memoir locates the origins of this social distance. As a Mexican who "passed" for "Anglo," he often had to hear jokes cracked at the expense of other Mexicans. There is a scene in this book when Rechy is invited to a lavish Texas ranch by two unsuspecting classmates (they think he is as "white" as they are). The lady of the ranch tells the young men that she can't eat if the Mexican servants lurk about and watch her. The lady, "Miz" Crawford, says, "I love their food, but I can't eat when they're in the room with me, and that's the Lord's truth."

Rechy, who has kept his ethnicity secret from them till now, stands up and says, "If you can't eat when Mexicans are in the room with you, ma'am, then I don't want to be here to ruin your dinner." As a pale, Anglo-looking Mexican and as a very masculine-appearing homosexual (who as a youngster dated a handful of women and even had sex with them), Rechy was often invited as an ally into the enemy camp. Since he did his coming out in the late 1940s and the 1950s, in the midst of the McCarthy years, under the eye of a sternly macho Latino father, and long before the advent of gay liberation, Rechy had an unusually hard time assuming his identity. As a hustler he sold himself as "straight trade," that is, as someone who pretended to be heterosexual but was willing to be fellated for money.

In Rechy's novels, most homosexuals are divided between the woodenly "butch" and the theatrically "femme," between gay men posing as macho tough guys and flamboyant queens, a recasting of the familiar gender dimorphism of our society into still more extravagant terms. Interestingly, the gay books of this period—Gore Vidal's *The City and the Pillar* (1948) with its campy, bitchy queens in hot pursuit of servicemen; Jean Genet's *Our Lady of the Flowers* (written during World War II but published in the US only in 1963) with its transvestite-prostitute hero, Divine; and Hubert Selby Jr.'s stories in *Last Exit to Brooklyn* (1964)—are all about low life, the world of petty criminals, pickpockets, prostitutes, jailbirds, and freaks. These books could be widely read by a hip audience precisely because their very exoticism made them fascinating but unthreatening, a kind of travel literature about the unseemly and seedy, a walk on the wild side. Later, when serious gay writers would picture middle-class gay life (I'm thinking of Alan Hollinghurst in *The Spell* or Andrew Holleran in *Dancer from the Dance*), their seemingly more conventional work was actually much more unsettling. The characters might include the man in the next office rather than the transvestite hooker on the waterfront, and readers found this proximity disturbing.

Although Rechy has written about his family several times, never before has he explored so thoroughly his painful adolescence. Early on in *About My Life* he tells us that even though he was considered very good-looking he had no friends. A classmate who stared at him all the time told him:

> You're like a ghost boy...You don't talk to anyone. You seem to be studying others around you, judging others. You act as if you're not where we are.

Part of the problem, no doubt, was that Rechy's father railed at the whole family in a constant rage but singled out his pretty-boy son for special scorn. He thought little John was not sufficiently athletic and was too attached to his mother. He should go out and play rather than staying at home alone, writing stories. The father was bitter because he now had to work as a hospital orderly but recalled his glory days by "conducting" an imaginary orchestra when his favorite opera, *Carmen*, was being broadcast on the radio. Rechy and his siblings and mother would have to sit attentively as his father waved a baton in the air.

Rechy has never been embarrassed by his own narcissism. In his new book he recounts how, when he became a gangly thirteen-year-old, he prayed: "Please, Blessed Mother Mary, make me handsome again." He describes one of his female high school teachers noticing his restored good looks and promptly seducing him; I don't doubt the seduction happened but it feels false, the sort of violent sexual appetite that gay writers often ascribe to women (think of Tennessee Williams's voracious women or Coleman Dowell's). A girl at school also flirts with him; it turns out that both of them are passing as "Anglos" and she is as Hispanic as he is—Isabel Franklin is actually Alicia Gonzalez—and just as ashamed to be Mexican. When Rechy invites an Anglo girl to the prom her mother shouts, "Over my dead body will my daughter go out with a Mexican." He stops to wonder only how she knew.

If complex feelings about his heritage are one part of Rechy's story, another aspect has to do with the sexuality he obviously radiates and feels both excited about and ashamed of. An older bohemian couple in El Paso pick him up at the laundry where he works and invite him to dinner. The wife retires as soon as the meal is over, leaving the teenager to her husband—except Rechy rebels during Mr. Kippan's reading of Henry Miller's *Tropic of Cancer* and, disgusted by the bawdy descriptions, runs out into the night.

Early on, Rechy showed signs of his literary vocation. With Barbara, a bright girl at school, he set about translating Lorca's play *Blood Wedding*. He edited the high school magazine and wrote an essay for it, "Modern Art: A Shattered Mirror." He began a novel called *Pablo!* Perhaps a breakthrough in the fulfillment of his cultural aspirations was his encounter with Wilford Leach, a theater director. Leach was witty, well known, interested in Rechy's writing—and obviously in love with Rechy himself.

All Rechy's early experiments in sex and art were put on hold when he was drafted into the army to serve in the Korean War. One day while he was proving he could do more sit-ups than anyone else in his unit, a message arrived that his father had just died. When he reported back to duty, he was sent not to Korea but to Frankfurt. After his term was up, the newly discharged Rechy headed for New York. He planned to attend school using GI Bill money, but on 42nd Street he began hustling—accumulating the experiences that would finally end up in his famous first novel, *City of Night*.

When I was twenty, I met John Rechy's character Miss Destiny in the pages of *Big Table*, a controversial magazine whose first issue had been suppressed as pornography (it contained ten episodes from William Burroughs's *Naked Lunch*). At that time, in 1960, Rechy was becoming known by publishing chapters of his book-to-be, *City of Night*, in the *Evergreen Review* and in *Big Table*, which had broken away over censorship issues from the *Chicago Review*. I was a student at the University of Michigan and was immersed in *Lolita*, which had come out four years earlier, and in Lawrence Durrell's tetralogy, *The Alexandria Quartet*, which was just then being published. I preferred smooth European fiction to American hipster lit. In the summer of 1960, I met Charles Burch, an ex–jazz musician ten years older than I, on the Oak Street Beach in Chicago, near my mother's apartment (it turned out he lived in the same apartment building). He was an ad man and became my first lover. The epitome of Fifties coolness, he was a published poet and had battled drug addiction; his fetish book was Alexander Trocchi's hymn to heroin, *Cain's Book*, just published.

Charles sneered at my reverence for Nabokov, whom he considered too literary and "square." Rechy he admired because he was obviously "hip." *City of Night* would eventually be published by Grove, in 1963. In those days, when literary matters were hotly debated, the *Evergreen Review*/Grove Press list (which included Samuel Beckett, Jack Kerouac, Allen Ginsberg, Lawrence

Ferlinghetti, and Alexander Trocchi) aroused either contempt or admiration. John Rechy came in for this blanket response as a Grove author; in the pages of *The New York Review* he was scorned and lambasted by Alfred Chester (a more "literary" gay writer) in the June 1, 1963, issue. The review began:

This is the worst confection yet devised by the masterminds behind the Grove *épater-la-post-office* Machine. So fabricated is it that, despite the adorable photograph on the rear of the dust jacket, I can hardly believe there is a real John Rechy—and if there is, he would probably be the first to agree that there isn't—for *City of Night* reads like the unTrue Confessions of a Male Whore as told to Jean Genet, Djuna Barnes, Truman Capote, Gore Vidal, Thomas Wolfe, Fanny Hurst and Dr. Franzblau. It is pastiche from the word go.

Witty as this is, the review invents a genre (the Grove novel) and then finds this particular case of it inferior—surely an indefensible critical practice. Nor does it make much sense to invoke the elaborate "iron whimsy" of Genet (as Sartre called it) in the same breath as the neoclassical coolness of Capote or the logorrhea of Thomas Wolfe. There is a similarity between one of Rechy's best characters, the Professor, and Djuna Barnes's Dr. O'Connor, one of the great talkers in American fiction, but I'd wager that both Barnes and Rechy based their characters on different real-life "originals." Indeed Rechy's biographer, Charles Casillo, asserts that the Professor was based on a well-known (but unnamed) writer whom Rechy knew in Los Angeles (in *City of Night* he lives in New York). And Djuna Barnes based her Dr. O'Connor on an Irish abortionist in Paris named Daniel A. Mahoney. Obviously gay life, then as now, included some spectacular monologists.

I met John Rechy in the late 1970s. "Gay fiction" had been invented recently (if by that one means unapologetic novels written by gays primarily for gay readers and consequently devoid of the earlier strategy of a let-me-be-your-Virgil-through-this-underworld narrator). Everyone in the newly established gay lit scene in New York wanted to meet Rechy, since he was clearly a sort of founding father. He gave a reading in one of the small legitimate theaters on West 42nd Street and I introduced him. We were impressed that he still hustled (in his mid-forties) and that he worked out so diligently and rolled back his sleeves to expose his huge biceps.

At the same time, Rechy had a lively sense of humor about himself. When I had dinner with him in Los Angeles a few years later, he showed me his elegant apartment in Los Feliz near cruisy Griffith Park and explained that he had to tell his "johns" that the apartment belonged to a friend; early on, as he explains in his memoir, he had been rejected by a hustling client for admitting he read Colette. He had learned his lesson and knew that johns wanted tough guys who couldn't dance or make quiche or read French lady novelists. With a laugh Rechy also told me that one night he'd greased up his torso to catch the headlights on Santa Monica Boulevard. As he was standing out on the curbside displaying himself to potential customers, he noticed a young man circling back again and again in his car. Finally, the young man rolled down his window and said, "Good evening, Professor Rechy, out for an evening stroll?" It was one of his creative writing students from the University of Southern California.

Rechy in person is as funny and frank about his own narcissism as he is in his books. I had dinner at Musso & Frank's with him and his beautiful student Melodie Johnson Howe, and the two of them argued over who was the more attractive and who turned more male heads. Given that she was a movie star who had worked extensively in TV and film in the 1960s and 1970s and he was a man twelve years older (in his fifties by that point), the debate was a bit strange, but Rechy has a truly obdurate egotism.

THE MAKING OF JOHN RECHY : 151

Although *City of Night* remains Rechy's best-known book (new acquaintances invariably tell him, "I've read your novel"), he has written many others. *Numbers*, which came out in 1967, reminds us that in the bad old good old days, a gay man's life was considered over at age thirty (I can remember when friends would stage a mock funeral for anyone passing that dreaded boundary). In *Numbers*, an "aging" hustler in his late twenties, Johnny Rio, after living away from Los Angeles for years, returns and needs to prove to himself that he can still sell his body on the open market. Johnny is admittedly "extremely vain" though he also has a "harrowing sensitivity about age." Luckily, he looks to be in his early twenties and has even had to prove his age in bars. The title, *Numbers*, works in several ways. It refers to the age, waist size, height, weight, and penis size so important to the male prostitute's desirability. In gay slang, a "number" is an erotic contender (as in "He's a real number"). And finally Johnny Rio is embarked on a project of selling himself to the highest number of bidders in a short time—he's playing a numbers game.

In *The Fourth Angel* (1972) Rechy returned to memories of his adolescence in El Paso though he set it in the late Sixties, the period when he wrote this novel, his least successful. As we learn in *About My Life*, one of Rechy's favorite places in El Paso as a teenager was Mount Cristo Rey with its fifty-foot-tall statue of Christ blessing the city below. A very similar mountain provides the setting for the melodramatic end of *The Fourth Angel*, in which two young male members of a gang (or "youngmen," as Rechy calls them) are forced by Shell, a bossy teenage girl, to have sex with each other—or rather one boy rapes another because the girl orders him to do so.

The whole story reads like a gay man's fantasy version of Nicholas Ray's 1955 James Dean vehicle, *Rebel Without a Cause* (a film that already had a strong gay subtheme). In Rechy's book it's as if he is trying to solve a riddle: how can two men have sex with each other and still remain straight (and thus desirable)? Genet had tackled this problem in his last novel, *Querelle* (1947), and James Baldwin had taken it up in *Giovanni's Room* (1956). By the time Rechy got around to the theme in 1972, it already felt old-fashioned, though he tries to make his book seem fresh by having the characters take LSD and refer to each other as "the dude" (as in "Shell's trying to *help* the dude!")

Three years earlier, Rechy's mother had died and he had tried to console himself by doing lots of drugs. His recent novels—*This Day's Death* (1969) and *The Vampires* (1971)—had been largely ignored by reviewers. By the late Seventies Rechy was back in the public eye with *The Sexual Outlaw* (1977), a "documentary" novel about three days and three nights of anonymous sex. Two years later, just two years before the onslaught of AIDS, Rechy wrote *Rushes*, a novel about a descent into a waterfront backroom bar obviously based on the notorious Mineshaft in New York. This book is marred by its constant references to Catholic ritual; it brings to mind many novels of the late twentieth century that invoke the prestige of religion without subscribing to its doctrines. It doesn't really help a chapter about the leather scene to have it titled "Bless this sacrifice prepared for the glory of Your holy name."

Sometimes Rechy has explored his own experience by casting it into new imaginative terms. His 1991 novel, *The Miraculous Day of Amalia Gómez*, for instance, could be read as what would have happened if his mother had lived in Los Angeles and not been burdened with her difficult husband. Not that Amalia's life is easy—in fact the sympathy that Rechy invests in his character often feels like "displaced" love for his downtrodden mother.

Rechy has never equaled in later novels the dynamism and freshness of *City of Night*. In that groundbreaking book he was inventing himself as a macho loner for sale and was observing a whole new array of characters: drag queens, the still-beautiful boy living dangerously beyond his sell-by date, the guilt-ridden married men eaten up by desire and remorse, the vice cops and fag hags—they're all there, many of them for the first time in American literature. As a genre the novel, as its name suggests, thrives on novelty. It's as if every time a writer opens up an entire new aspect of experience the page begins to vibrate. *City of Night* is in some ways a road novel like Kerouac's. The language is hip, and sometimes excessive, but the energy of the whole long prose poem is undeniable. Like Kerouac himself, Rechy had discovered that Americans had no need of Surrealism; for them, their country itself was the *au-delà*, more exotic and frightening than any fantasy. The last pages of his memoir recount how Rechy—rather reluctantly, almost in spite of himself—came to write this classic American novel.

PORTRAIT OF A SISSY

The novel *Belchamber*, first published in 1904, is the portrait of a sissy and as such it was initially disliked by everyone, including Henry James and Edith Wharton, who should have known better. Curiously, the author, Howard Sturgis, was a beloved, amiable sissy who made no effort to hide his embroidery frame and the basket of silk thread he kept beside him at all times. Just as "Sainty," the hero of his novel, finds the only happiness of his boyhood in his "work," so Sturgis plied his needles with modest contentment and unremitting application.

Sturgis, however, had arranged his life much more satisfactorily than did his miserable character. Sainty has to give up his sewing. As his boisterous, athletic younger brother Arthur blurts out, "You're jolly bad at games, and you like to sit and suck up to an old governess, and do needlework with her, like a beastly girl." Whereas Sainty has no friends of his own and must submit to the wishes of his iron-willed Scottish evangelist of a mother, in real life Howard Sturgis surrounded himself with a family of distinguished and scintillating friends who adored him.

Sturgis was an American from a rich Boston family. His father, Russell Sturgis, had made money in the Philippines, but when he returned to Boston to enjoy his success he found the cost of living had become dauntingly high. He decided to go back to Asia with his family, but in transit they all stopped in London for several weeks— and never left. A bank, Baring Brothers, offered to make him a partner. Russell Sturgis accepted and soon was successful enough to maintain three houses, including a big country place, Givons Grove at Walton-on-Thames. He was wonderfully hospitable and was soon known as the "entertaining partner" at Baring's (just as a character in Ford Madox Ford's *No More Parades* is called "Breakfast Duchemin" after his splendid morning spreads).

Through his parents little Howard met such American luminaries as Charles Francis Adams and Edward Boit (a Boston artist who'd settled in Paris and whose daughters were painted by John Singer Sargent in one of the most technically astonishing canvasses of all time). Howard also met writers such as Thackeray (to whose fiction his own "caste-ridden" *Belchamber* has been compared) and Henry James, who was introduced to the family in the 1870s.

Howard was extremely attached to his parents, especially his mother. As a child he made his mother's boudoir into his playroom, and she refused to correct him for his effeminacy. She murmured that he was "sweeter as he was." As Howard's cousin, the philosopher George Santayana, remarked:

As if by miracle, for he was wonderfully imitative, he became save for the accident of sex, which was not yet a serious encumbrance, a perfect young lady of the Victorian type.

For instance, when he would step over a puddle he'd automatically lift the edge of his coat "as the ladies in those days picked up their trailing skirts."

He attended Eton and Cambridge (like Sainty), but unlike his character he courageously affirmed his effeminacy before his jeering classmates. His brothers had hoped Eton would make a man of Howard, but the plan came to nothing. Santayana praised his "inimitable honest mixture of effeminacy and courage, sensibility and wit, mockery and devoted love."

Howard also attended art school but soon was entirely occupied with nursing his father and then his mother through long illnesses. Russell Sturgis died in 1887, when Howard was thirty-two, and his mother died the following year. Suddenly, Howard was in possession of a large fortune—and had no direction in his life. As his friend A.C. Benson recalled, "He was almost in the condition of a nervous invalid, suffering from the long strain as well as from the shock of the double bereavement." He made a year-long trip to America, where he met Edith Wharton and Santayana. He returned to England the following year, in 1889. He then sold a remote country house in Wales and bought a much more accessible and commodious one in Windsor, right next to Windsor Great Park and not far from Eton. It had been built only twenty years earlier and was cozy and comfortable with its wide verandas, vermillion brick walls, *oeil-de-boeuf* windows, and its single acre of rather frowsy gardens.

Inside, however, everything was perfectly tended—small rooms with deep chintz-covered armchairs and couches and little side tables and coal fires glowing in every grate. It was the height of comfort and Howard, who disliked exercise, would leave it only for the occasional "toddle" with Misery, his dog, into Windsor Park. Howard was envied for Mrs. Lees, his cook, and his expert, attentive butler. Perhaps he was even envied for his stolid, pleasant lover, William Haynes-Smith, known simply as "the Babe," a man's man who preferred cigars and the racing results in "the Pink 'Un" to literary chat and *The Golden Bowl*. Eventually, the Babe inherited what was left of Howard's sadly depleted estate—and moved a wife in.

But for years and years, Howard and the Babe ruled over Queen's Acre, which was always called "Qu'Acre." They received Howard's many friends in such an unending stream that Howard confessed, "I feel at times like the unctuous manager of a smart hotel!" Most of the friends were male, many of them younger homosexuals, often from Eton, and they gathered in adulation around Henry James (after all, they had literary careers of their own to launch). They included Percy Lubbock, who would go on to enshrine James's and Wharton's ideas about the novel in *The Craft of Fiction*—he also wrote book-length portraits of James and Wharton. Another was the good-looking portly young writer Hugh Walpole (who purportedly once made an—unsuccessful—pass at the elderly and virginal James. Staggered by the initiative, James blubbered, "I can't, I can't").

Arthur Benson, Edmund Gosse, and Gaillard Lapsley were all regular guests (Lapsley shared Edith Wharton's enthusiasm for A.E. Housman and Proust). Wharton was one of the few women in the inner circle. She would travel with her fairly crazy husband Teddy over from France in her chauffeur-driven motorcar and swoop down on James in Sussex and whirl him off to Qu'Acre. She called the habitués of the house her "male wives."

Everyone seems to have been happy there with the lively conversation, the alternate currents of stylish bitchiness and genuine affection, and the studied luxuries. Some of the guests would go on outings to nearby stately homes. They all loved reading aloud; James put aside his habitual stammer to cry forth with eloquence the rolling periods of Walt Whitman. James called Qu'Acre "a sybaritic sea." Wharton was happy enough to leave behind the "anxious frugality" of James's Lamb House for the "cheerful lavishness" of Qu'Acre. Santayana called Sturgis "host and hostess in one" and dubbed him a "universal mother." Sometimes, of course, there were complaints in such a close-knit circle. As Hermione Lee puts it in her biography of Edith Wharton, "Hugging and yearning went along with satire and malice."

Many of the guests were transplanted New Englanders or New Yorkers who were delighted to affirm among themselves their very American form of exclusiveness. It was a relief for them, who were so often condescended to by the superior English, to mock the King as an emperor of India who lived at neighboring Frogmore. They liked calling Edward VII an arch-vulgarian (the great French chef Escoffier claimed that the King—then Prince of Wales—liked to have caviar scattered over every dish, a preparation known as "à la Prince de Galles"). As fellow expatriates, Wharton and Lapsley would swap clippings from American papers with their favorite headlines about adultery, murder, and felony.

These New Englanders at Qu'Acre included Walter Berry (Wharton's best friend and mentor), Morton Fullerton (a bisexual who became her lover—perhaps her first, since her marriage may have been sexless), Henry James, Lapsley, and Sturgis himself. As Percy Lubbock remarked, it was the only house in England where James was completely at home. In *A Backward Glance*, her memoir, Wharton writes that Sturgis sat next to the fire in a chaise lounge,

his legs covered by a thick shawl, his hands occupied with knitting-needles or embroidery silks, a sturdily-built handsome man with brilliantly white wavy hair, a girlishly clear complexion, a black moustache, and tender mocking eyes under the bold arch of his black brows.

Such was Howard Sturgis, perfect host, matchless friend, drollest, kindest and strangest of men, as he appeared to the startled eyes of newcomers on their first introduction to Queen's Acre.

The contrast of tenderness and mockery was noticed by all his friends, who remarked on his almost tearful kindness; after Sturgis's first visit to Lamb House James asked him to live with him and years later Sturgis asked James the same thing—both unsuccessful bids. James once compared Sturgis to a big sugar cake that everyone— all his friends—feasted on. But Sturgis could also waspishly imitate his friends, especially James, including his maddening way of stammering as he groped after *le mot juste*. Just as Marcel Proust could reduce everyone to helpless laughter with his mimicry of *his* mentor, Robert de Montesquiou, in the same way Sturgis could "do" James—and perhaps this art of mimicry was linked to both men's novel-writing talents.

In 1903, Sturgis passed along to James the first 160 pages of the proofs of *Belchamber*, his third—and as it turned out his last—novel. His first, *Tim*, had been the tale of a schoolboy crush at Eton. In his second, *All That Was Possible*, an epistolary novel, Sturgis had impersonated an actress who flees London for the peace and authenticity of Wales only to discover that Welsh men are as caddish as those in the capital.

Belchamber was altogether more ambitious. Sturgis worked on it intermittently for more than ten years. In it, he draws the portrait of an English marquis who is also Baron St. Edmund and is nicknamed "Sainty," a diminutive that is at once trivializing and an acknowledgment of his basic goodness. Just when Sainty is about to be sent to Eton and pushed onto the brutal playing fields, he is providentially injured in a riding accident. Lame and feeble, a partial invalid anchored to a raised shoe, Sainty is unable to participate in ordinary male games and the gentlemanly rites of hunting, much to his relief. From the beginning he was effeminate (more feminine than his bossy, controlling mother), but now he has an excuse for it.

Sainty is a complete contrast to his macho younger brother Arthur. When Arthur enters Eton he takes the place by storm with his frank and friendly manners, hatred of books, love of games, and perfectly obvious and understandable type of beauty.

Arthur remains uppermost in Sainty's thoughts throughout the novel, first as an endearing but easily corrupted and brainless boy whom Sainty must look out for, then as someone who has been corrupted by his feline French cousin Claude Morland, who has introduced him to gambling and actresses. Claude—well-mannered and penniless—is suspiciously polite, a Gallic smooth operator:

Claude's smile was a caress, the grasp of his hand an embrace; in later years a lady once said of him, that she always felt as if he had said something she ought to resent when he asked her how she did.

Whereas Henry James worked out his "international theme" of Americans versus Europeans, Sturgis pitted his supersubtle, suave, and immoral French characters (Claude against his grandmother, who was Lady Belchamber and now, *en secondes noces*, the Duchess of Sunborough) against his English elite, who are either puritanical (Sainty and his mother) or selfish and unbridled in their lust, covetousness, and capriciousness (Arthur and the woman who will become Sainty's wife, Cissy Eccleston).

Sturgis brings up his big guns to satirize these English profligates. When Sainty attends one of his brother's routs he thinks:

If this was the sort of entertainment Tannhäuser found in Venusberg, he thought the pilgrimage to Rome must have been an exhilarating change.

Elsewhere Arthur is supposed to be cramming in order to be admitted to the army but he keeps being lured away by the pleasures of the hunt. As Sturgis puts it:

It might be all very necessary that he should help to slaughter his fellowmen by and by, but the immediate duty was the destruction of pheasants…

If Sainty's mother is a zealous evangelist whose faith is at odds with what English society expects of such a wealthy, titled woman, Sainty's uncle is not troubled by his brand of Christianity:

His religion was of that comfortable, rational kind in which there is more state than church, and which is first cousin to agnosticism, but infinitely more respectable.

Perhaps because Howard Sturgis was so androgynous and such a keen observer and impersonator of women, he could be most unchivalrous in his descriptions of them:

She presented him to her mother, a terrible warning of what she was on the high road to become. This lady was a shorter and twenty years' older edition of Lady Arthur, more coarsely painted, more frankly vulgar, more consentingly fat, and she wore an olive green wig of Brutus curls.

Sainty is the incarnation of everything the English gentleman was not supposed to be. He is bookish and is happiest during his years at Cambridge. He dislikes sports and hunting but adores gardening and interior decoration. He accuses himself of being a coward, though the reader is not so sure; often he seems quite daring in espousing his eccentric beliefs. He is a great landowner who faints when he's meant to address his tenant farmers. He admires boys, especially thoughtless, rugged ones like his brother, but he is hoodwinked into marrying a fortune-hunting girl remarkable for her acting abilities before the wedding and her cruelty after it. He is, worst of all, a virgin and a cuckold who does not take punitive action when his wife becomes pregnant by another man.

Sainty's spinelessness, his refusal to fight back against his dictatorial mother and his mocking, abusive wife, are what James and Wharton both objected to. Perhaps if Sainty had been provided with Sturgis's own acerbic wit or literary friends or stolid Babe they would have forgiven him. But even if Sainty has a satirical eye he keeps his own counsel and seldom translates his thoughts into speech.

Wharton was kinder than James. She reviewed the book favorably and in her memoirs she allowed how Sturgis had chosen a "difficult" subject and that this unfortunate choice revealed his "relative inexperience as a novelist." Then, in a more ambivalent vein, she went on to say:

> He has shown us, in firm, clear strokes the tragedy of the trivial, has shown us how the susceptibilities of a tender and serious spirit may be crushed and trampled underfoot in the mad social race for luxury and amusement.

The modern reader takes exception. Maybe because of our own gender explorations we ask why the problems faced by an effeminate man constitute "the tragedy of the trivial." Why is Sainty a "difficult" subject except insofar as he isn't conventionally masculine? Nor can we quite see how Sainty is crushed by the race for luxury, since he himself is rich enough to absorb his losses and quite indifferent to all his possessions and, at least initially, eager to hand them over to his brother, who he's sure will make a more suitable Lord Belchamber.

Sainty's great disappointment is not with his beautiful wife, whose superficiality he recognizes from the beginning though he hopes that somehow, miraculously, she might love him in spite of his ugliness. He thinks:

> Jewels, clothes, a house in town, the means to feed the thankless rich, the power to walk out of the room before older women—if these things could make her happy, as far as they were his to give, let her take them in full measure. They were freely hers. He had no particular use for them himself.

No, Sainty's real disenchantment comes when he discovers that his Cambridge mentor Newby is an unconscious hypocrite. Although

Newby presents himself as an idealist tending toward socialism, he turns out to be overimpressed with Sainty's wealth and lands as well as with the titles of the guests who attend Sainty's coming-of-age festivities (one of the best sections of the book).

James wasn't quite sure that Sturgis, as a mere American and commoner, had mastered all the details of the milieu of an English marquis and wondered if he shouldn't have lowered everyone's rank a notch or two; which was strange since Sturgis's brother-in-law was a marquis (but maybe James had forgotten that). Then James found the end terribly rushed since (according to him) what is interesting in a novel is not the events (and the end of *Belchamber* is very eventful) but how they strike the governing central intelligence. To James, one gathers, Sainty was not sufficiently alive to his circumstances. No, he was nothing but a "poor rat."

James's objections are for the most part cryptic, as if he didn't want to assault Sturgis too directly, but he seems to want Sainty to be more a man, even a sexually performing man:

> You *keep up* the whole thing bravely—and I recognize the great difficulty involved in giving conceivability to your young man's marriage. I am not sure you have taken *all* the precautions necessary—but one feels, in general, that Sainty's physiology, as it were, ought to be definitely and authoritatively established and focused: one wants in it a *positive* side—all his own—so that he shall not be *all* passivity and nullity.

Elsewhere James comments on a scene where Cissy halfheartedly attempts to seduce Sainty so that she'll have an excuse for being pregnant:

> I wish [Sainty's] failure to conjoin with [his wife] about 2 a.m. that night on the drawingroom sofa, could for his sake have

been a stand-off *determined* by some particular interposing, disconcerting, *adequate* positive fact...something not so merely *negative* for him.

In another letter, James elaborates: "Suffice it for the present that I am perhaps just a wee bit disappointed in the breadth of the celebrated nuptial night scene..." Does he mean it's too long or too short? Too detailed or not specific enough?

Would James have been happier if Sainty had insisted on his conjugal rights? If, improbably, he had raped Cissy? But that would have been another novel and another character. It seems almost ludicrous that Wharton and James, who may have both been virgins at this point, should be bullying Sturgis about his lack of heterosexual expertise.

Amazingly, James writes in a later letter, "Start next year *another* book and let me anonymously collaborate." This is the same strange offer he made to several other writer friends, so certain was James that he alone knew how to write a proper novel. Still, in spite of all his objections, James predicts that the book, which was "never for a moment dull," would be a roaring success—a dubious compliment since he was certain that the public was ignorant ("no one notices or understands *any*thing, and no one will make a single intelligent or intelligible observation about your work"). But even so James can't resist adding that Sainty lacks a self and that as a result the reader keeps asking, "To *whom* is it happening?"

This criticism was sufficiently damning that Sturgis threatened to withdraw the book from publication. James shrieked:

If you *think* of anything so insane you will break my heart and bring my grey hairs, the few that are left me, in sorrow and shame to the grave.

Repeatedly, James assures him that the book would be very successful with the British public (which he calls "the BP").

It wasn't. Typically the *TLS* wrote that *Belchamber* "is a literary work rather than a work of literature," which presumably means it was uninspired and unpersuasive if carefully elaborated. The other critics were equally harsh, objecting to Cissy as a disagreeable woman and Sainty as a weakling, and the book sank quickly out of sight. It had to wait until the 1930s, a decade and more after Sturgis's death, to be hailed as a classic by E.M. Forster in an essay he collected in *Abinger Harvest*. One critic, George Thomson, even argues that Sturgis may have influenced Forster's earliest fiction. Thomson points out that *Belchamber* is intimate (in its direct access to the pathos of Sainty's feelings) and ironic (in its satirical portraiture of most of the other characters). Thomson argues that Forster adopted the ironic tone but rejected being on an intimate footing with the main characters—what we might call "doting." Forster never dotes on his characters but rather treats them all with a bracing dose of ironic distance.

Santayana was clearly influenced by *Belchamber* in *The Last Puritan*, "a memoir in the form of a novel" that he took forty years to write. By 1966 the anonymous reviewer of the *TLS* was calling a reissue of *Belchamber* "a remarkable book." The supporting cast, the reviewer wrote, "was a collection of deplorable though intensely lifelike characters, which include some of the most appalling women to be encountered in all fiction." In fact they seem no worse than the women in the slightly later *Guermantes Way*.

After *Belchamber*, Sturgis wrote almost nothing except a short story in which a younger writer is severely criticized by his imperious mentor and commits suicide. In the story, "The China Pot," a stand-in for James called John Throckmorton lets slip several half-uttered but damning criticisms of an unfinished novel by Sturgis's double, Jimmy. Mortally wounded, Jimmy withdraws from society. He cannot go on living while knowing that his hero,

Throckmorton, thinks he is talentless. He kills himself. At the funeral, Throckmorton pretends that he can't fathom why Jimmy, who had "everything," would have committed suicide. Jimmy's best friend also pretends out of politeness to be mystified.

In real life Sturgis was much more sanguine about giving up his writing career. His friend A.C. Benson said that he thought Sturgis had all the makings of a great writer except the drive. Perhaps he was right. Though Sturgis ran through his fortune and fell on hard times toward the end of his life (he even proposed that Santayana live with him as a paying guest), he still seemed to be enjoying himself. He told Wharton after he underwent unsuccessful surgery for cancer, "I'm enjoying dying very much."

ROBERT MAPPLETHORPE

Paradoxically, Robert Mapplethorpe is both a link in a long photographic tradition and someone who was startlingly original, without precursors. And his place on the artistic map was entirely something conscious and chosen; although he was not a reader, his visual culture was probably deeper than that of any other contemporary photographer, due to his own interests and those of his companion of two decades, Sam Wagstaff, one of the most ambitious private collectors of photographs of our time. Mapplethorpe, moreover, imposed his personal visual style on every element in his environment, from his simple, sturdy, virile Stickley furniture to his collections of glass and pottery to his own clothes, his saturnine leathers, which, when I knew him in the late 1970s and early 1980s, were never stiff, shapeless, clunky jackets out of a Brando film but rather supple, form-fitting Dutch black leathers elegantly seamed in blue.

In those days Robert lived in a loft on Bond Street just a few blocks away from me in the no-man's-land between the West Village and the East Village and north of SoHo. The exact historical and cultural moment of the late 1970s in gay New York is hard to re-create, partly because it was overshadowed after 1981 by the dark and ever-growing anxiety generated by AIDS, which not only cast a pall over an earlier exuberance but also changed values so radically that we can scarcely understand that vanished era.

Mapplethorpe was conspicuously apolitical and obsessed with his own career, with a degree of self-absorption friends might have called anarchic individualism and enemies might have labeled narcissism.

Even he, though, was inevitably influenced by contemporary political events, if for no other reason than that his stated ambition to raise gay male pornography to the level of high art plunged him into the turbulent and quickly changing moral values of the epoch.

In its first decade gay liberation (which began in 1969 in New York during the Stonewall Uprising) was all about sexual freedom. In preceding years, gays had been afraid to assemble lest their bars be raided and their names printed in the paper—a common practice, and one that usually resulted in losing jobs and apartments, not to mention friends and the sympathy of family members. What impelled lesbians and gay men to get together was sexual urgency, and these sexual encounters were what the police and psychiatrists were intent on stopping. For Mapplethorpe, gay life began and ended with sexual opportunity, always of the most urgent importance to him. As he explained in 1988 without a trace of irony, referring to the late 1970s: "I had many affairs during that period, but I was never into quickie sex. I've only slept with maybe a thousand men." Even today older gays have trouble understanding what "gay culture" means and what "gay identity" might represent, since for them gayness was only a matter of sexual necessity best forgotten once desire was sated.

But by 1969, the year Mapplethorpe moved to Manhattan, the mood was changing in response to a general social ferment. As

Michael Bronski, one of the founders of the Gay Liberation Front, has written: "The Stonewall riots and the Gay Liberation Front would not have happened in 1969 had it not been for the enormous social vitality of the times. If it were not for the presence of the Black Power movement, the second wave of feminism, the youth culture, the civil rights movement, the drug culture, the hippies, the yippies, and rock and roll, the raid on the Stonewall Inn would have been petty police harassment against one more mob-owned drinking hole that housed another dozen queens."

Indifferent as Mapplethorpe might have been to sloganeering, his work became celebrated because it flourished precisely during this period of heady freedom—from censorship and from received ideas about gender, race and sexual orientation. As he later said, "My life began in the summer of 1969. Before that I didn't exist." If he was later able to investigate perversion; to take self-portraits of himself as man and as woman; to picture a black man and white woman embracing naked; to coolly observe self-mutilation; to mix pictures of flowers, society women, and fist-fucking, this visual daring and promiscuity was endorsed and even empowered by the epoch. Ezra Pound once wrote that "the age demanded an image of its accelerated grimace," and Mapplethorpe provided his age with the very image it required.

In its first decade, 1969 to 1979, the one that formed Mapplethorpe's art and sensibility, the battle for gay liberation was still a violent one. For instance, on October 1, 1971, Connecticut became only the second state, after Illinois, to decriminalize homosexuality between consenting adults. In some states sodomy was still a capital offense. Early in 1972 the New York City Council vetoed a gay rights ordinance that would have prohibited discrimination against lesbians and gay men in employment, housing and public accommodations. In 1973 the Supreme Court decided that communities could censor works of art that might offend local standards of morality—which led, for instance, to a raid in New

Jersey on six allegedly obscene movies, including Warhol's *Flesh* and *Lonesome Cowboys*. The continuing closetedness this persecution brought about even in the gay artistic community in New York had a direct effect on Mapplethorpe's career. Dealers in the early 1970s might have been enthusiastic about Robert's explicitly homosexual art, but they all shrugged and said they couldn't sell it. Patti Smith, Robert's girlfriend, would show his work to gay dealers who'd reject it; as she recalled, "Several of them told me, 'I think the work is really interesting, but how can I exhibit it without making a statement about who I am?' Robert was really hurt by that."

As Michael Bronski points out, the original impetus behind gay liberation was the fight for the right to behave homosexually— to commit homosexual acts. This is no longer the case. Now in response to the pressures of the religious right, the anxiety and stigma associated with AIDS and the ambitions of lesbian and gay assimilationist political leaders, the goal has shifted from sexual liberation to identity politics. We are no longer defending our right to behave homosexually but rather our right to *identify as* homosexuals. The army's "Don't Ask/Don't Tell" policy reflects this shift, alas; gay sexuality is still illegal, although the right to identify as homosexual is now permitted; yet even there, the assimilationists argue, the question of identity should ideally be kept a private matter of self-identification in silence.

Although Mapplethorpe set out to incorporate explicit gay imagery into high art, he was reluctant to be identified "simply" as a gay artist. In the 1970s and 80s (and in many gay circles today), the term "gay artist" was considered a restriction, not just commercially but also esthetically, although it could be pointed out that a presumed membership in a dominant culture ("white writer," say, or "heterosexual painter") does not strike anyone as a limitation. But whether Mapplethorpe wanted to be considered gay or not, retrospectively he has been thrust into this role. The unfortunate shift today away from an emphasis on sexual freedom to gay identity has made the explicit sexual content of Mapplethorpe's photos look sleazy, politically incorrect, even racist.

Gay history evolves so quickly that the particular moment Mapplethorpe so fully inhabited and indeed helped to shape is in danger of being lost. What should not be forgotten is that when his photos became famous in the late 1970s, the gay community was one of the few entities in which white racism and black separatism were not yet in full control; in fact, back then the gay organization of Black and White Men Together seemed to hold out at least the faint possibility of healing the schisms of race through love. Of course, this trend was a minor one. Many white-dominated gay bars barred black customers from entering by asking for five pieces of identification at the door. Even in the gay pornographic press there were very few pictures of black men. I can remember that when I was interviewing black gay men in Atlanta in 1978 several told me that Mapplethorpe was virtually the only photographer who was giving them exciting and beautiful images of their race, a fact I mentioned in my 1980 book, *States of Desire: Travels in Gay America*.

Today, of course, all that is changed. Gay assimilationists want to play down the troubling question of sexuality altogether. The prevalence of identity politics rules that only blacks can photograph blacks; for whites to do so is considered invasive at best, exploitive at worst. A talented black gay poet, Essex Hemphill, attacked Mapplethorpe (after his death) in 1990 by singling out his famous photograph *Man in Polyester Suit*, in which the subject's head is not shown although his immense penis protrudes from his fly. He writes: "What is insulting and endangering to Black men is Mapplethorpe's *conscious* determination that the faces, the heads, and by extension, the minds and experiences of some of his Black subjects are not as important as close-up shots of their cocks." Quite rightly he adds a paragraph later: "It has not fully dawned on white gay men that racist conditioning has rendered many of them no different from their heterosexual brothers in the eyes of Black gays and lesbians.

Coming out of the closet to confront sexual oppression has not necessarily given white males the motivation or insight to transcend their racist conditioning."

At the time I tried to argue back in print that the subject was Mapplethorpe's lover Milton Moore, who forbade the photographer to show his body and face together; he was afraid family members would see the pictures and figure out he was gay. He gave Mapplethorpe permission to photograph his body alone, without the head, or the head alone without a nude body.

Of course, I realize this is just an anecdote, but I think it's a telling one. The subject dictates the very terms of the photo, an unusual situation except, perhaps, in the portraits of royals, corporate executives and movie stars. Yet Mapplethorpe's remarkable acquiescence in this matter reflects his more general attitude towards photography. His portraits were almost always shot in the studio under controlled conditions and with the full cooperation and even complicity of the sitter; not for him the shadow-stealing of the unauthorized snapshot. If I underline this point I do so because he has sometimes been compared to the white ethnographic photographer of the last century, the very symbol of exploitation.

One glance at his pictures, of course, belies this absurd accusation; his models are not people caught unawares at their folkloric habitual activities. Rather, they are carefully lit and posed bodies, sometimes placed against backdrops or sculptures Mapplethorpe designed. Sometimes their bodies are also oiled, although Mapplethorpe himself disliked this look, believing it to be reminiscent of corny physique photography of the 1950s, and shot oiled bodies only when the subjects insisted. Moreover, Mapplethorpe was an adept of the cult of beauty and rejected the freakish photo a la Diane Arbus or the unmasked-celebrity photo a la Avedon.

Of course, one could say that he was "objectifying" these bodies, but I would contend that photography by its very nature objectifies (the French word for "lens" is *objectif*). A photograph is always one person's glance at another, and the model never speaks or in any other way expresses his or her opinion about the results. It strikes me as not coincidental that so many of the general debates about exploitation that have wracked America have involved photography—women against pornography and the Native American critiques of early ethnographic photographers are but two examples. Photography is by its very nature an invasion and, to the degree that a portrait suggests an insight into another person, a definitive likeness, a revelation of character, it is an imposition of one person's vision on another person's identity.

If objectification is at the heart of photography, the visual arts in general conceal precisely in their very formal categories certain built-in prejudices and conservative social agendas. Take the genre distinction between "nudes" and "portraits," as old as sculpture and painting in the West. I would contend that this very distinction, one that Mapplethorpe observed and perpetuated in his work, is inherently insulting, as though only notables merit a careful, respectful depiction of their personalities and faces, whereas less important if usually more beautiful men and women are to be prized for their bodies alone. An emperor poses for his (admittedly idealized) portrait bust; he chooses the sculptor. A sculptor, however, chooses a woman to represent a muse, say, or an abstraction such as Justice, and if he accomplishes his purpose the actual identity of his model will not be recognizable from the nude statue. As Marina Warner has pointed out in *Monuments and Maidens*, one reason sculptors in the nineteenth century used a woman to represent Justice was because in so doing there was no danger that the woman would resemble any actual judge. A good portrait is an unforgettable likeness, whereas nude figures—naiads or bathers, for instance—are generic figures, virtually interchangeable. Most nudes invite the viewer's desire; as feminist critics have shown, even seemingly consecrated images such as the Polynesian bare-breasted women Gauguin painted are actually soft-core porn. Since

Gauguin's figures are women, the traditional and conventionally "formal" subject of figure painting, we do not even register the erotic element invoked by the round fruits they hold beneath their breasts (although this strategy became more obvious when art critic Linda Nochlin created analogue paintings of men with large penises holding trays of bananas).

I enter into these genre distinctions and the class prejudices and sexual politics behind them because some critics have questioned why Mapplethorpe so often gives us portraits of white society women, for example, and impersonal nude studies of black men. The question, I would concede, is a legitimate one, but I'd also argue that the supposedly demeaning attitudes expressed by Mapplethorpe are linked to desire. He desires black men and studies their bodies; he is fascinated by women "only" as personalities and therefore makes portraits of them. If Mapplethorpe is inherently racist (in this sense alone), he is certainly not sexist. He "exploits" men's bodies in nude photos and renders women the full (if finally hollow) honors of portraiture. Interestingly, when his sensibility was truly engaged by either a man or a woman (Bob Love or Lisa Lyon, for instance), the distinction between nude and portrait breaks down; his figures may be naked, but the subjects' personalities are intensely rendered. Nevertheless, it remains disconcerting that in the National Portrait Gallery show in London, *Mapplethorpe Portraits*, only ten of the seventy-one images in the catalogue were of black men or women, whereas in a corresponding book of nudes more than half the photos would have been of black men.

In some ways photographs are like music—likely to awaken strong but not very specific emotions. Most people respond with intense feelings to a Mozart piano concerto, but if a roomful of people were asked to write descriptions of what they feel while listening to a largo, no two descriptions would be the same. Similarly, images in general and photographs in particular evoke strong reactions, but seldom the same ones. The written word, by contrast, conjures up much more precisely defined feelings, but usually those feelings are somewhat milder and slower to be evoked. The French novelist Jean Genet, for instance, never had any problem with the law until his fourth novel, *Querelle*, was given sexy illustrations by Jean Cocteau; perhaps censors prefer glancing at disturbing images to reading long books. Or, to give another example, hundreds of books can be bought in the United States that are far more sexual or even more sadomasochistic than the most extreme images produced by Mapplethorpe, but none has awakened the rage elicited by his photographs.

Why?

Not only can a photograph be quickly apprehended, but it can also be seen inadvertently and by anyone who happens to glance at it; seeing it does not depend on a decision by the viewer, whereas reading a text is a project that must be voluntarily embarked on. Of course, one could argue that this problem is eliminated when these potentially disturbing images are restricted to a book or an exhibition one must pay to see, or when the most extreme images are relegated to a particular part of the exhibit or to a sealed book available only to adults.

But the problem does not end there. Whereas words are symbols that evoke visual images provided by the reader's own imagination (and presumably no two readers' images are the same), a photograph provides the viewer with a ready-made image of a specific individual; no participation on the part of the spectator other than looking is required.

Moreover, that photographed individual has a history, a scar, an age, a name (Mapplethorpe usually gives us his subject's names, or at least, depending on the model's preference, his first name). If one man is photographed urinating in another's mouth, that picture gives the participants' names, a date on which the event occurred and the name of the site (Sausalito in this case). We are not dealing with a fantasy invented by a writer or a painter but with a real event staged for the camera. In the case of Mapplethorpe's sadomasochistic pictures, real people are presumably being shown practicing their real vices: they have been recruited because they are already adepts of, say, bondage or water sports. No matter that these pictures are rather cold, formal, even static and, at least for this viewer, decidedly unexciting and therefore nonpornographic; some of them make one think less of enslavement and possession than of the banal pride of the deep-sea fisherman posing beside the day's stupendous catch.

When we look at a photo, we're always aware of time; for that reason we speak of "old photos" and even "old movies" but never "old paintings" or "old novels." When we look at Thomas Eakins's paintings of boys jumping into a swimming hole, we never stop to ask questions about the models, whereas when we look at the photos he worked from we say, "I wonder what his name was?" or "How old would he be if he were still alive?" or "I wonder if Eakins made it with him?" Roland Barthes said that photography is always about death; because we're confronted with a living person, we wonder about when he died in the past or will die in the future. In this sense, as Marina Warner has argued, photos are descendants of wax death masks, and even their glossiness reminds us of the shininess of wax itself.

But if photos arouse ideas of death, of real individuals, and consequently awaken feelings of outrage that writing does not usually evoke, by the same token their instantaneous availability means that they can elicit an enthusiasm denied to literature. Mapplethorpe became much more famous and rich, for instance, than any gay writer of the same epoch. To read Larry Kramer's *Faggots*, for example, involves a week-long immersion in a very specific ghetto life, one that the reader must re-create in his own mind, drawing upon his own supply of memories, psychological knowledge and visual experience; the book must enter into the very fiber of its reader, whereas the photograph can be glanced at without being assimilated. The photo, of course, also has an inherent value as a precious object. And it can travel faster, farther, easier than a text; in that way it is like music. No need to translate it. Patti Smith's records are known the world over, whereas her poetry is read by only a cult, just as everyone knows Gauguin's paintings but not his book, *Noa Noa*.

Mapplethorpe's most disturbing images, those of bondage, sadism, humiliation, scarification, are somehow appropriate both to his particular moment as a gay man and to a more general, less time-bound American sensibility. When I speak of that American sensibility, what I have in mind is a puritanical hatred of pleasure. Sex cannot be esteemed by Americans as an art, a form of dalliance, an expression of affection; no, it must stand for a transcendent search, a quest for self-revelation or self-perfection. The early Christian martyrs excoriated the flesh in the name of the spirit; the modern American puritan unites the flesh and the spirit and excoriates both. Pain is a guarantee of spiritual mission; self-destruction is a form of martyrdom.

The particular gay moment of the 1970s I referred to was one of virilization; as gay men rejected other people's definitions, they embraced a new vision of themselves as hypermasculine—the famous "clone" look. Soldier, cop, construction worker—these were the new gay images, rather than dancer or decorator or ribbon clerk. A new tribalism replaced the isolation of the self-hating queer individual; a kind of body fascism came into vogue, as muscular bulk took precedence over boyish slimness, as the weathered thirty-five-year-old man instead of the hairless ephebe became the ideal.

The very success of this revolution brought its own problem: conformity. Whatever its shortcomings might have been, at least preliberation homosexuality had been guaranteed to be irrevocably marginal, transgressive, scandalous. What Mapplethorpe (and Pasolini) found in sadism and scatology was a practice, a world, so revolting that even (or especially) other homosexuals were horrified by it. Like every good Catholic, both Pasolini and Mapplethorpe were attracted to Satanism (indeed Mapplethorpe reportedly would whisper into his lovers' ears, "Do it for Satan"); the torture Mapplethorpe documented in his photos and Pasolini in *Salò* will smell eternally of brimstone. In the gay movement the two ver- boten subgroups are still sadists and pedophiles; it is no accident that Mapplethorpe alluded to both.

Of course, for Mapplethorpe there were precedents for homosexual photography—F. Holland Day, von Gloeden, Herbert List—just as there were influential homosexual painters of an earlier period, including Paul Cadmus, Jean Cocteau and Pavel Tchelitchew. Mapplethorpe also had important photographers as contemporaries, including George Dureau, Arthur Tress, Bruce Weber and Duane Michals. But the most relevant to an appraisal of Mapplethorpe seems to me to be George Platt Lynes.

Born in 1907 in New Jersey, Lynes traveled to France when he was just eighteen, where he met Cocteau and Tchelitchew as well as Gertrude Stein. From the age of twenty until his early death in 1955 at age forty-eight, Lynes worked as a photographer. He did fashion work, celebrity portraits—and homoerotic photography. He took pictures of erect penises, of black and white male couples, of a suffering man in bondage; he paired nude men with classical sculpture. In all these ways Lynes set an important precedent for Mapplethorpe. Lynes, too, isolated body parts and fetishized sexual organs. He, too, photographed other gay men, usually dancers or artists; in this way Lynes and Mapplethorpe differ from photographers such as Bruce Weber, whose subjects (cowboys, greasers, professional athletes, fashion models) are usually heterosexual. They may awaken gay desire, but the desire is not reciprocated. Quite a contrast with Mapplethorpe, who often had sex with his subjects on the same night he photographed them. In fact his usual procedure was to pick up someone or other for sex and then only later ask if they'd pose for him (he'd always give them two prints as payment, which as the years went by and his prices rose astronomically turned out to be very handsome recompense indeed). Mapplethorpe was always frank about and even proud of his own sexual involvement with his models. As he told *American Photographer* in 1988, "Let's face it, most photographers are living their lives vicariously by taking pictures. When they get into sex or pornography it's often a sort of cover-up for their own sexual inactivity or inadequacy. They'd rather do it through the camera and sublimate their desires in order to take pictures."

In Mapplethorpe's case his sexual encounters with models preceded taking their picture.

If Mapplethorpe was linked to earlier photographers and painters, he was also genuinely original, especially in his simplicity, his directness, his unapologetic curiosity, the unwavering force of his regard. As any look at gay art, whether literary or plastic, reveals, nothing is so difficult, so recent, so evolved as the simplicity of unmediated vision. Early gay fiction, for instance, is set in ancient Greece or in another country or occurs between innocent schoolboys or touches on the subject of forbidden sexuality only on the last page or takes place between an aristocrat and a peasant on fog-swept island or involves a doomed couple living far from other gay people. Madness or suicide or accidental death is usually the conclusion. (But Michael Bronski's *Pulp Friction* collection contests this general view and sees gay fiction of the 1940s and 1950s as more nuanced and cheerful than I do.) Similarly, the alibi of early gay photography is the classical world of ballet or mythology or "scientific" studies of motion or degeneration. Sleeping boys or the dead Christ or the martyred Saint Sebastian or mud-larks fishing coins out of the Thames or naked wrestlers or exotic Arab dancing boys dressed as girls—these are just a few of the pretexts for earlier gay photography.

What is extraordinary about Mapplethorpe is his abandonment of all these contexts, this window dressing for, if you will, the naked fact of sexual curiosity and erotic intensity.

Mapplethorpe once said that all his photographs were altars.

When he first started to work, this adulation of the body was still staged in Catholic terms; only later did he eliminate the element of Catholic kitsch, although what remained was a sense of ceremony, of mystical transformation. He liked to say that S&M stood for "sex and magic," and certainly the first and last article in his faith became sex, and the principal mystery in his cult that of the magical transubstantiation of the naked into the nude, the fallible body into the perfection of flesh.

"I guess you could say I have a certain Catholic aesthetic," he confided to his biographer, Patricia Morrisroe, to whose book I am indebted for some of the information in this essay.

He was born in Hollis, Queens, on November 4, 1946, the third child in a pious middle-class family. As a boy he attended the local church, Our Lady of the Snows, and did Cubist portraits of the Madonna. Later, as an adult, he told Ingrid Sischy, the editor of *Artforum*, "A church has a certain magic and mystery for a child. It still shows in how I arrange things. It's always little altars. It's always been this way—whenever I'd put something together I'd notice it was symmetrical."

He attended art school in Brooklyn at the Pratt Institute. In 1967, when he was twenty, he met Patti Smith, with whom he lived for years and with whom he shared an intense period of creative discovery. They each worked part-time, and for a while Patti was earning enough money selling books at Scribner's to be able to support Robert entirely, liberating him to work nonstop on his art. He did not become a photographer right away, although from almost the beginning he used sexy gay photos he found in magazines as collage elements.

He and Patti both read Rimbaud's poetry and Genet's novels, the work of two writers who resorted to Catholic imagery, usually for profane purposes. Genet was the first writer to break with the earlier evasiveness regarding homosexuality and to present himself under his own name as a gay protagonist and narrator living not in some never-never land but, in the case of *Our Lady of the Flowers*, in the gay ghetto of Montmartre itself. In Genet's novels there are no medical or psychological or genetic explanations of the origins of homosexuality. Unlike most middle-class writers of his day, he did not present homosexuality as a malady calling for compassion from the reader; no, Genet always presented homosexuality as a sin and a crime.

Mapplethorpe, like Genet, would invert Catholicism and would emphasize the satanic side of homosexuality. His self-portraits would become the equivalent to Genet's various first-person narrators, always named Genet. And Genet's erotic fascination with violence and torture would find an echo in Mapplethorpe's hard look at physical brutality.

When Mapplethorpe would work beside Patti Smith in the early 1970s, he would wear a monk's robe; as he said, "When I work, and in my art, I hold hands with God." In their room Mapplethorpe set up an altar that included his own drawing of a pentagram, a black cloth draped over a table, statues of the Virgin purchased at a Puerto Rican bodega, bronze figures of the devil, and the skull of a monkey he had named Scratch (one of the devil's names) and later decapitated and boiled down.

During these early years he would devise collage pieces from gay pornography, and on November 4, 1970, he opened his first one-man show of twelve "freak collages," as he called them. But the religious theme was never far from his mind. He referred to his collages as "altarpieces from some bizarre religion." In 1969 he tacked a tie rack onto a found lithograph of the Virgin. At home he put together an altarpiece by covering a nightstand with Patti's wolf skin, a magic talisman for both Robert and her. On the table he placed a statue of the Sacred Heart with black tape covering the eyes. He bought a conventional Advent calendar but replaced all the holy images with pictures of Patti. He created two Cornell boxes in which he placed a statue of the Sacred Heart, a crucifix and a skull.

This religious theme was paralleled by—and sometimes even mixed in with—pornographic images, some of them self-portraits. He appeared in a thirty-three-minute movie called *Robert Having His Nipple Pierced.* Among the first photos he took were the 1972 black-and-white Polaroids he shot of David Croland, which he later photostatted and hand-colored. They show Croland crouching naked under a net, his back to us, or again lying down, face up, under the same wide-mesh net. He did a nude self-portrait in 1971 which he placed behind a piece of wire mesh, the whole affixed to a paper bag. The bag may suggest disposable garbage, but the Saint Sebastian pose alludes to martyrdom, whereas the wire mesh evokes the screen in a confessional. Some of these works, as well as four nude self-portraits in which the body is juxtaposed against classical sculpture, were shown in his earliest shows (his first photography show was held in January 1973).

Mapplethorpe learned from the men he attached himself to. Through his intense friendship with Metropolitan curator John McKendry, Mapplethorpe was introduced to Thomas Eakins's photographs of naked boys and Alfred Stieglitz's photos of Georgia O'Keeffe nude. Since Stieglitz and O'Keeffe were married, this encounter may have suggested to Mapplethorpe the idea of photographing Patti Smith nude. Thanks to Sam Wagstaff, Mapplethorpe first saw the nudes of von Gloeden (which Wagstaff collected) as well as the magisterial portraits of nineteenth-century artists and writers photographed by Nadar.

By the late 1970s Mapplethorpe had become a mature artist. He had entirely eliminated the last tacky bit of collage or Catholic kitsch, although his early orientation towards creating unique pieces led him sometimes to fashion elaborate frames out of silk panels and wood and even to make stylized crosses out of white shag carpet and wood or of frosted mirror in a shaped frame. As his taste became purer he eschewed anything juvenile or ironic or sacrilegious, but his urge to adore and his sense of reverence are still transparent in his awe-inspired portrait of say, Bob Love, the enthroned African deity, the Ur-principal of fertility. Even his flowers, far from being an escape into the natural or the decorative, are meticulously posed organs—"New York flowers," as Mapplethorpe called them. As he once remarked, "Sex is magic. If you channel it right, there's more energy in sex than there is in art." He made the two so interchangeable, and mingled them both so intimately with his life, that in the end neither he nor we need to choose between them.

THE DESERT OF SOLITUDE

In an essay about the Sahara, "Baptism of Solitude," Paul Bowles tells us many interesting things about oasis towns (where the fertility of cultivated plants is all-important and birds are hated as seed-stealers) and about the Touareg, a desert-dwelling tribe whose name in Arabic means "lost souls" but who call themselves the "free ones." But what Bowles prizes above all else about the desert is its absolute solitude. "Why go?" he asks.

The answer is that when a man has been there and undergone the baptism of solitude he can't help himself. Once he has been under the spell of the vast, luminous, silent country, no other place is quite strong enough for him, no other surroundings can provide the supremely satisfying sensation of existing in the midst of something that is absolute. He will go back, whatever the cost in comfort or money, for the absolute has no price.

As his novel *The Sheltering Sky* suggests, the absolute solitude of the desert may exert a strong appeal, but that magnetism is not necessarily salutary. In it two young Americans, Kit and her husband Port, head farther and farther into the desert, even though he is seriously ill and will soon die. When they finally arrive at a remote outpost, Kit observes that at last there is no "visible sign of European influence, so that the scene had a purity which had been lacking in the other towns, an unexpected quality of being complete which dissipated the feeling of chaos." Here Port dies and Kit enters her own slow process of abjection and self-destruction. "Purity" is the quality Bowles's characters cherish, but it is a purity that destroys them.

Bowles embraced the desert as a Christian saint embraces his martyrdom. His self-abnegation and his love of traditional culture made him one of the keenest observers of other civilizations America has ever had. Unlike some of his countrymen, he did not brashly set out to improve the rest of the world. For Bowles, Americanization was the problem, not the solution. As for many intellectuals of his generation, civilization was equivalent to its discontents; for Bowles, however, third-world culture was also equivalent to its dehumanizing poverty. A situation where there are only two alternatives and both are bad is one definition of tragedy. Bowles had a tragic vision.

Although *The Sheltering Sky* was a first novel, it reads like the work of an experienced master. Bowles was in his late thirties when he wrote it; he had long been living in a sophisticated milieu; and he had carefully edited the remarkable novel *Two Serious Ladies* by his wife, Jane Bowles. *The Sheltering Sky* has none of the awkwardness or variability of a maiden effort.

It is also surprisingly adroit technically. Novels need different openings than stories do; a novel needs an opening that is inviting, engaging but not too definitive or even too satisfying. *The Sheltering Sky* opens with a narrative that wavers between the point of view of Port and Kip without giving away too much about either character. And in just a few pages it establishes the seedy, menacing atmosphere of a North African port.

After Port's initial awakening, we're given a tableau on the terrace of the Café d'Eckmühl-Noiseux (the German-French name in an Arab country suggests the cultural confusion of colonialism) where three Americans—two men and a girl (as Bowles calls her)— are observed from a distance. One of the men is looking at a map. Then we suddenly are privy to the fact that maps bore Kit whereas they fascinate Port. They've been married twelve years and are constantly in motion. When they're not traveling maps continue to attract him. Now they're in North Africa with a great deal of luggage.

We switch from access to her thoughts to an external observation of her: "Once one had seen her eyes, the rest of the face grew vague, and when one tried to recall her image afterwards, only the piercing, questioning violence of the wide eyes remained." A strict follower of Henry James would object to all these shifts of point of view, but in fact they give a strong inside-outside sense of Kit and Port. It's important that we know that Kit is slightly mad—and this objective snapshot of her eyes gives us our first clue.

Kit says that she fears everything throughout the world is getting homogenized, and Port is quick to agree that indeed everything is becoming grayer and grayer. "But some places'll withstand the malady longer than you think. You'll see, in the Sahara here…" At this point we're only on page eight but already the Sahara has been introduced. It will be one of the main characters in the novel. And its introduction is ironic; it will turn out that the desert will be monochromatic, literally, and that the oasis towns will be dirty, dusty, almost featureless.

Afterward Port wanders through the town on his own. Prefiguring the central movement of the book—the steady push inland—in this opening scene he keeps walking farther and farther—away from the sea, toward the desert—into dangerous zones of the town. This contact with "a forbidden element" elates him. "The impulse to retrace his steps delayed itself from moment to moment." Someone throws a small stone at him and hits him in the back. But still he plunges on into the terra incognita of the town: "He sniffed at the fragments of mystery" in the wind boiling up out of the desert, "and again he felt an unaccustomed exaltation."

Port meets a man who appoints himself his guide; he arranges for Port to have sex with a very young girl in a tent in a foul-smelling dump at the bottom of a steep hill. Port catches her trying to rob him of his wallet and he flees into the darkness; he then becomes completely lost and only with great difficulty finds his way home to the hotel. Being endangered and lost foreshadows Port's fever-dream "travels" at the end of the book when he is dying and fears he won't be able to find his way back to the room where his physical body is lying and suffering.

The young girl-prostitute tells him a tale that becomes emblematic and gives its name to this section, "Tea in the Sahara." In her story three prostitutes suffer the attentions of their ugly customers because once they met a handsome, tall nomad and they long to follow him someday to the Sahara where he lives, but they never earn enough. Finally they decide to pool their resources, take a bus south, and then join a caravan. Once they are in the Sahara they sneak away from the caravan and keep climbing one dune after another, always looking for the highest one. They've brought along their teapot and cups and plan to drink tea in the desert. But they're so exhausted they fall asleep, die, and are found days later with their tea glasses full of sand.

200 pages later, after Port's death, Kit joins a handsome nomad and, like the man in the tale, he is mounted on a *mehari*, a tall, slender, fawn-colored camel with a small hump. There are other parallels to the fable: the awful British tourists, the Lyles, drink tea no matter where they go; tea-drinking is their proof that they are better than the savages they live among. They carry with them the tea and tins of English biscuits. Finally, the annihilation that the three girls endure in the Sahara is really what Kit and Port are both courting.

Both Kit and Port are passive and fatalistic, but in a curious way they are extremely active in pursuing their very self-destruction. Just as Port is about to get his stolen and all-important passport back (and thus recover his Western identity), he flees with his wife to an even more remote town. He should be heading back north to the coast and an airplane that will convey him to the hospitals of Europe or America; he is very ill and a return to the first world is his only hope of recovery. But he flees the promise of recovery. After his death Kit flees—not once but twice. In fact, the book ends with her melting into the crowd and escaping her well-meaning if slightly dim escort from the American consulate; at least we presume she's boarded the tram that is inching through the crowds and heading out to the very edge of the city. She is inarticulate with madness and even smells bad.

On the level of plot and motivation, one could argue that Port is fiercely, if silently, jealous of Tunner, the American who is traveling with them, and that Port flees him because he is afraid of him as a rival, just as one could argue that Kit feels so guilty about not being with Port at the moment of his death that she cannot bear to contemplate what she has done. As she looks at his dead body, Bowles writes, "These were the first moments of a new existence, a strange one in which she already glimpsed the element of timelessness that would surround her...now she did not remember their many conversations built around the idea of death perhaps because no idea about death has anything in common with the presence of death." Only when she surrenders herself to people who hold her captive, keep her drugged, turn her into a sex object, and whose language she cannot understand can she push aside all thoughts of her responsibility. Bowles does not, however, resort to the language of psychology; his vocabulary is metaphysical ("the element of timelessness" and "the presence of death"). Most novelists are careful to "motivate" their characters with plausible explanations of their behavior; Bowles submits Kit and Port to eternal philosophical principles, much like the characters in Greek drama.

But there are some faint traces of motivation or at least consistency. Kit has been portrayed throughout the text as a woman who has irrational fears and superstitions, who sees omens and portents everywhere, and is, in a word, slightly crazy. Port, who is presented as being in love with his wife and longing for a rebirth of their sexual intimacy, does nothing to achieve this goal. On the contrary, he is the one who invites Tunner, his rival, to join them. And he never speaks openly of his love to Kit.

This deep passivity, we could even say this obstinate passivity, was an earmark of Bowles's personality and oeuvre and is so far from the average person's experience and behavior that it remains a permanent puzzle for most readers. One of Bowles's friends said to me once, "Paul was as passive as some of his characters." For instance, he refused to encourage or discourage a woman who was courting him after Jane's death. In *You Are Not I*, her portrait of Bowles, Millicent Dillon quotes Bowles as saying, "I never said anything. Well I never do. I don't know why you have to say something. You just have to go on living. People can guess for themselves whether it's yes or no." Elsewhere, when Dillon asks him if his feelings were hurt when one of his Moroccan lovers left him for a rich woman, Bowles says in his best Zen manner, "I don't know. I don't know what it feels like to have your feelings hurt." In his most troubling short story, "Pages from Cold Point," the father who has just slept with his son says, "Destiny, when one perceives it clearly from very near, has no qualities at all." In the story "You Are Not I" the narrator says, "I often feel that something is about to happen and when I do I stay perfectly still and let it go ahead. There's no use wondering about it or trying to stop it." Halfway through *The Sheltering Sky* Port says:

Yet everything happens only a certain number of times, and a very small number, really. How many more times will you remember a certain afternoon of your childhood, some afternoon that's so deeply a part of your being that you can't even conceive of your life without it? Perhaps four or five times more? Perhaps not even that. How many more times will you watch the full moon rise? Perhaps twenty. And yet it all seems limitless.

I mention this passage—which is a striking and original thought in any event—partly because it is the way I feel toward *The Sheltering Sky* itself. I read it once in my twenties and I remember being impressed by the seamless beauty of the writing, the way the constant pressure of the narrative drives forward into disaster after disaster, much as the characters at every point make the wrong choice, precisely the one that will doom them. I also admired the largely hidden, offstage working of the narrative strategies; so much is left out. We don't know where Kit's and Port's money comes from, how they met and married, why they feel so attached to one another despite the sexual stalemate they've arrived at, what the attraction of the desert and Arab culture is for Port (Kit would be just as happy, if not happier, in Italy or Spain), how he survived the war without serving in it; they both seem not merely rich but old-rich in American terms—they have lovely manners, they speak fluent French, they have beautiful clothes, they are in no way jingoistic. But how did they get to be this way? Bowles explains nothing; the constant forward impetus leaves us so breathless with anticipation that we never stop to ask all these unanswered questions. There is no willful obscurity in the way the tale is told; it's just that there are big omissions that we forget to worry about.

I suppose because most readers knew that both Paul and Jane Bowles were homosexual (or was it bisexual?), *The Sheltering Sky* was sometimes read, especially in the beginning, as a story that arose out of the sublimation or the concealment of the author's homosexuality. Port's dalliances with the dangerous young girl in the first port town and with a blind girl whom he never succeeds in seducing despite his frantic efforts—these misfired but obsessive meetings feel much more like the kinky homosexual behavior of the period than normal heterosexual adventuring. The 1940s were the time of the "danger queen" in search of sex with "straight trade" who might turn "dirt" (that is, become dangerous) at any moment; Tennessee Williams recounts dangerous encounters with "dirt" in his *Notebooks* from the same period.

And then Port's ambivalence about the conventionally handsome Tunner seems to dramatize his mixed feelings about his marriage. On the one hand he appears to be encouraging Kit to cheat on him with Tunner—but at the same time he is sarcastic, even openly hostile, about Kit and Tunner's nightlong train ride together (the one moment when they do in fact betray him). Although Port says he intends to revive his physical affair and his love for Kit, he is too deeply passive and even perverse ever to act. He prefers to wait—not for anything she might do or any sign she might give, for he feels confident that she is receptive to his love at every moment and does not need to be propitiated—no, he is waiting for the shifting of his own inner machinery.

My memory is so bad that I didn't recall much about *The Sheltering Sky* when I came to write my novel *The Married Man*. It is in some ways an autobiographical novel, never more so than in the closing section that takes place in Morocco. I had a French lover, Hubert Sorin, with whom I lived mostly in Paris for the last five years of his life. After less than a year together we learned that he was HIV-positive and already far advanced in the illness. A few months before he died he said he hated the cold and damp of Paris and begged me to accompany him to Morocco. We spent some time in Marrakesh; Hubert wanted to come back a month later and to please him I tried to rent a beautiful *riyadh* in the heart of the old city. The lease was about to be signed, but then the owners got a glimpse of Hubert. They must have been shocked by his appearance; he was blade-thin, tottering, obviously dying. The deal fell through and to console him I said we'd fly the next month to Agadir, rent a car, and drive inland to the small beautiful town of Taroudant. We did so despite the warnings of all our friends in Paris, who said he wasn't well enough to travel. He was already suffering from pancreatitis and unable to keep food down. But Hubert insisted—he wanted to get to the Sahara. And I was almost hysterically in denial. We spent a few days in a hotel, formerly a wonderful old pasha's palace in Taroudant built right into the town walls—and then started heading west and south, toward the desert.

Foolishly, I imagined that traveling in a car couldn't be all that tiring. But Hubert had no flesh left on his body and even sitting was very painful for him. To hide his thinness he started wearing long white Moroccan robes. One of the medications he was taking made him turn much darker in the sunlight. Soon, because of his darkness, his Mediterranean features, his starved-looking body, and his robes, people began to assume he was Moroccan.

Of course, we should have turned back and returned to France, but Hubert insisted we go farther and farther. We reached Ouarzazate, then headed south for Zagora. Then we drove across the desert on a dirt road to Erfoud. There he could no longer walk and he'd become incontinent. It was a miracle that the hotel manager gave us a room.

I realized in Erfoud that we must try to get a flight back to Paris— but first we had to return to Ouarzazate or possibly Marrakesh. As I wrote in *The Married Man:*

When they arrived in Ouarzazate at last, Julien said he couldn't walk into the hotel.

"You can and you will!" Austin shouted angrily. "We just need to get to the room, and you'll feel better."

"No, " he whispered. "I can't. Don't you see it's over?"

"It's *not* over. We're going to get that plane back to Paris—"

"I hate you!" Julien hissed. "*Je te déteste!*" was what he said in French, the exact words. "Don't you see? I'm covered in shit."

"I'll clean you up." Austin lifted him up, stood him beside the car, threw his dirty robes on the ground and helped him step into trousers.

"Now we're just going to walk normally past the desk and to the room."

"I can't," Julien wailed. "Can't you see? It's over. Why won't you let me go?"

Austin, grim and determined and cold with fury, put his arm around Julien's waist and walked him toward the entrance to the hotel, but suddenly Julien fainted and crumpled onto the grass. A Frenchman who was walking by said, "What happened? Call an ambulance, for God's sake. I'll call an ambulance," and he ran into the hotel and insisted the clerk phone the hospital.

Austin looked down at this tiny, shit-stained effigy in the grass and he sobbed. "I can't, I don't—" but he didn't know what he was saying and his whole body was seized with a violent fit of trembling which was only more sobs and at last tears. It was as if his will, so long screwed up to its tightest, tautest pitch, had at last snapped and now was hanging down as useless as a violin string. After so much tuning and sawing and plucking, after so much rapture and suffering had been wrung out of it, at last it had snapped and no one was more surprised than the instrumentalist himself.

I suppose if someone had asked if I'd been influenced in writing this book by *The Sheltering Sky* I might have nodded vaguely. But I would have protested that everything I described had actually happened to us. We were not a neurotic couple tempting fate—and yet we were. Hubert's illness wasn't psychogenic, but Port's illness wasn't, either. Our persistence in fleeing help was similar. Even one particular detail was similar. After Port dies, Kit walks through the oasis town as drums beat. "The season of feasts had begun," Bowles writes; exactly as the beginning of the very end for my character occurs during the festive end of Ramadan.

We eventually hired an ambulance to take us through the freezing Atlas Mountains to Marrakesh and a crummy Arab clinic, the Clinique du Sud. I should have insisted we go to the good European clinic at the Mamounia Hotel but I didn't know about it. Hubert died while I was asleep in the bed beside his in his hospital room. His last words to me had been those he'd said a day before—"I hate you." Just as Kit was not present when Port died, I was asleep when Hubert passed away. I awakened to see his drip had stopped and then, when I looked closer, I saw that his face was startled, exactly as if he'd seen something horrifying.

The second time I read *The Sheltering Sky* three years ago I was mainly struck by the deliberate perversity of the characters. I didn't notice that Bowles provides at least a few motivations for their behavior. But I'm sure I wasn't letting myself absorb very much of the text—it was too close to home.

Then I read the book for probably the last time. It took me the whole month of January to get through it—so painful was it. I became quite depressed reading it. Port's coldness reminded me of my own. Kit's madness was also like the breakdown I'd had when Hubert started to slip away from me. The feeling of living through a death in an utterly alien world was all too familiar.

I was also struck by how different our books are, not to mention that Bowles's book is a work of genius. There is lots of humor in my novel and none in *The Sheltering Sky*. Bowles gives a dry gray picture of postwar Morocco whereas my book is a lot more colorful—a critic might say it's the picture-postcard approach. Bowles writes in a cool metaphysical dialect, whereas mine is all human, circumstantial, psychological. All of which is a way of saying how extreme and unusual Bowles's book is, which is also what is remarkable about it.

Was I influenced by Bowles's book? Yes, in the sense that it gave me permission to narrate my personal drama against the unfolding of the Moroccan landscape. In the sense that I counted on that landscape to do my feeling for me, just as Bowles had done. In the sense that the interaction between first-world characters and third-world "extras" was crucial to both books. But it would be mere superstition to suggest that my life was inspired by a half-forgotten reading of *The Sheltering Sky*. For one thing I wasn't that much in control of my life at the time. Hubert, who never read the book, was the one endlessly pressing us toward the desert. He was the one who wouldn't turn back.

Oddly enough, he was not the first person dying of AIDS whom I'd accompanied toward the Sahara. What is it about the desert that attracts the ill and the dying? Could Bowles be right that it represents a taste for the absolute? And what does that mean?

A DIFFERENT PERSON

James Merrill had a great sense of friendship. I once wrote a blurb for his memoir *A Different Person* in which I mentioned his efforts to trade in the family drama for the human comedy, and indeed he did seem in his poetry to be constantly searching to be rid of his childhood and to embrace the adult family of his friends.

Often when he spoke or wrote of friendship he envisioned a *circle* of friends rather than a tête-à-tête with an individual friend. In *The Changing Light at Sandover*, his book-length epic poem, there is a whole milieu of friends—W.H. Auden and a Greek friend Maria Mitsotaki and his recently deceased neighbor Robert Morse and a host of other American and Greek comrades—and this throng of voices seems to drown out the sound of any single friendship.

In this way Merrill was very European. He prized the milieu more than the individual friend; that must be why he was a peacekeeper and so diplomatic in village cultures such as Stonington, Connecticut and Key West, Florida, two places where he lived. In such places everyone has to agree to be friendly; a feud is a terrible waste of energy and time and threatens to destroy the sense of harmony. I don't know if such a policy of agreement works in Stonington but after spending thirty winters in Key West I can attest that it's an unspoken policy down there.

But Jimmy wasn't just being discreet or diplomatic when he envisioned a circle of friends. I think he prized the idea of a small crowd of amiable spirits for itself. He seemed to vibrate faster when he wrote about friends and their multiple connections one to another, even across the barriers of time and space, even across the greatest barrier, that of life and death. Of course this love of an ideal society shows up throughout *Sandover* in the exchanges between Merrill and his companion David Jackson and their heavenly interlocutors. But it is also the tone of a much earlier poem, "The Summer People," which is about Stonington and, roughly speaking, about his friendships with Eleanor Pirenyi and her mother Grace Stone, two Stonington neighbors and stalwarts. We watch the cavortings of the newcomer Jack and his Asian servant Ken, of Andrew and the painter Jane and Nora and her mother Margaret and the cat Grimes. As Merrill writes:

That summer was the model
For several in a row—
High watermarks of humor
And humankindness, no

Discord at cards, at picnics,
Charades or musicales,
Their faces bright with pleasure might
Not have displeased Frans Hals.

The reference to charades or musicales gives a clue to what Merrill liked in friendship. He wanted people to be amusing and amused, to play games with each other, to keep things light, though in his poetry he could transform the light into the dark, the trivial into the profound and the ludic into the tragic.

Nor did Jimmy require his friends to be brilliant—thank God, I might add, having been one of the duller bulbs around him. Whereas a coterie, such as the one that constituted the New York School of poets (John Ashbery, Kenneth Koch and Frank O'Hara), was made up of friends who were all major poets, who reinforced each other's artistic standing and served as first readers of each other's work, the circle that surrounded Merrill was quite different. Some of his friends were poets—especially J.D. McClatchy and Elizabeth Bishop and Richard Wilbur—and some were critics, such as David Kalstone and his old teacher Reuben Brower, but most were not observers but players on the stage of village life, not professional allies but rather action figures he could gently satirize or memorialize or narrate. Even their faults played into Jimmy's hands.

It was no accident that he loved to read the Mapp and Lucia books by E.F. Benson, those hilarious novels , written in the 1920s and 30s, about village life among the idle—Lucia and her admirer Georgie as they play "Mozartino" on the piano, the very same Mozartino who shows up under that name in *Sandover* when Robert Morse is reborn in Bombay and his older Hindu sister is practicing the piano. How Jimmy loved the ferocious Mapp determined to expose Lucia as an imposter incapable of speaking a word of Italian despite her reputation for fluency or the antics of the eccentric lesbian Quaint Irene cycling through the town. Benson lived in Henry James' old house in the village of Rye, and his observations of his feuding and loving friends provided him with all the material he needed.

Just as Merrill needed nothing more than Stonington to fuel his white-hot imagination, in the same way he could turn his card games and word games and above all his Ouija board sessions into great verse. In Key West he played anagrams with Rust Hills, the former fiction editor of *Esquire*, and with the poets Richard Wilbur and John Ciardi; in Stonington he and David Jackson filled page after page with dictation from the spirit world culled from the Ouija board.

The uninitiated always found Merrill's highly rehearsed and thrillingly effective readings to be revelations, because only Merrill himself could authorize the young and the naïve and the overly serious and respectful to laugh. The tone in Merrill's poems is mercurial, turning on the dime of an enjambment or a pun from droll to sad, from particular to universal, from social to personal. He once said that Jung was right, there is a collective unconscious, and it is language itself. The pun was the magic road into the secret heart of the unconscious unity of language. Baudelaire's correspondences were all verbal for Merrill.

Another poem, even earlier, that tells us more about Merrill's ideas of friendship is "A Tenancy" (characteristically dedicated to David Jackson). This is the conclusion:

From the doorbell which rings,
One foot asleep, I hop
To let my three friends in. They stamp
Themselves free of the spring's
Last snow—or so we hope.

One has brought violets in a pot;
The second, wine; the best,
His open, empty hand. Now in the room
The sun is shining like a lamp.
I put the flowers where I need them most

And then, not asking why they come,
Invite the visitors to sit.

If I am host at last
It is of little more than my past.
May others be at home in it.

In a certain sense Merrill is an autobiographical poet, but only in the Proustian sense. Proust took the main outlines of his life and assigned them to his characters but changed sexes, chronology, religions and even generations. His male chauffeur became Albertine, his Jewish mother became Catholic, what happened to his mother he ascribed to his grandmother—and his own gay identity was traded in for heterosexuality. Merrill rather remarkably for a man of his generation accepted his homosexuality—it's a subject frequently discussed in *Sandover*—and his few lovers get a lot of play in his poems. But like Proust he arranged events and trimmed the dramatis personae in order to make more effective artistic wholes. And like Proust he had a palpable, visceral sense of his own past, of which he was the host, offering it up to his reader-guests.

Jimmy's love of games and frivolity could be bewildering to his thick-thighed, slow-moving Puritanical fellow Americans. Even Helen Vendler, the great poetry critic and defender of Merrill's reputation, felt obliged to say, somewhat defensively, that Merrill knew how to keep it light and to stress that lightness was a virtue. I remember The Little Players, a troupe of Victorian hand puppets who put on plays they turned into ballad operas. Two men manipulated a whole family of puppets who, in turn, put on plays about Phaedra and Hippolytus, for instance, which were interrupted by songs sung to popular tunes. "Hello, Phaedra," for example, was sung to the tune of "Hello, Dolly." Jimmy had given a grant to the Little Players and I remember attending a performance and then a dinner afterwards at the apartment of Arthur Gold and Robert Fizdale, the duo-pianists. Again Jimmy was the host there too. It was he who paid for the dinner, though he sat back and pretended to be surprised and delighted by everything he himself had so carefully planned and bankrolled.

In my 1997 novel, *The Farewell Symphony,* I wrote a few pages about Merrill. In the book I gave him a new name but here I'll restore the original one:

Jimmy was a genius who corralled into the sacred paddock of poetry his irreverent social tone and his sense not only for how things look and taste and smell but also for how they wriggle and crawl and soar. On the page his puns and acrostics and palindromes, even his calculated written-out stuttering, were so freighted with feeling that I didn't know whether to smile in acknowledgment of his skill or cry because he'd passed an electrode over the neurons in which my strongest emotions were stored...

As a young poet he'd written bejeweled verse full of poetic props (swans, lutes), and his favorite poet of the recent past had been Elinor Wylie. But to this overwritten, turn-of-the-century formula, which made the poet weep but left the reader dry-eyed, Jimmy brought a sudden new intensity generated by touching together the two least likely wires— autobiography and allegory. Everyone else of his generation, following Robert Lowell's example, was beginning to write confessionally, with a new straightforwardness that felt as exciting as sin after years of the monastic discipline of impersonality imposed on poets by Eliot and the New Critics. Jimmy's early poems had conformed to this austere ideal, but now he was slowly inserting his life into his work— with this difference, that he couldn't resist allegorizing even his own parents' divorce, which instantly became a quarrel between Mother Earth and Father Time, a marriage on the rocks.

If Jimmy could count friends in the hundreds, I belonged not to the first hundred but to the second. I wasn't a poet, I wasn't his type, I wasn't a neighbor, I didn't play bridge and I was too stupid to play word games. What I could do was admire—and as a performer Jimmy had a modest need of admirers. So much poetry seems inferior to fiction in my eyes—less involving, less comprehensible, even less well written. But Jimmy's best verse (and almost all of it was good, better or best) outshone most of the fiction I knew. It told a story, it was funny and unpredictable, it traced out the lives of characters, it was about the great subjects of love and death and transcendence, about the loneliness and confusion and magic of an artist's childhood, about the exaltation and disappointments of adult love, about the poet's progress, about homosexuality—which I would contend is in itself a great subject since it is the reverse side of normal life and love and enables us to understand normality from a useful distance. The reverse side of a Persian rug allows us to see the pattern.

To observe Jimmy was to watch an artist at work and at play. He was often up at six in the morning and at his desk, no matter how sodden had been the night before. There in the alchemy of his verse all the elements of his life—the imperfect loves and silly games and the lives only glimpsed through peripheral vision—were all brought center stage and given the dignity and focus of art. As a friend he was fun—so much fun that he could make me feel leaden by contrast. He had a merry chortle and as a wit he could hear a double entendre in every other sentence, even if it was in reality single and unintended.

He saved my life three of four times during the impoverished 1970s by giving me Merrill grants, small sums from his foundation that I didn't need to feel grateful to him for (though I did). He always said it had nothing to do with him, that the foundation awarded the grants, he was only one voice among many. The other judges I think were Irma Brandeis and John Hollander but David Kalstone told me that they always went along with Jimmy's decisions.

I think he was only vexed with me once and that was when I wrote something about him in a British newspaper. They had a column called Heroes or Villains and I chose Jimmy as my hero. I devoted the whole column to praising him but just to lend myself an air of objectivity I dared to tease him about his clothes, though I myself, as you can see, know nothing about fashion and someone who does know, Alison Lurie, later praised him for the fabrics and colors he chose. Jimmy, however, was already sick and depressed, though I didn't know that—almost no one did. He sat with me in his study in Key West and huge silences installed themselves between us, as they never had before. He said, angrily, "If you think I dress so badly I'll give you carte blanche to dress me as you see fit. You can use my credit card." I was bewildered—hadn't he realized that I'd chosen him as my hero? I learned from that experience that you can say someone is the best poet since Dante but if you mention in passing that he should stop dying his hair or lose ten pounds he will never ever forgive you. In recent years I've certainly had to endure endless comments about my own weight, for instance, and I never forgive them.

Jimmy's playfulness and kindness and antic sense of humor kept him eternally young. He was our young man and will always be our young man. People say that before a certain age we have the face god gave us but after a certain age we have the face we've earned. The same might be said about age. Before forty we are the age time gave us; after forty we have the age we've chosen. Jimmy chose to remain a boy forever—the *puer aeternus*. And only a youth has the energy to invent and sustain a friendship; only a boy can believe in it.

SENSUAL IN THE SOUTH

Reynolds Price once said in an interview:

I think I had as miserable an adolescence as any human being can ever have had—at least outside the novels of Dickens...My problems were simply the problems of being an unpopular kid in a small town who was always being beaten up—partly through my own fault but to a large extent through just the malice of my contemporaries.

No wonder Price exulted when he escaped his native North Carolina on a Rhodes scholarship and attended Merton College, Oxford, for three years, from 1955 to 1958 (he returned to Merton for a fourth year in 1960–1961). *Ardent Spirits*, which recounts his years at Oxford and his first years of teaching in North Carolina, is heady in tone, starting with the title. Price delighted in everything—from the college's special vocabulary (the Thames is called "the Isis" where it flows past Oxford, and "sconcing" is the punishment of drinking a full tankard of beer at a single go for daring to talk about studies over dinner). He made scores of friends, including some famous ones—Stephen Spender, W.H. Auden, and John Gielgud, among others. Spender published in *Encounter* an early story of Price's and over the years would write him some three hundred letters. Auden drank endless amounts of tea and gin with him and rewarded him with his ceaseless eloquence, almost always fairly impersonal.

Price traveled throughout England to see the best productions of Shakespeare. He fell in love with a young straight man, Michael Jordan, a fellow student, and had a sexless romance with him, a relationship that turned into an enduring fifty-year friendship. Price asks himself in this memoir if Auden and Chester Kallman were the first "admittedly queer couple I witnessed in public life." (I myself can remember that ten years later, even in New York in the mid-1960s there were very few openly gay couples to be met or even seen.)

Although Americans, especially Southerners, pride themselves on their friendliness, Price quickly discovered that American hospitality could scarcely rival Oxford sociability—the endless invitations to tea, to drinks, to elevenses, to supper, eventually to High Table. When Price buys a Volkswagen he's suddenly free to go careening down narrow roads to country houses for long weekends. He even travels with his "bromance" to Italy in the Beetle.

Perhaps because he teaches at Duke University and has done so for half a century, Price is careful to recognize with gratitude his old teachers. In an earlier memoir, *Clear Pictures*, he renders homage to Crichton Davis, an unusual young woman teacher in his small-town North Carolina high school who made him memorize reams of poetry and improve his drawing skills, and to Phyllis Peacock, an English teacher in high school for whom Price wrote his first real short story. At Oxford he studied with Nevill Coghill, Helen Gardner, and David Cecil.

His portrait of Cecil is perhaps the most affectionate. Lord David, the biographer of Max Beerbohm and Lord Melbourne, was also a champion of Hardy. He was a famously eccentric don in his antics before an audience, with long, long fingers that would stretch upward like feelers while he spoke. He would spray his listeners out of enthusiasm and sometimes stand on tiptoe while making some excruciatingly interesting observation. Helen Gardner, best known for her studies of Donne and T.S. Eliot, is pictured as a tough scholar who worked with enormous drive and discipline to prove herself in a world in which women intellectuals were rare.

One of the joys of Oxford was its extraordinary libraries. While writing a study of Milton's *Samson Agonistes*, for instance, Price was able to take home and peruse Milton's own copy of Euripides, complete with the young poet's annotations (this copy had also belonged a hundred years later to Doctor Johnson).

Price has written two of his three memoirs (*Ardent Spirits* and *Clear Pictures*) in a rapid, casual style, entirely at odds with the careful, almost lapidary eloquence of his fiction. The third memoir, *A Whole New Life*, is a more meticulous account of his battle with cancer of the spine, which left him unable to walk. In that book about his illness he must have wanted to give a precise record of his despair and ultimate optimism, of the medical procedures and mishaps he had to undergo, and of his intense if unchurched religious faith and the saving power of his friendships.

By contrast, *Ardent Spirits* feels appealingly breezy and almost slapdash. Because Price did not keep notes or a journal he has little to say, for instance, about Auden beyond remarking the quantities he drank and the filthiness of his rooms and his comment on Emily Dickinson, "Very little-bitty at times, don't you feel?" His essential response to Auden was awed admiration, a conviction that the poet was one of the supreme artists of our times:

Even in the most relaxed moments in his Christ Church rooms, coming to the end of our first half-quart of martinis, he'd fall silent for two long draws on his endless cigarette; and in the brief silence that fell around us, I could hear his great mind turning like the wheels of a vast locomotive. Surely the barrels of alcohol and the kegs of amphetamines were, in part, mere means of damping that motion, the heat and light it steadily induced as it did its work...

We get a general impression that there was a lot of dazzling and witty conversation at Price's Oxford. Of course, nothing is more elusive than humor, and even if Price had been a note-taker the remembered repartee of even the greatest wits invariably sounds disappointing. David Cecil was the best conversationalist Price has ever heard (and he has met everyone over the years), but he can recall only one real zinger. When a famous bore interrupted himself and said to David's uncle Hugh Cecil, "I *hope* I'm not boring you, Lord Hugh," the kindly Lord Hugh replied, "Not *yet.*" That's stretching it a bit, isn't it, to quote someone's clever *uncle?*

What does come across is Price's sheer joy in living at Oxford, in doing textual criticism with eagle-eyed scholars, in being punted down the Isis by a broad-shouldered youth, in complaining cheerfully about the eternal cold and rain while scurrying through medieval rooms built by kings. Even the appalling food has the appeal of tradition.

Of course, Price's main focus while at Oxford was on his own fiction. He had written several stories, he had an agent, his teachers and even Eudora Welty had all encouraged him—and he was convinced that he had a genuine vocation. While at Oxford and then back in America one of his stories grew into a novella and eventually became a short novel, *A Long and Happy Life*. Nothing could be more homegrown Southern than this elegantly economical book with its rural cast of black and white characters and its country idioms. How strange that he wrote it mostly at Oxford; it's as though Faulkner had written *As I Lay Dying* at Versailles. In *Ardent Spirits* Price gives us a running account of how and where he came to develop and perfect this darkly lyrical first novel. "Perfect" is the telling word, since we learn how painstaking the young author was in fashioning each scene and how perilous the whole venture must have felt.

Reynolds Price was born in Macon, North Carolina, in 1933—not to be confused with the much larger and more thriving Macon, Georgia. Though middle-class, his family had been impoverished like most others by the Great Depression. His father, Will, was a drinker and had only a high school education; he drifted from being a train conductor to a clerk in the freight office to a door-to-door salesman of life insurance. He courted his wife-to-be for six years and then, after six years of marriage, a first child, little Reynolds, was born. The birth was so difficult that Will made a bargain with God—if Reynolds and his wife Elizabeth survived, he'd never take another drink. They survived and, eventually, Will sobered up. The child had terrible convulsions during his first three years of life, possibly as a result of the forceps that had dug deep into his skull trying to rescue him from a breach birth.

Soon after Reynolds's birth his father got his first real job as a salesman of electric appliances. Elizabeth's parents had died when she was young but Will's mother was a bit of a tyrant and only when he got his job selling appliances were they able to move fifty miles away from her—a saving distance that afforded them all some quiet and independence. Reynolds was an only child for the first five years of his life; then a baby brother Bill was born and his extreme closeness to his parents came to an end.

Reynolds as a child spent hours and hours listening to older relatives "visit," as we say down South. "Visiting" means trading family anecdotes with an eye to astounding and amusing one's listeners; that everyone knows the stories by heart only enhances rather than lessens their charm. Even relatives living in the same state might not see each other more than once or twice a year; the occasional reunions would call for lots of eating, teasing, and endless laughing and visiting. These stories of friends, neighbors, and relatives are the source of Price's fiction and drama, not so much as tales copied from life as myths that resemble those he had listened to over the years. In *Clear Pictures* Price recalls that he and his aunt Ida would go through her box of old photos and she would describe each one: "That's Mama in the awful hat she bought to wear on a trip to Portsmouth."

While Price was still a youngster he saw and heard a recital given by the great African-American contralto Marian Anderson. His father accompanied him as he paid a call on the singer, whom he worshiped. She invited him back for a twenty-minute "audience" the next day and signed his copy of her recording of Brahms's *Alto Rhapsody*. The year was 1948 or 1949 and that such an unruffled exchange could have taken place in Raleigh at that time is a tribute to how civilized the two races could be under the right (and all too rare) circumstances:

> She'd paid me the highest compliment you can pay a stranger, patient courtesy. What she couldn't have begun to sense was how far the respect with which she received a young white Southerner went toward validating my own ambitions to make—like her, with only the strengths of my body and the Spirit's inspiration—works of art.

Except for his four years at Oxford, Price has never lived outside North Carolina, which, as he points out, "sent more men to the Confederate Army than any other. Unlike a number of Southern writers in my generation, I never felt driven out of my region, whatever its wrongs." Racial strife, however, did turn him into an alienated observer and caused him to adopt James Joyce's motto, "silence, exile and cunning." The only problem, morally, with the silence of the internal exile is that it can rather take one off the hook. In the 1960s I can remember how we "radicals" would say that though we were keeping our corporate jobs we were really undermining the "system" from within—something we'd say with defensive conviction but with a sheepish smile at the ready.

As a little boy Price had been interested in drawing and painting but by the age of thirteen he had started writing. As an adolescent he became addicted to books and read constantly—a habit his parents indulged to the best of their means. Although we think of Reynolds Price as someone who never left his home state, in fact he lived in thirteen different places in North Carolina in fourteen years as a youngster. After his family moved to Raleigh he began to write poetry, plays, and fiction. Throughout his life he has continued to write in all the genres, including essays, a book of interviews, and another volume called *Learning a Trade: A Craftsman's Notebooks, 1955–1997*.

Price attended Duke as an undergraduate but during his first three years there his studies and the riotous socializing of that campus left him no time to write fiction. And then, when he was a junior, his beloved father died of cancer in his fifties. Only in his last year of university, after his father's shocking death and encouraged by a professor who had the knack for validating those few students he found to be gifted, did Price write about forty pages he was able to keep. It was on this foundation that he built his first novel while at Oxford.

A Long and Happy Life, which appeared in 1962, is just 195 pages long. It is a love story between a young man, Wesley, and a woman who has the curious name of Rosacoke. Typical of the hushed and somewhat mannered prose is this passage:

> Wesley was on his feet at the corner of the porch nearest Rosacoke, leaning one shoulder on the last post, facing the road but looking down. From the trees Rosacoke could see three-fourths of him—the dark blue trousers he had worn all summer, the loose white shirt, his hair lighter from the sun at Ocean View—all but his face. He covered most of that with

his hands that quivered tight on the harmonica till the music stopped for awhile. Then one hand opened and it started again—not songs or tunes and like nothing she had known since she was a girl and heard old Negroes blowing harps as if they remembered Africa and had been grand kings or like Milo [her brother] that summer he grew up (when his beard arrived, the color of broomstraw) and went past telling her his business and every evening sat in the dusk after supper before he would leave the house, whistling out his secrets in tunes she never understood and planning back of his eyes what he would do with the night when it fell altogether (which would be to walk three miles to see an Abbott girl who was older than him—and an orphan that lived with her uncle—and was taking him in dark tobacco barns, teaching him things too early that some folks never learn).

It's all here—the infinite regress of stories, the sexual passion Rosacoke feels for Wesley displaced onto a nested tale of her brother's adventure with the Abbott orphan, the gnarled syntax, and the simple words that convey complex meanings ("teaching him things too early that some folks never learn"). Expressions such as "when his beard arrived" and "back of his eyes" look like plain speech but in fact require the reader to pause and parse.

Although Price is sometimes compared to Faulkner, inevitably, they are different in most ways, especially in their use of the language. Faulkner redoubles all his effects and keeps piling them on, whereas Price, a much edgier stylist, advances one square only to swerve off to one side with the next move (that "too early" that moves like a knight into "never"). Faulkner can be obscure, whereas Price realized early on that he wanted his country cousins and aunts to be able to make sense of his prose ("These were not highly educated, supremely literate people, and yet I wanted to be understood by them").

By the time twenty-five years later that Price was writing his best-known novel, *Kate Vaiden* (for which he received the National Book Critics Circle Award in 1986), he'd cut back the underbrush of the run-on sentences but preserved the queer Southern turns of phrase. In this novel you can hear a country woman sizing herself up as if she were an animal: "I'm nothing but a real middle-sized white woman that has kept on going with strong eyes and teeth for fifty-seven years"—the "that" instead of "who" properly objectifies her. Despite his Oxford education, worldly connections, and endowed chair at Duke, Reynolds Price has remained true to the impoverished gentility of his childhood, the women's way of talking in elegant periphrases ("she had died on him before he was grown"), the men's charming, hopeful bluntness ("If you'd started earlier, and I knew enough, we could have you singing on big-time stages before you vote—Madame Butterfly!"). People in his fiction have a hard time getting anywhere because they can't scare up the bus fare. They are happy to have a room "with bathroom privileges." Price knows intimately the old South as it was before it became prosperous in the 1970s and he has remained true to it, both as subject and as audience.

In 1984, when he was fifty-one, Price was diagnosed with a large tumor in his spinal column. He ended up having three surgeries—and his lower body was left paralyzed by the radiation treatments. He had lived alone out in the country for years but now he was helpless, entirely dependent on around-the-clock nurses and assistants. He was also plagued with constant and excruciating pain, which was relieved only when he learned how to hypnotize himself and employ biofeedback techniques.

In the midst of his pain he had either a dream or a vision, though he himself opts for it having been a vision. Christ appeared to him, beckoned him to follow. Price stripped down and, naked, entered the water. Jesus cupped water in his hands and poured it over Price's head and said to him, "Your sins are forgiven." But sin wasn't what was worrying Price. "Am I also cured?" Price asked. Jesus said, "That too."

Reynolds Price is an admirable man. His beautiful books, his tremendous productivity, his spirituality and cheerfulness, his abiding friendships with former students (Anne Tyler is the most famous one) and other writers his age (including the late William Styron)—all these generous traits and dynamic accomplishments have characterized him over the decades despite the constant pain and the loss of physical independence he has had to endure.

Ardent Spirits is an innovation in that it seems to be the first time that Reynolds Price has acknowledged his homosexuality in print. In his fiction and poetry he has touched on homosexuality as a theme, but lightly and seldom at length. In his 1995 novel, *The Promise of Rest*, a male character comes home to die of AIDS. In *Good Hearts* (1988) Wesley Beavers (like Mayor Giuliani) takes refuge from a bad marriage with a gay male friend. In *Tongues of Angels* (1990) a summer camp experience between a boy and a counselor (never openly expressed sexually) forms a bond between the two men. In several poems there is a Housman-like lyricism about the beauty of young men's bodies.

As a writer who wants to be read by his friends and relatives and neighbors, Price has never been explicit about his own desires and has seldom touched on queer life. But his deep sensuality, which he freely acknowledges, has worked its way into all his evocations of heterosexuality and his Tiresias-like double vision of the two sexes. It would certainly be crudely reductive to suggest that he could have written better if he'd been more open about his own homosexuality. All one can say is that if he'd been less closeted his fiction might have been as effervescent as his new memoir and perhaps just as insouciant.

SONS AND BROTHERS

We now have the first two volumes of what will eventually be a 140-plus-volume set of the complete letters of Henry James. The entire collection of some ten thousand letters will be published by the University of Nebraska Press over the coming years. (The largest previous collection was Leon Edel's four volumes of 1,084 letters published between 1974 and 1984.) This set will bring together letters scattered across many different archives and from many different books, some out of print; a quarter of the letters have never been published previously. The volumes are beautiful, solidly put together, with big type, wide margins, and copious annotations remarking on cross-outs and misspellings and new words written over old ones. All the foreign phrases are translated and potted biographies of the people mentioned are supplied. If James refers, for instance, to a story he's written, the editors provide the reader in a note with the full name of the story and where it was published and when. At the end of each volume are an index, a bibliography of works cited, a biographical register, and even genealogical charts of the families intertwined with the James family.

In an effort to make the printed letters as close as possible to the holographs, the editors have adopted a system called "plaintext editing," originated by Robert H. Hirst in his version of *Mark Twain's Letters*. There are no emendations to correct spelling or punctuation errors or just errors of fact (though the mistakes are flagged in the notes). A simple line indicates where a word has been crossed out. Drawings that James included are rendered. The result of all this faithfulness to the original letters may seem a bit fussy but the text is easy to read, and scholars who can't consult the holographs or microfiches will be grateful for the variants. The net effect is to bring a high seriousness to letters that were usually dashed off; certainly the scholars preparing these volumes will have spent many more hours on each letter than did either James or the recipients he was addressing.

The letters are to close friends such as Minny Temple, the whole Sedgwick clan, Charles Eliot Norton and his various family members, and Thomas Sergeant Perry (one of Henry's—and William's—best friends, someone to whom Henry would write faithfully for nearly fifty years). Many of the letters, however, are addressed to his mother and father, his sister Alice, his older brother William, and occasionally to his two younger brothers or his Aunt Kate. Of course people write letters when they are traveling or when their friends and family members are abroad, which was the case of the letters in these two volumes, which cover the years from 1855 to 1872 and are devoted mainly to Henry's European wanderings through England, France, Switzerland, and Italy, with time out for visits back to the United States.

Like all travelers, he falls into the bad habit of comparing the characters of the various nationalities. He is a snob about Americans and their "vulgarity" and "commonness." He sometimes refers to them wearily as "the *dear* Americans," though he admits he is incurably and indelibly American himself. Similarly, William James could complain that English and French literature is "provincial" as compared to German literature. Europeans in general Henry reduces to "idlers & starers & self-absorbed pleasure seekers." Paris he dislikes in its new streamlined aspect created in the immediately preceding years by Baron Haussmann. Rome he dubs "terrible serious Rome," though he is fascinated by it and writes, "I went reeling & moaning thro' the streets, in a fever of enjoyment." He is put off by Pope Pius IX ("I'm sure I saw one of the pontifical petticoats hanging out to dry"), and he prefers the bracing masculinity of the ancients to the Pope's supposed effeminacy:

When you have seen that flaccid old woman waving his ridiculous fingers over the prostrate multitude & have duly felt the picturesqueness of the scene—& then turn away sickened by its absolute *obscenity*—you may climb the steps of the Capitol & contemplate the equestrian statue of Marcus Aurelius.

The English he is fond of and admires, though he dislikes their anti-intellectualism:

The English have such a mortal mistrust of any thing like "criticism" or "keen analysis" that I rarely remember to have heard on English lips any other intellectual verdict (no matter under what provocation) than this broad synthesis— "how immensely clever." What exasperates you is not that they can't say more, but that they wouldn't if they could. Ah, but they are a great people, for all that.

Of course, European travel was something James had known from his earliest childhood. Born in 1843, he was taken to Europe when he was one (his earliest memory was of the Place Vendôme in

Paris). By the fall of 1844, the family was sailing back to New York, but from 1855 to 1858 (when Henry was age twelve to fifteen), they were in Europe again. Except for one childhood note that has been preserved, the earliest surviving letter was sent in 1858 from Boulogne on the English Channel to a pal, Ed Van Winkle, who'd written him a get-well letter (James was fourteen and was recovering from a grave case of typhus). The second move to Boulogne, after a crash of the American stock market, reminds the reader of James's story "The Pupil," in which *nouveau pauvre* American gentry keep moving through Europe just ahead of their bills.

Henry and William James were constantly being pulled out of one school (and country) and pushed into another institution or culture all through their childhoods. In Henry's autobiography, *A Small Boy and Others*, he writes about his first schools (for there were often two or three in a given year):

We were day-boys, William and I, at dispensaries of learning the number and succession of which today excite my wonder; we couldn't have changed oftener, it strikes me as I look back, if our presence had been inveterately objected to, and yet I enjoy an inward certainty that, my brother being vividly bright and I quite blankly innocuous, this reproach was never brought home to our house.

The problem was their father's extremely changeable (even capricious) ideas about what would benefit his children. Henry James Sr. was "imperious" and "mercurial," as Robert D. Richardson describes him in his magisterial recent biography, *William James: In the Maelstrom of American Modernism*. The elder James was the son of one of the richest men in America, though in later years Henry Jr. would wonder what had happened to those "golden three millions." Henry Sr. had lost a leg when he was young and hobbled about on a wooden prosthesis (in Henry Jr.'s letters there are many anxious questions about the cyst that temporarily made wearing the wooden leg impossible). By turns generous-hearted and irascible, Henry Sr. had undergone in 1844 a terrible spiritual crisis (a "vastation" as he called it, using the Swedenborgian term) and after that he became a Swedenborgian, though not of the sort that any other Swedenborgian would have recognized.

His new philosophy provided him with strange and seemingly contradictory ideas. He used an intensely spiritual vocabulary—exalted, transcendental, morally demanding—but this otherworldliness did not distract him from interfering on nearly every mundane subject. He was opposed to his oldest son, William, pursuing painting and did everything to steer him toward science. He himself spoke French and not a word of German, but he pushed his boys constantly toward the study of German. He talked about sensual fulfillment with all the fervor of an earlier fellow Swedenborgian, William Blake, but counseled chastity until marriage. He'd enroll his boys in school in New York but change them from one institution to another. In 1853, for instance, when Henry was ten, he was sent to the Vergnès Institute for Young Gentlemen on East 10th Street, and then yanked out and enrolled at the school of a Mr. Richard Pulling Jenks on Broadway. The next year Henry Jr. and William were transferred to yet another school, this one on 14th Street. But their father was displeased with the possibilities in America for what he called, in a characteristically cryptic way, a "sensuous education."

In 1855, he accordingly bundled the family off to Europe—to Geneva (surely the least sensuous city on the Continent), where little Henry was taught by French-speaking governesses, then sent to the Pensionnat Roediger. When their father's enthusiasm for this institution inevitably waned, they all moved to London, where tutors were engaged again, though their governess Mlle Cusin was retained and brought over from Geneva to continue teaching them French. It was during these years that the boys acquired their nearly perfect and certainly idiomatic French; the self-critical James could say, "My French astounds me—its goodness is equalled only by its badness. I can be terribly *spirituel*, but I can't ask for a candlestick." In later years, Henry would be guilty of Gallicisms ("the actual President of the United States") and would scrawl hasty notes to himself in French. His letters in these two volumes are peppered with French phrases, two or three a page. After addressing Thomas Sergeant Perry in French for a full page, Henry (at age twenty-four) switches back to English but deplores the loss of the intimate *tu* ("How detestable this *you* seems after using the Gallic *toi!*"). Some of the strangeness of James's prose in these early letters can surely be explained by his translating back into English from French. For instance, when he writes Perry in 1860 from Paris he describes what he sees out the window of his hotel and refers to "a grasp of warriors" passing by (a phrase which surely began life as *une poignée de guerriers*). Or when James talks of a Swiss mountain trail that took eighteen years to "pierce," he's obviously translating back from *percer*. Richardson remarks on similar mistakes in William's English, though in his case the source of the errors was German.

These years were a blur of constant toing and froing—a move to Paris in the summer of 1856, several transfers back and forth between Paris and Boulogne in 1857, a year in Newport in 1858 at the Berkeley Institute (named after the philosopher Bishop Berkeley, who had lived in Newport for three years in the eighteenth century), a return in 1859 to Geneva, a year later a new experiment—enrollment in a German school in Bonn—though by the end of 1860 they were all back in Newport.

The result of this jagged, caprice-driven education was that William and Henry Jr. finally ended up knowing very little that was taught in ordinary schools. They were good in French, and William had a smattering of German (though Henry Jr. resisted learning the language, maybe as a form of silent rebellion against his father and older brother, both of whom were so keen on it).

They had been exposed to Latin and Greek but little Henry was "so backward in Latin" that he was refused entry in the Académie de Genève and was enrolled in a polytechnic school instead, where he was incapable of following the curriculum of mathematical and scientific courses and finally was limited to studying nothing but French and French literature.

As an adolescent, William, intent on becoming an artist, had studied painting and anatomy and drawing in Paris and later in Newport with William Morris Hunt. In fact, it was William James who had insisted they all leave Paris, improbably, and move back to Newport so that he could become a painter there, of all places. When William was sixteen he wrote his friend Ed Van Winkle:

> We have now been three years abroad. I suppose you would like to know whether our time has been well spent. I think that as a general thing, Americans had better keep their children at home.

In later years, William would rebel against his father's beliefs (of the five children he was the only one to tackle seriously his father's nearly unreadable books of philosophy). As Richardson, speaking of a letter William wrote in 1867, puts it:

> William's own views were now, and had been for some time, almost diametrically opposed to those of Henry Senior. Father believed that just the spiritual was real; he had so little use for what he thought of as "low information" that he would not read his friend Wilkinson's biography of Swedenborg, believing as he did that a narrative can be valuable only when read symbolically. William believed that the natural and the physical were what were real. Father had a private language in which he defined words such as "moralism" to mean what he said they meant, no more, no

less. William was trying to master the accepted languages and methods of science and philosophy...

In some ways, Henry Jr. remained more faithful to his father's ideals—he, too, would see narrative in a symbolic light, and he, too, would put every moment of his tales and novels under a constant moral pressure—though his moral judgments remained elusive. And he, too, would practice a description, as Peter Brooks puts it,

> that one might call "hypersignificant." It doesn't simply record the appearances of the real, it asks about their meaning, what they suggest and perhaps conceal, the context they provide for human thought and action.

When they were both still adolescents, Henry Jr. echoed his brother's anti-European sentiment ("The more I see of this estrangement of American youngsters from the land of their birth, the less I believe in it") but in fact he was not so dissatisfied. He might know little Latin and less Greek but he had his impressions. Throughout his life (and quite dramatically in these two earliest volumes of letters) James was to insist on the value of stored-up impressions; for him the picturesque counted heavily, in the double sense of something visual and something curious and foreign and yet typical. Speaking of his younger self in the third person, James wrote in his moving *A Small Boy and Others* about his unsupervised wanderings at a very young age around New York as he hoarded impressions:

> For there was the very pattern and measure of all he was to demand: just to *be* somewhere—almost anywhere would do—and somehow receive an impression or an accession, feel a relation or a vibration.

He became at an early age addicted to "wondering and dawdling and gaping" and he was convinced he was profiting from his peregrinations. "What it at all appreciably gave him—that is gave him in producible form—would," he writes, "be difficult to state; but it seems to him...an education like another; feeling... that no education avails for the intelligence that doesn't stir in it some subjective passion..." William James, who received an MD at Harvard and went on to conduct rigorous scientific experiments, to be one of the founders of Pragmatism, and to study religious and psychic phenomena, might have raised an eyebrow about his younger brother's "impressions" and "subjective passions," but Henry (or "Harry" as he was called at this time) rejoiced in acquiring just such intangible capital.

Throughout the two volumes of letters there are many, many "impressions." At sixteen he is writing Perry a detailed account of his teachers and unfriendly classmates in Geneva, and rather priggishly summarizing:

Here are five pages all about myself, but the reason I have written so much is because I like nothing better than for you to write about your own manners & customs...

Though James complains that his own letters are "lugubrious" and "egotistical" and that he has a heavy hand and can never rival Perry's lightness and brilliance, nevertheless he begs Perry to keep them. In fact, James informs his brother William, "You know, by the way, that I must economize & concentrate my scribblements & write my diary & letters all in one." He hesitates in one letter to talk about Geneva for it "has not yet been fertile in sensations." He writes to Charles Eliot Norton:

On the whole I try to make the most in the way of culture, of all my present opportunities. I think it is less of a privilege to see England than to see Italy, but it is a privilege nevertheless, & one which I shall not in future years forgive myself for having underestimated. It behooves me as a luckless American diabolically tempted of the shallow & the superficial, really to catch the flavor of an old civilization (it hardly matters which) & to strive to poise myself for one brief moment at least, in the attitude of observation.

Observing, estimating, tasting, absorbing—these are the cultured traveler's duties, especially if he comes from such an intellectually impoverished country (and such an exalted, spiritual family). Of course, in the day when postcards and photographs were still a rarity and a family could spend an entire evening studying a handful of photographs, a verbal description of a great painting still counted as an important document. James had seen no major Renaissance paintings before he traveled to Europe as an adult, and he is constantly astonishing and delighting his parents back in Newport or Cambridge with his battle reports from Florence or Venice or even the familiar Louvre.

When Grace Norton sends to William James a few photos of Siena, Henry Jr. tells her that his brother was enraptured and "that to him, for several days, they have been as meat & drink." Henry adds that with her five or six months in Siena "you will have had a rich experience." "Sensations" and "impressions" are what he values most, as well as "the thrilling, throbbing present" and "the rich acquisitions of these inestimable days." This emphasis on experience in the abstract (rather than on concrete knowledge) would later become characteristic of James's fiction. These youthful letters are already full of an unspecified sense of morality and of intellectual adventure devoid of content; as T.S. Eliot famously said, Henry James had "a mind so fine that no idea could violate it."

James certainly wasn't much interested in politics. He barely refers to the Civil War, in which his younger brothers participated and which he lived through in America. He writes to Perry from Northampton on October 28, 1864, that he's heard they will be giving Colonel Lowell a "grand funeral" in Boston. He adds:

I hope it may be some comfort to his poor wife. By Jove, by moments what an awful thing this war is! I mean for wives, etc. I went up Mount Holyoke t'other day for the 2d time. Of all the concentrated vulgarities it is the greatest.

So much for the war. We can see in this edition that James struck out the phrase "by moments," but the impulse was trivializing in any event, and the sentiment is false and rushed.

He is no more impressed by the reunification of Italy in 1870 or in the same years the collapse of Napoleon III's Second Empire, the brief reign of the French Commune, and the subsequent establishment of the Third Republic (which he predicts won't last). Alfred Habegger writes in his graceful and enlightening introduction:

If one compares what the young traveler saw in fourteen months of Europe to what Tocqueville picked up during nine months of America (both writers having been about the same age), it becomes clear that James's vision was confined to a small arc of the visible spectrum...In fact, as he admitted more than once, he was unprepared for much of what he saw.

When it came to painting, one of the great themes of his youthful correspondence, his loyalties shift from Titian to Tintoretto to Michelangelo, but he is grudging about Raphael. He is particularly inspired about Tintoretto, whom he describes almost as if he were a realist novelist:

His especial greatness, I should be tempted to say lies in the fact that more than any painter yet, he habitually conceived his subject as an *actual scene*, which could not possibly have happened otherwise; not as a mere subject & fiction—but as a great fragment wrenched out of life & history, with all its natural details clinging to it & testifying to its reality.

He is awestruck by Tintoretto's *Miracle of Saint Mark* "with life enough in it to animate a planet." Just as he would later delight in the many rooms in the "house of fiction," in Venice, he was struck by the juxtaposition of Bellini and Tintoretto and

> the vastness & strangeness of art,...to reflect upon their almost equal greatness & yet their immense dissimilarity, so that the great merit of each seems to have been that he possesses just those qualities the absence of which, apparently, ensures his high place to the other.

James had begun to write fiction during the period covered by these letters—a few short stories and a first novel, *Watch and Ward*. In the beginning he was extremely modest and a bit fearful about his literary future. To Perry he said in a letter:

I write little and only tales, which I think it likely I shall continue to manufacture in a hackish manner, for that which is bread. They *cannot* of necessity be very good, but they *shall not* be very bad.

To his sister he refers facetiously to "a slight romance from my facile pen."

During his twenties, most of James's writerly efforts went toward turning out book reviews for *The Nation* and *The Atlantic Monthly*. At first he devoted an enormous amount of energy and subtlety to reviewing ephemeral books, but soon enough he began to tackle more serious things, Thoreau's letters, new French fiction, and especially nonfiction by two of his favorite French writers, Charles-Augustin Sainte-Beuve (the very critic whose literary analyses Proust attacked as absurdly biographical in his *Contre Sainte-Beuve*) and Hippolyte Taine (whose influential history of English literature James reviewed for *The Atlantic*). As James told Perry in a letter":

Deep in the timorous recesses of my being is a vague desire to do for our dear old English letters and writers *something* of what Ste. Beuve & the best French critics have done for theirs.

Often James in these years speaks as if he wants to be a critic, not a novelist.

How different this young, hesitant James is from "the Master" of many years later. The University of Michigan Press has just re-released *Henry James at Work* by his secretary, Theodora Bosanquet, to whom he dictated many of his late books and his three memoirs (one unfinished). Bosanquet emphasizes how utterly dedicated James was to his work and to his "scenic" method, which he had derived from his unsuccessful ventures into playwriting. She says he was "unusually impervious to everything which is not an impression of visual images or a sense of a human situation." She cites passages from James's notebooks in which he makes triumphant claims for his neglected art:

I simply make an appeal to all the powers and forces and divinities to whom I've ever been loyal and who haven't failed me yet—after all; never, never yet!...

A comparison of James's youthful letters with those of Marcel Proust (recently reissued in a charming 1949 translation by Mina Curtiss) reveals that both authors, though at different periods, were obsessed with visual art (as a young man Proust, born about thirty years after James, was translating two of Ruskin's books), with their own health, and with society. Afflicted by asthma, Proust could never have climbed Swiss mountains as James did—though he did serve in the army, which James avoided doing during the Civil War. Proust was a stay-at-home except for a famous trip to Venice and his jaunts around Normandy. James had contempt for Boston and Cambridge society; his social ambitions were all to play themselves out eventually in Paris and London. For Proust letter writing was mainly a way of staying in touch with the *beau monde* despite his invalidism—or a way to social-climb. Whereas James adopts a heavy-handed, teasing gallantry with his women friends, Proust is a shameless flatterer—in fact he raises flattery to grotesque new heights unusual even in the Belle Époque. In 1903 (when he was thirty-two), Proust writes the Comtesse de Noailles, in response to her letter after the death of Proust's father:

> You are too kind. In ages of faith, how natural it was to love the Holy Virgin—for she let the cripples touch the hem of her gown, and the lepers, the blind and all the sad of heart. But you are kinder still, and every new proof of the infinite generosity of your heart gives me a clearer understanding of the unshakeable foundation of your genius, rooted, as it is, in eternity. And if it annoys you a little to be an improvement on the Holy Virgin, I shall say that you are like the Carthaginian goddess who inspired lascivious ideas to many and longing for holiness in a few.

Was there ever a less appropriate response to a condolence note?

James has his own brand of camp ("the Florentines have great cheap brown eyes"), but nothing to compare with this silliness. James can refer to date palms as "perfect debauchees of light & heat" in a phrase that anticipates Ronald Firbank's style of humor, just as he can plead that his bedroom be removed from its place over the family kitchen in Cambridge since he's becoming "a little overdone." At moments one doesn't know if James is being camp, sententious, or just fatuous: "That Pompeii should be interesting I of course expected: it's a way so many things have!" And, writing before the Oscar Wilde trial of 1895, he could afford to describe passing young men with drooling admiration while addressing his unsuspecting New England friends; Proust, writing after 1895 and to a cynical and fully advised Paris, was far more cautious.

The most peculiar letters in this collection are about James's health. It seems that everyone in the James family (except the mother) was almost permanently ill, usually with back pains. Henry Jr. had injured his back in Newport as a volunteer firefighter, and his entire European hegira in 1869 and 1870 is justified as a way of overcoming his weak back. The cure is walking and more walking and mountain climbing—miles and miles every day. What is forbidden is reading or (even worse) writing, but of course this does not stop him. While Henry is suffering constant backaches and taking sitz baths in Malvern, a spa in England, or contemplating purchasing a corset, he is copiously consoling his brother William for his back problems.

But much weirder are Henry James's complaints to his brother about his constipation. Pages and pages are devoted to detail about his lack of "movements," the (literally) back-breaking burden of full bowels, the need for pills of all sorts, constant exercise, dietary restrictions, enemas, even electricity. ("I shall be glad enough to try it, if there is any prospect of its helping me," he writes, asking if William himself has yet started to use "battery" with good results.) Henry announces to his brother that he has "a *passionate* desire for a reformation in my bowels." As he tells his brother with a hushed sense of intimacy:

At this present moment of my writing, I know neither how

I'm to do without a stool, nor how (in spite of the doctor's pills, as yet) I am to get one. The whole matter occupies perforce (how gracefully!) the foreground of my thoughts & oppresses equally my mind & my body.

The bowel problem ("my moving intestinal drama") only aggravates the problems with his back. If Peter Brooks in *Henry James Goes to Paris* is right in speculating that James had strong romantic attachments to men but never acted on them, then we might be tempted to think that this endless dithering about his bowels in extremely long letters to his beloved older medical brother represents a sort of displacement of erotic energy.

To be sure, health and money are inevitably tied together in the strange James family. James's mother, for instance, will reproach her son for spending too much of his father's money during his travels; James will then argue back that the whole trip is an important investment culturally and hygienically. As Brooks comments:

It was a typical James Family double-binding operation: on the one hand, paternal largesse and encouragement to pursue a writerly vocation, on the other hand the maternal censure for lack of thrift.

Brooks's study begins with a discussion of 1875, the year James spent in Paris. He was writing *The American*, which takes place in Paris, and was meeting Turgenev (whom he idolized) and the most prominent French writers, including Flaubert, Maupassant, Zola, and Alphonse Daudet. He was going to the theater almost every night because he had so little society, even if he did for a while dine frequently (and improbably) with his fellow American Charles Sanders Peirce, a founder of Pragmatism. (Imagining their table talk might make a good subject for Tom Stoppard.) Brooks's main thesis is that when James lived in Paris he "missed" much that was new and exciting. He didn't really like Flaubert's writing, he dismissed the Impressionists, and he found Wagner's music "boring." But twenty or more years later, Brooks argues, what James failed to appreciate at the time came back to haunt him and to affect his later great work. Though James was more of a Romantic realist in the tradition of Balzac (with a large taste for melodramatic kitsch and wild and improbable plot twists), he came to appreciate Flaubert's exquisite style and measured realism and to write several important essays on him.

There are three great letters in these two volumes. On September 20, 1867, James tells Perry that there is nothing better than being an American. Then he adds:

We have exquisite qualities as a race, and it seems to me that we are ahead of the European races in the fact that more than either of them we can deal freely with forms of civilization not our own, can pick and choose and assimilate and in short (aesthetically etc.) claim our property wherever we find it. To have no national stamp has hitherto been a defect and a drawback; but I think it not unlikely that American writers may yet indicate that a vast intellectual fusion and synthesis of the various national tendencies of the world is the condition of more important achievements than any we have seen.

On May 10, 1869, he writes his father about meeting George Eliot—in a rushed, dramatic encounter, since the son of her companion George Lewes was howling in pain and writhing on the drawing room floor as his father went out searching for morphine; the young man would die a few months later from tuberculosis of the spine. James found Eliot fat ("she has a larger circumference than any woman I have ever seen") and "magnificently ugly—deliciously hideous" with her "vast pendulous nose," strong jaw, and huge (and nearly toothless) mouth. Then James adds:

Now in this vast ugliness resides a most powerful beauty which, in a very few minutes steals forth and charms the mind, so that you end as I ended, in falling in love with her.

James was to salute her last novel, *Daniel Deronda*, as the masterpiece that it is, though his reactions were so complex that he had to assign his various feelings to three different speakers in a shockingly anti-Semitic review. (One of the speakers talks of "a hard, big, Jewish nose.")

The third great letter is about the early death of his spirited young cousin Minny Temple. Here he betrays the gift of noble and quirky phrase that would characterize his mature style. "The more I think of her the more perfectly satisfied I am to have her translated from this changing realm of fact to the steady realm of thought":

Her presence was so much, so intent—so strenuous—so full of human exaction: her absence is so modest, content with so little. A little decent passionless grief—a little rummage in our little store of wisdom—a sigh of relief—and we begin to live for ourselves again.

He laments his fruitless attempt to transmute "a hard fact into a soft idea."

Prophetically he writes (to his brother William, his most intimate correspondent):

Among all my thoughts & conceptions I am sure I shall never have one of greater sereneness & purity: her image will preside in my intellect, in fact, as a sort of measure and standard of brightness and repose.

And indeed his memories of this "pure American growth...locked away...within the crystal walls of the past" would inspire many of his most attractive American heroines, from Daisy Miller to Isabel Archer. Typically it is in these inspired metaphorical passages that James is most visual and visionary as he thinks of "my youth" that is "turning to gold in her bright keeping."

NABOKOV'S PASSION

Nabokov is the high priest of sensuality and desire, the magus who knows virtually everything about what is at once the most solemn and the most elusive of all our painful joys—the stab of erotic pleasure, that emblem of transitory happiness on earth. As Proust observed, ardor is the only form of possession in which the possessor possesses nothing.

But if passion is the treasure (that is, the absence) that lies at the heart of the great pyramid of Nabokov's art, he has been careful to protect it from the vulgar, the prying, the smug; he has surrounded his secret riches with a maze of false corridors, of precariously balanced, easily triggered, almost lethal megaliths. These are the notorious traps, the crushing menhirs of Nabokov's wit, his scorn, his savage satire. Nonetheless I'd insist that passion, not brilliance or cruelty or erudition or the arrogant perfection of his craft, is his master motif, that his intelligence is at the service of the emotions.

In a superb story, perhaps his best, "Spring in Fialta," first written in Russian and published in 1938, the love between the narrator and the heroine, Nina, is contrasted with—I'm tempted to say safeguarded by—the contempt directed at her husband, Ferdinand. Nina is an impulsive, generous, but negligent woman who has often given herself to the narrator (and to many other men along the way); just as suddenly and often she has forgotten the gift she's conferred on them. The narrator first meets Nina in Russia "around 1917," as he says with an eerie casualness, and they exchange their first embrace outdoors in winter:

Windows light up and stretch their luminous lengths upon the dark billowy snow, making room for the reflection of the fan-shaped light above the front door between them. Each of the two side-pillars is fluffily fringed with white, which rather spoils the lines of what might have been a perfect ex libris for the book of our two lives. I cannot recall why we had all wandered out of the sonorous hall into the still darkness, peopled only with firs, snow-swollen to twice their size; did the watchmen invite us to look at a sullen red glow in the sky, portent of nearing arson? Possibly. Did we go to admire an equestrian statue of ice sculptured near the pond by the Swiss tutor of my cousins? Quite as likely. My memory revives only on the way back to the brightly symmetrical mansion towards which we tramped in single file along a narrow furrow between snowbanks, with that crunch-crunch-crunch which is the only comment that a taciturn winter night makes upon humans. I walked last; three singing steps ahead of me walked a small bent shape; the firs gravely showed their burdened paws. I slipped and dropped the dead flashlight someone had forced upon me; it was devilishly hard to retrieve; and instantly attracted by my curses, with an eager, low laugh in anticipation of fun, Nina dimly veered toward me. I call her Nina, but I could hardly have known her name yet, hardly could we have had time, she and I, for any preliminary; "Who's that?" she asked with interest—and I was already kissing her neck, smooth and quite fiery hot from the long fox fur of her coat collar, which kept getting into my way until she clasped my shoulder, and with the candor so peculiar to her gently fitted her generous, dutiful lips to mine.

When the narrator sees Nina indoors a minute later, he is astonished "not so much by her inattention to me after that warmth in the snow as by the innocent naturalness of that inattention..."

In this passage, the visual memory turns instantly into visual invention, when the lit doorway nearly becomes an ex libris. The seemingly innocent description soon enough resolves itself into an emblem—"out of books," indeed, since the scene that follows is reminiscent of Chekhov's "The Kiss"—the same mansion, a similar party, the same passionate kiss between strangers. Moreover, the quality of the narrator and Nina's intermittent affair is always novelistic and the language used to recount it is invariably the language of literature: "Again and again she hurriedly appeared in the margins of my life, without influencing in the least its basic text."

If this marginal romance—lusty, a bit sentimental, not quite honest, genuinely moving but also tinged with *poshlust*—is related by a narrator who is a writer *manqué*, then the ghastly Ferdinand, Nina's husband, is nothing but a writer—diabolic, coldly technical. In fact, he is one of those many grotesque versions of himself Nabokov planted throughout his fiction, a sort of signature not unlike Hitchcock's fleeting appearances in his own films. This particular double is particularly unappetizing, driven as he is with a "fierce relish" for ugly things and woebegone people: "Like some autocrat who surrounds himself with hunchbacks and dwarfs, he would become attached to this or that hideous object; this infatuation might last from five minutes to several days or even longer if the thing happened to be animate."

In "Spring in Fialta," which is just twenty-one pages long, Nabokov manages to generate as dense a sense of lived-through time as can be found in many novels. He achieves this narrative density by two means: a complex but rigorous time scheme; and the juxtaposition of highly contrasted moods. I won't dwell on the time scheme now except to mention that the story progresses on two planes: connected episodes at Fialta in the present that alternate with memories of past trysts with Nina in many cities over the years. Both the present and the past are told sequentially and the last flashback to be presented is the narrator's most recent memory of Nina. In other words, these two systems of time converge to produce the final scene, in which Nina is killed when her car crashes into a traveling circus company, whose arrival has been heralded throughout the tale by dozens of tiny details, as at sea the approach of land is promised by a quickening flux of grass, twigs, and land birds. The two time schemes and the payoff of the circus's appearance at the end tie everything together.

But the actual sense of time passing also depends on the rapid alternation of contrasted scenes, a technique perfected by Tolstoy. These scenes are either satirical or romantic. Some of the romantic scenes are not scenes at all but instead beautifully rendered telescopings of time:

Once I was shown her photograph in a fashion magazine full of autumn leaves and gloves and wind-swept golf links. On a certain Christmas she sent me a picture post card with snow and stars. On a Riviera beach she almost escaped my notice behind her dark glasses and terra-cotta tan. Another day, having dropped in on an ill-timed errand at the house of some strangers where a party was in progress, I saw her scarf and fur coat among alien scarecrows on a coat rack.

In a bookshop she nodded to me from a page of one of her husband's stories…

The tone of these passages is elegiac, tender, and sensual; it is Nabokov's genius (as one might speak of the genius of a place or of a language) to have kept alive almost single-handedly in our century a tradition of tender sensuality. In most contemporary fiction tenderness is a sexless family feeling and sensuality either violent or impersonal or both. By contrast, Nabokov is a Pascin of romantic carnality. He writes in "Spring in Fialta": "Occasionally in the middle of a conversation her name would be mentioned, and she would run down the steps of a chance sentence, without turning her head." Only a man who loved women as much as he desired them could write such a passage.

What makes the narrator of this tale a writer *manqué* is his uncritical—one might say his uninjured—ease in the world of the sentiments. There is no bite, no obliqueness, no discomfort in his responses, and though he is in no danger of becoming vulgar, he is close to that other Nabokovian sin, philistinism. No wonder he is repelled by the real writer, Ferdinand, the center of the satirical scenes with their passages that send up the culture industry, the fatiguing milieu of art groupies. Ferdinand sounds a bit like a combination of the sardonic Nabokov and, improbably, a naive Western European devotee of Russian communism. But instead of focusing on Ferdinand's bad politics, let us concentrate instead on his peculiarities as a writer:

Having mastered the art of verbal invention to perfection, he particularly prided himself on being a weaver of words, a title he valued higher than that of a writer; personally, I never could understand what was the good of thinking up books, of penning things that had not really happened in some way or other; and I remember once saying to him as

I braved the mockery of his encouraging nods that, were I
a writer, I should allow only my heart to have imagination,
and for the rest rely upon memory, that long-drawn sunset
shadow of one's personal truth.

I had known his books before I knew him; a faint
disgust was already replacing the aesthetic pleasure that
I had suffered his first novel to give me. At the beginning
of his career, it had been possible perhaps to distinguish
some human landscape, some old garden, some dream-
familiar disposition of trees through the stained glass of his
prodigious prose...but with every new book the tints grew
still more dense, the gules and purpure still more ominous;
and today one can no longer see anything at all through that
blazoned, ghastly rich glass, and it seems that were one to
break it, nothing but a perfectly black void would face one's
shivering soul.

In this remarkable, and remarkably sly, passage, the narrator's
relationship to the reader (and to the writer Nabokov) becomes
intricate. We know that Nabokov's own art is not autobiographical
in the simple photographic sense, and we resist the narrator's
assumptions about the sufficiency of memory to art. The narrator
sounds too sincere, too Slavic, to our ears, although his objections
to Ferdinand are phrased with all the suavity and eloquent
conviction at Nabokov's command. Since we, the readers, know
that a figure much like the diabolical Ferdinand has written even
this argument for sincerity, our relation to the text is slippery. The
nastiness of these passages contrasts vividly with the tenderness of
the alternating scenes to produce an almost topographical sensation
of traveling though time, as though the landscape below the tip of
the wing were either a mountain peak or a shadowed gorge, never
a flat plain.

Many writers proceed by creating characters who are parodies of themselves or near misses or fun-house distortions, or they distribute their own characteristics across a cast of characters, and some especially like to dramatize their conflicts and indecisions by assigning them to different personages. One thinks of Proust, who gave his dilettantism to Swann, his homosexuality to Charlus, his love of his family to the narrator and his hatred of his family to Mlle. Vinteuil, his hypochondria to Aunt Leonie, his genius to Elstir and Bergotte, his snobbism to the Guermantes, his Frenchness to Françoise. In this sense (but this strict sense only) every novel, including Nabokov's, is autobiographical. Indeed, the notion of a parallel life that does, impossibly, converge with one's own may have suggested the concept of two worlds and two histories slightly out of sync—the moiré pattern of Terra and anti-Terra woven by *Ada*.

But it was Nabokov's particular delight to invent sinister or insane or talentless versions of himself, characters who are at least in part mocking anticipations of naive readers' suspicions about the real Nabokov. For all those innocents who imagined that the author of *Lolita* was himself a nympholept, Nabokov prepared a hilarious response in *Look at the Harlequins!* in which the narrator's biography is composed from nothing but such crude suppositions: "As late as the start of the 1954-55 school year, with Bel nearing her thirteenth birthday, I was still deliriously happy, still seeing nothing wrong or dangerous, or absurd or downright cretinous, in the relationship between my daughter and me. Save for a few insignificant lapses—a few hot drops of overflowing tenderness, a gasp masked by a cough and that sort of stuff—my relations with her remained essentially innocent." *Essentially* innocent—that's the kind of essence that lubricates our villainous society.

Nabokov's model for inventing such characters, the author's disabled twin or feebler cousin, mad brother or vulgar uncle, was surely Pushkin among others, for it was Pushkin, following Byron's lead in *Don Juan*, who fashioned a distorted portrait of himself in Eugene Onegin, the young man of fashion whose attitudes and deeds sometimes draw a crude outline of the poet's own silhouette and just as often diverge completely. Of course, Pushkin scrupulously disowns the resemblance (I use Nabokov's translation):

> I'm always glad to mark the difference between Onegin and myself, lest an ironic reader or else some publisher of complicated calumny, collating here my traits, repeat thereafter shamelessly that I have scrawled my portrait like Byron, the poet of pride.

Before Pushkin establishes their differences he points out the similarities. He tells us that he likes Onegin's "sharp, chilled mind" and explains their friendship by saying, "I was embittered, he was sullen."

Wit, scorn, and the parody of romance can be a way of rescuing romance. Just as Schoenberg remarked that only the extreme recourse of his twelve-tone system was able to provide German Romantic music with another fifty years of life, so Nabokov might have asserted that only by casting *Lolita* into the extreme terms of a Krafft-Ebing case study, the tale of a European nympholept and his gum-snapping, wise-cracking, gray-eyed teen-age enchantress—that only by making such a radical modulation could he endow the romantic novel with new vitality.

That vitality is attributable to obsession, the virtue that is shared by vice and art. As Adorno observes in the *Minima Moralia*: "The universality of beauty can communicate itself to the subject in no other way than in an obsession with the particular." The lover, like the artist, loathes the general, the vague, the wise, and lives only for the luminous singularity of the beloved or the glowing page. Everything else is insipid.

Lolita, as all the world knows, is full of parodies—parodies of literary essays, of scholarly lists of sources, of scientific treatises, of psychiatric reports, and especially of the confession and the legal defense. It is also a compendium of sometimes serious, but usually jocular, allusions to key works of nineteenth-century Romanticism, especially French fiction and verse (Humbert's first language is French, of course, and *Lolita* is more Gallic than American or Russian, at least in its explicit references and models). But the function of this brilliant panoply of literary allusions is not to disown Romanticism but to recapture it. As Thomas R. Frosch remarks in "Parody and Authenticity in *Lolita*":

> In relation to romance, parody acts in *Lolita* in a defensive and proleptic way. It doesn't criticize the romance mode, although it criticizes Humbert; it renders romance acceptable by anticipating our mockery and beating us to the draw. It is what Empson calls "pseudo-parody to disarm criticism." I am suggesting, then, that *Lolita* can only be a love story through being a parody of love stories.

To be sure, the entire history of Romantic verse and fiction has been self-consciously literary. One could go further and insist that romantic passion itself is literary; as La Rochefoucauld said, no one would ever have fallen in love unless he had first read about it. Humbert and Lolita's mother, Charlotte Haze, represent two quite distinct romantic traditions, the courtly versus the bourgeois. For the courtly lover love is useless, painful, unfulfilled, obsessive, destructive, and his very allegiance to this peculiar, seemingly unnatural ideal is proof of his superiority to ordinary mortals. As Frederick Goldin has remarked about the origins of courtly love in the Middle Ages:

> Ordinary men cannot love unless they get something in return—something they can get hold of, not just a smile.

If they do not get it they soon stop loving, or, if the girl is from one of the lower orders, they take it by force. But usually, since ordinary men love ordinary women, they get what they want; and then, their mutual lust expended, they go their separate ways, or else, if they are restrained by some vulgar decency, they mate and settle down. In this wilderness of carnality and domesticity, nobility declines; there is no reason, and no chance, for the longing, exaltation and self-discipline of true courtliness. This is one of the basic creeds of courtly love.

One of the most amusing paradoxes of *Lolita* is that the satyr Humbert Humbert becomes the minnesinger of courtly love for the twentieth century. To be sure, before he can fully exemplify the "longing, exaltation and self-discipline of true courtliness" Humbert must lose Lolita and kill his double, Quilty. If Humbert and Quilty have mirrored each other in the first half of the book, in the second half they turn into opposites, as Humbert becomes leaner, older, more fragile, more quixotic, and Quilty grows grosser, drunker, fatter, and more corrupt; the murder of Quilty expiates Humbert of everything base.

If Humbert embodies courtly love, Charlotte comes out of the more recent tradition of bourgeois marriage. It is a sign of Nabokov's compassion that he is so gentle in his treatment of the ridiculous Charlotte, who in spite of her constant smoking, her bad French, her humorlessness, her middlebrow cultural aspirations, and her cruelty to her daughter he also shows is lonely, touching, decent: "To break Charlotte's will I would have to break her heart. If I broke her heart, her image of me would break too. If I said: 'Either I have my way with Lolita, and you help me to keep the matter quiet, or we part at once,' she would have turned as pale as a woman of clouded glass and slowly replied: 'All right, whatever you add or subtract, this is the end.'" Even Humbert describes her, poetically, as a creature of "clouded glass," an impression denoting nothing but connoting beauty.

Charlotte has been shaped by reading women's magazines and home-decoration manuals and popular novels. Her pious expectations of the monogamous and "totally fulfilling" marriage in which sex, sentiment, and even religious faith coincide are at odds with Humbert's stronger emotions and more desperate aspirations. The best Humbert can do by way of a domestic fantasy is to imagine marrying Lolita, fathering a daughter, and living long enough to indulge in incest not only with that child but with *her* daughter as well: "—bizarre, tender, salivating Dr. Humbert, practicing on supremely lovely Lolita the Third the art of being a granddad." Even when he attempts for a moment to abandon his own brand of romantic literature, the script of his courtly and obsessive passion, for Charlotte's kind of pulp, the attempt fails: "I did my best; I read and reread a book with the unintentionally biblical title *Know Your Own Daughter*…"

Nabokov wrote in *The Gift* that "the spirit of parody always goes along with genuine poetry." If "genuine poetry" is taken to mean romantic literature about passion, one can only concur, since passion is parody. *Don Quixote* is a parody of tales of knightly adventure; in Dante the lovers Francesca and Paolo discover their mutual passion when they read "of Lancelot, how love constrained him." The pump of Emma Bovary's ardor has been primed by her reading of cheap romantic magazine stories. In *Eugene Onegin*,

Tatiana is besotted by romantic fiction: With what attention she now reads a delicious novel, with what vivid enchantment drinks the seductive fiction!But her reading, alas, is different from Onegin's, for Tatiana reads Rousseau's fiction and Goethe's *The Sorrows of Young Werther* (as Nabokov comments in his notes, "Werther weeps on every occasion, likes to romp with small children, and is passionately in love with Charlotte. They read *Ossian* together in a storm of tears"). Immersed in her own brand of Lachrymose Lit,

Tatiana sighs, and having made her own another's ecstasy, another's melancholy, she whispers in a trance, by heart, a letter to the amiable hero.

That letter sounds like Charlotte Haze's avowal:

"I am nothing to you. Right? Right. Nothing to you whatever. *But* if, after reading my 'confession,' you decided, in your dark romantic European way, that I am attractive enough for you to take advantage of my letter and make a pass at me, then you would be a criminal—worse than a kidnaper who rapes a child. You see, *chéri. If* you decided to stay, *if* I found you at home…"

and so on. Charlotte's letter seems a parody of Tatiana's far more touching but no less fervent appeal:

My fate henceforth I place into your hands, before you I shed tears, for your defense I plead. I'm waiting for you: with a single look revive my heart's hopes, or interrupt the heavy dream, alas, with a deserved rebuke.

Humbert may fake his acceptance of Charlotte's avowal, but Onegin rejects Tatiana in rolling Byronic phrases:

But I'm not made for bliss; my soul is strange to it; in vain are your perfections: I'm not worthy of them.

This understanding, fatal to the future happiness of both characters, is not so much owing to character differences as to different reading lists. Whereas Tatiana has read of lovers given to sacrifice, duty, and devotion, Onegin has been coached by Byron's egotistical and disabused Don Juan:

My days of love are over; me no more\The charms of maid, wife...Can make the fool...The credulous hope of mutual minds is o'er.

Years go by, Tatiana suffers, becomes stoic, and then one day is drawn to Onegin's deserted country house. She enters his library, reads the books he once read, and in a stunning passage she wonders whether Onegin might not be "a glossary of other people's megrims, a complete lexicon of words in vogue? Might he not be, in fact, a parody?" Just as Charlotte recognizes Humbert's criminal passions for Lolita once she reads his diary, so Tatiana understands Onegin is a fraud once she peruses his books.

The Byronic hero could, in his most degraded form, become coldly indifferent to women and with men murderously touchy on points of honor. If the calculating seduction is the way the Byronic monster approaches women, his characteristic exchange with other men is the duel. Here again Humbert executes a grotesque parody of the duel in stalking down Quilty; this is the final sorry end to the already shoddy, senseless business of the Lenski-Onegin duel.

So it is not surprising that *Lolita* is a parody of earlier works of Romantic literature, including not only *Onegin* but much more obviously a succession of French novels devoted to the anatomy of the passions—that line that runs from *La Princesse de Clèves* through *Les Liaisons Dangereuses, Adolphe, Atala* and *René* and on to *Mademoiselle de Maupin, Carmen*, and *Madame Bovary*—a tradition, moreover, that Humbert specifically alludes to again and again. His mind is also well stocked with French poetry from Ronsard to Rimbaud. Whereas some Russian Formalists (I'm thinking of Tynyanov's *Dostoevski and Gogol: Remarks on the Theory of Parody*) argued that parody is a way of disowning the past in an act of literary warfare, in Nabokov's case we see that parody can be the fondest tribute, the invention of a tradition against which one's own originality can be discerned, a payment of past debts in order to accrue future capital.

In his treatment of love, Nabokov points the way beyond parody and convention. At their best his characters act out of character, transcend their roles. The most sublime moment in *Lolita*, of course, occurs when Humbert sees the "hugely pregnant" Lolita after searching for her for several years.

> There she was with her ruined looks and her adult, rope-veined narrow hands and her goose-flesh white arms, and her shallow ears, and her unkempt armpits, there she was (my Lolita!), hopelessly worn at seventeen, with that baby, dreaming already in her of becoming a big shot and retiring around 2020 AD—and I looked and looked at her, and knew as clearly as I know I am to die, that I loved her more than anything I had ever seen or imagined on earth, or hoped for anywhere else.

Here the pervert breaks through the narrow confines of his perversion, the connoisseur of *le fruit vert* looks longingly at the no-longer-ripe apple in a now vanished Eden. Passion—fastidious, tyrannical, hostile—has given way to compassionate love. Correspondingly, Lolita shrugs off her own grudges and forgives Humbert for having taken away her youth; when Humbert asks her to leave with him, she says, "No, honey, no." In a heartbreaking line, Humbert writes: "She had never called me honey before."

A similar moment when love transcends passion, when sentiment exceeds sexuality, occurs in *Pale Fire*. The exclusively homosexual Kinbote—who, had always treated his wife with "friendly indifference and bleak respect" while drooling after "Eton-collared, sweet-voiced minions"—begins to *dream* of Disa, his queen, with throbbing tenderness:

He dreamed of her more often, and with incomparably more poignancy, than his surface-like feelings for her warranted; these dreams occurred when he least thought of her, and worries in no way connected with her assumed her image in the subliminal world as a battle or a reform becomes a bird of wonder in a tale for children.

These heart-rending dreams transformed the drab prose of his feelings for her into strong and strange poetry.

The transcendent virtue of love is seen again in *Ada* when the aged rake Van Veen is reunited after many years with his now plump and no longer appealing Ada: "He loved her much too tenderly, much too irrevocably, to be unduly depressed by sexual misgivings." *This* from the great sensual purist! Of course this very passage, in which love goes beyond its conventional limits, is, paradoxically, itself a parody of the end of *War and Peace* and the marriage of Natasha and Pierre.

Andrew Field writes, "All of his novels, Nabokov told me once, have an air—*not quite of this world, don't you think?*" Field didn't take the remark seriously; he thought it was just more leg pulling. But I think the hint that his novels are "not quite of this world" should be taken seriously. After boyhood Nabokov was not conventionally religious, although the poetry of his early twenties continued to rely occasionally on religious imagery. Nevertheless, he retained within his pages a quick, visceral sense of disturbing spiritual presences. His is a haunted world, and to prove it W.W. Rowe recently published an entire volume to that effect: *Nabokov's Spectral Dimension.* Inspiration itself is such a specter, of course; in *The Gift* when Fyodor begins to write, he is conscious of "a pulsating mist that suddenly began to speak with a human voice." Vera Nabokov, the writer's wife and the dedicatee of virtually every book from his pen, has said that a main theme in all of Nabokov's writing is "the hereafter." Of Fyodor's father, the boy thinks: "It was as if this genuine, very genuine man possessed an aura of something still unknown but which was perhaps the most genuine of all."

The luminous unknown, this aura of the ghostly genuine, is always bordering the picture Nabokov presents to his reader. The narrator of his last novel, *Look at the Harlequins!* is afflicted with recurrent bouts of madness. His perception of space is so personal and so harrowing that at one point he becomes paralyzed. "Yet I have known madness not only in the guise of an evil shadow," he tells us. "I have seen it also as a flash of delight so rich and shattering that the very absence of an immediate object on which it might settle was to me a form of escape."

It is in those flashes of delight, which illuminate almost every passage, that Nabokov's glimpses of another world can be detected. Lolita's smile, for instance, "was never directed at the stranger in the room but hung in its own remote flowered void, so to speak, or wandered with myopic softness over chance objects." In *The Gift*, the hero imagines returning to his ancestral home in Russia: "One after another the telegraph poles will hum at my approach. A crow will settle on a boulder—settle and straighten a wing that has folded wrong." That straightened wing—the precision of an imagined imaginary detail—is worthy of a Zen master. In "Spring in Fialta," we encounter "that life-quickening atmosphere of a big railway station where everything is something trembling on the brink of something else"—a phrase that might well serve as Nabokov's artistic credo (and that recalls Quine's notion that a verbal investigation of language is akin to building a boat while sailing in it).

Mythology in Nabokov does not (as it does in Joyce's *Ulysses*) limit the neural sprawl of a stream of consciousness. Nor is it there to provide a plot (as in the neoclassical drama of Anouilh and Giraudoux). Nor is it there to lend unearned dignity to an otherwise dreary tale, as in the plays of Archibald MacLeish or Eugene O'Neill. In Nabokov the vocabulary of religion, fairy tales, and myths is the only one adequate to his sense of the beauty and mystery of the sensual, of love, of childhood, of nature, of art, of people when they are noble. It is this language that metamorphoses the comic bedroom scene in *Lolita* into a glimpse of paradise. Once they're in the hotel room:

> Lolita walked up to the open suitcase as if stalking it from afar, in a kind of slow-motion walk, peering at that distant treasure box on the luggage support. (Was there something wrong, I wondered, with those great gray eyes of hers, or were we both plunged in the same enchanted mist?) She stepped up to it, lifting her rather high-heeled feet rather high, and bending her beautiful boy-knees while she walked through dilating space with the lentor of one walking under water or in a flight dream.

Nabokov's novels are not of this world, but of a better one. He has kept the romantic novel alive by introducing into it a new tension—the struggle between obsessive or demented characters and a seraphic rhetoric. Given his inspired style, no wonder Nabokov chose to write not about the species or the variety but about the mutant individual. Such a subject gives his radiant language something to overcome. In one story, "Lance," Nabokov relaxed this tension and indulged in his verbal splendors with chilling abandon. In that story the young hero, Lance Boke, ascends into the heavens as his old parents watch through field glasses: "The brave old Bokes think they can distinguish Lance scaling, on crampons, the verglased rock of the sky or silently breaking trail through the soft snows of nebulae." I like to think of Nabokov himself, the supreme alpinist of the art, ascending those new heights.

He must be ranked, finally, not with other writers but with a composer and a choreographer, Stravinsky and Balanchine. All three were of the same generation, Russians who were clarified by passing through the sieve of French culture but were brought to the boiling point only by American informality. All three experimented boldly with form, but none produced "avant-garde trash," as Nabokov called it, for all three were too keen on recuperating tradition. In a work such as the *Pulcinella* ballet score, the baroque mannerisms of Pergolesi are aped, even insisted upon, but baroque squares are turned into modernist rhomboids and scalenes, and mechanical baroque transitions, the yard goods of that style, are eliminated in favor of a crisp collage built up out of radical juxtapositions. Everything is fresh, new, heartless—and paradoxically all the more moving for the renovation. Similarly, Balanchine eliminated mime, a fussy port de bras, story, and decor to make plotless ballets that distill the essence of the Petipa tradition. As parodists, all three artists loved the art they parodied and make it modern by placing old jewels into new settings.

Most important, all three men had a vision of art as entertainment, in the sense of wooing shrewder, more restless though robust, sensibilities. Sartre once attacked Nabokov for his lack of political content, but one could reply to that charge without hesitation that the paradise Balanchine, Stravinsky, and Nabokov have made visible to us is one of the few images of happiness we have, that very happiness politics is working to secure, the promise of harmony, beauty, rapture.

In "Fame," a poem he wrote in Russian in 1942, Nabokov bitterly echoed the 1836 poem *Exegi monumentum* of Pushkin, which in turn echoed the poem by Horace and those of many other poets. Whereas Horace and Pushkin could well consider their verse a monument they had raised to their own eternal glory, Nabokov, writing in exile for a tiny Russian-speaking audience that would soon be dying cut, could only imagine a fantastic, garrulous visitor:

"Your poor books," he breezily said, "will finish by hopelessly fading in exile. Alas, those two thousand leaves of frivolous fiction will be scattered..."

As we know now, and know with gratitude, the prophecy was not fulfilled. More glorious and surprising in his metamorphosis than any butterfly he ever stalked, Nabokov, the Russian master, turned himself into a writer in English, the best of the century.

ACKNOWLEDGMENTS

I wish to thank Don Weise who had the idea of doing this book and who selected and arranged all these essays.

Most of these essays appeared in the *New York Review of Books*:

Nabokov: March 29, 1984

Henry James: October 11, 2007

Edith Wharton: April 26. 2007

Howard Sturgis: March 6, 2008

John Rechy: April 3, 2008

Marguerite Duras: June 26, 2008

Glenway Wescott: Feb 12, 2009

John Cheever: April 8, 2010

Martin Amis: June 24, 2010

The Beats: August 19, 2010

Ford Madox Ford: March 24, 2011

The essay on Paul Bowles appeared in the *New York Review of Books*; July 14, 2011.

The essay on E.M. Forster appeared in the *New York Times*; January 17, 2010.

The essay on Christopher Isherwood appeared in the *New York Times*; December 9, 2010.

The essay on Robert Mapplethorpe was originally the introduction to the 1995 collection of his pictures, *Altars*.

The essay on Truman Capote appeared in *The Burning Library: Essays*, edited by David Bergman under the title "Sweating Mirrors: A Conversation with Truman Capote." The piece combines an interview published in *After Dark*, 1980, with a review of *The Capote Reader* in the *Times Literary Supplement*, May, 13, 1988.

The essay on Rodin was published in 2008 in *The Museum as Muse* by the Princeton University Art Museum.

ABOUT THE AUTHOR

Edmund White is a 2010 National Book Critics Circle finalist for his memoir *City Boy*. He is also the author of many works, including the autobiographical novel *A Boy's Own Story* and a popular travel book titled *The Flâneur*. He was a recipient of the Lambda Literary Foundation's 2009 Pioneer Award in recognition of his tremendous contributions to LGBT literature. White lives in New York City and teaches in the creative writing department at Princeton University. Visit the author online at www.edmundwhite.com.